GREAT CHICKEN DISHES

READER'S DIGEST

GREAT CHICKEN DISHES

325 DELICIOUS RECIPES—FROM LIGHT SALADS TO HEARTY STEWS

The Reader's Digest Association, Inc.
Pleasantville, New York • Montreal

GREAT CHICKEN DISHES

READER'S DIGEST PROJECT STAFF

Editorial Director
Carol A. Guasti

Senior Design Director
Elizabeth L. Tunnicliffe

Production Technology Manager
Douglas A. Croll

Editorial Manager
Christine R. Guido

READER'S DIGEST ILLUSTRATED REFERENCE BOOKS

Vice President, Editor-in-Chief
Christopher Cavanaugh

Art Director
Joan Mazzeo

Copyright © 1999 The Reader's Digest Association, Inc.
Copyright © 1999 The Reader's Digest Association (Canada) Ltd.
Copyright © 1999 Reader's Digest Association Far East Ltd.
Philippine Copyright © 1999 Reader's Digest Association
Far East Ltd.

Printed in the United States of America

Address any comments about Great Chicken Dishes to
Reader's Digest, Editor-in-Chief, U.S. Illustrated Books,
Reader's Digest Road, Pleasantville, NY 10570

To order additional copies of Great Chicken Dishes,
call 1-800-846-2100

You can also visit us on the World Wide Web at:
www.readersdigest.com

Library of Congress Cataloging in Publication Data

Great chicken dishes: delicious recipes from light salads
to hearty stews/Reader's Digest.
    p.cm.
ISBN 0-7621-0238-1
 1. Cookery (Chicken)

TX750.5.C45 G74 1999
641.6'6—dc21   99-045682

PRODUCED BY REBUS, INC.

Publisher
Rodney M. Friedman

Director, Recipe Development & Photography
Grace Young

Editorial Director, Food Group
Kate Slate

Writer
Bonnie J. Slotnick

Associate Editors
James W. Brown, Jr., John P. Lynch

Art Director
Timothy Jeffs

Design Assistant
Yoheved Gertz

Senior Recipe Developer
Sandra Rose Gluck

Recipe Testers
Iris Carulli, Michelle Steffens,
Maggie Ruggiero, Megan Schlow

Photographers
Mark Ferri, Lisa Koenig, Michael Grand

Photographers' Assistants
Katie Bleacher Everard, Shari Milzoff,
Lisa Rutledge

Food Stylist
Paul S. Grimes

Assistant Food Stylists
Margarette Adams, Jonathan Leff,
Maggie Ruggiero, Megan Schlow

Prop Stylist
Debrah Donahue

Nutritionists
Hill Nutrition Associates

Foreword

"A chicken in every pot" once meant prosperity and plenty. Today, that phrase means much more: You can bake, sauté, stir-fry, roast, and poach chicken—so you really can cook chicken in every pot! Whether you're looking for great appetizers, delicious salads and sandwiches, or tempting main dishes, chicken is amazingly adaptable, varied, and nutritious. Chicken is also the economical choice, and is sold in so many forms that whether you have hours to cook dinner, or just minutes to get a meal on the table, you can confidently make chicken your choice.

Contents

Chicken Basics

About this book:

Did you know Americans consume about 70 pounds of chicken per person per year? It's easy to see why. Certainly it has to do with chicken's versatility as an ingredient, as well as its budget-friendly price. And who doesn't like its flavor? Plus, there are other important features that make chicken a top choice for cooks: It's low in fat and calories, many cuts cook quickly, and you can make great dishes with leftovers! Accordingly, this book was designed to highlight recipes that satisfy these great features. Any recipe that derives 30 percent or fewer of its calories from fat is marked with a colored flag labeled "**Low-Fat.**" Recipes that can be quickly prepared—30 minutes or less, from start to finish—are marked with a flag labeled "**Quick-to-Fix.**" And when the dish can be prepared with cooked chicken that you have in the fridge (or buy from the deli department), it's marked with the flag labeled "**Leftovers.**"

At the Market

Chicken comes in more different forms than ever—whole, cut-up, in your choice of parts and portions. In addition to the familiar choices shown in the chart on the opposite page, there are many other chicken products, among them pre-seasoned and ready-to-cook; already roasted, rotisserie-cooked, and in the form of cold cuts and sausage. So serving chicken need not always require turning on the oven or stove: You can pick up some cooked chicken at the supermarket and combine it with other fresh ingredients to make a quick, satisfying meal. Here, a rundown of some of the chicken choices available.

TENDERS These are the tenderloins of the chicken breast—the narrow strips at the side that can be separated from the rest of the breast meat. Note that when you buy chicken tenders you pay a premium for the labor involved in preparing them.

WHAT IS IT?

DEFINING A CHICKEN TENDER

The tender or fillet (bottom) is a narrow, tapering strip at the outer edge of a chicken breast half (top). Tenders are often sold already separated from the chicken breast, and they are the priciest chicken parts of all.

GROUND CHICKEN The already-ground chicken sold at the supermarket is often thigh meat and skin. For lower-fat ground chicken, buy boneless chicken breasts, cut them into chunks, and chop them in the food processor, using an on/off pulse.

CHICKEN NUGGETS These are small pieces of chicken breast, breaded and flash-fried, fast-food style. They can be reheated in the oven or microwave. Children go for chicken nuggets, but note that this product's fat content is quite high.

PRE-SEASONED (UNCOOKED) CHICKEN For a fresh hot meal with minimal preparation, you can buy pre-seasoned chicken packaged by several large companies. The options are seasoned whole chickens, chicken parts, boneless breasts, breast strips for stir-fries or fajitas, or chunks for skewering. The chicken has been prepared with a spice rub or a marinade. All you need to do is cook it.

CHICKEN SAUSAGE (FRESH & FULLY COOKED) Many of the same types of sausages traditionally made with beef, veal, or pork are now made from chicken. Both fresh and fully-cooked sausages are available. Look for Italian (sweet or hot), sun-dried tomato, cilantro,

Fresh Chicken: Basic Options

These are the most popular market forms of chicken, the ones you'll find in most supermarkets. These cuts are also available frozen.

CHICKEN PART	MARKET FORM	HOW MUCH?
Whole and Half Chickens	*Roasters* weigh 5–8 pounds *Broiler-fryers* average 3–4 pounds *Broiler-fryer halves* are split lengthwise	allow ½ pound per person
Quarters	*Breast quarters* consist of a split breast with the wing and back portion—all white meat *Leg quarters* consist of a drumstick, thigh, and back portion—all dark meat	allow ½ pound per person
Breasts	*Whole breasts* have the breastbone and both sets of ribs *Split breasts, or breast halves,* are just one side of the rib cage; they are sold bone in, with skin, and skinned and boned	1 bone-in breast half, or 1 or 2 skinless, boneless halves, per person
Legs	*Legs* consist of the drumstick with the thigh attached *Thighs* are the meaty portion above the knee joint, bone in, with skin, or skinned and boned *Drumsticks* are the lower portion of the leg	1 leg, 2 thighs, or 2 drumsticks per person
Wings	*Whole wings* consist of the little drumstick, the two-boned midjoint, and the short wing tip *Drumettes* are the meaty little drumsticks	as an appetizer, 1 whole wing or 2 drumettes
Livers	Sold in tubs or trays; or, save up the single livers that come with the giblets of a whole chicken (store them in the freezer)	¾ pound for 8 appetizer servings

THE ANATOMY OF A CHICKEN WING

A chicken wing consists of three parts: The meatiest part, with only 1 bone, is the little drumstick, or drumette (left). The middle part, with 2 bones, has less meat. And the bony wing tip has no meat, but can be saved for making stock.

apple, lemon, or basil-flavored sausage; and even andouille- and chorizo-style sausages. If you don't find them at your supermarket, check at a gourmet shop, butcher shop, or in a mail-order specialty foods catalog.

CHICKEN FRANKS Hot dogs made from chicken may be slightly lower—or much lower—in fat than their beef or pork counterparts; it depends upon whether dark meat and skin are included. Like all franks, chicken hot dogs are high in sodium. Be sure to read the label.

Grasp the skin at the edge of the thigh and pull the skin off. Remove any loose pieces of fat.

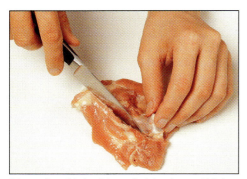

Place the thigh skinned-side down. With a paring knife, cut along the bone, from end to end, on the thinner side of the thigh. Cut around one end of the bone to free it.

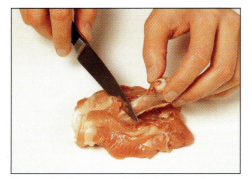

Grasp the free end of the bone and scrape the flesh away from it. Finally, cut around the opposite end of the bone and pull it free.

READY-TO-SERVE ROASTED OR BARBECUED CHICKEN

You can buy these at supermarkets, delis, and restaurants, but they're also distributed by large national firms. Choose from whole or half chickens, legs, or breasts; reheat the chicken in a conventional oven or microwave, or serve it cold.

ROTISSERIE CHICKEN The

popularity of rotisserie chicken—whole chickens cooked on a turning spit—has skyrocketed in the past few years. Many supermarkets feature rotisseries that turn out juicy, crisp-skinned roasted birds all day long. Follow your nose to the deli department to find these, and be sure to choose one that's plump and not dried out.

PRECOOKED, CUT-UP

CHICKEN Seasoned, cooked chicken breast cut into strips or chunks that are ready to go into salads, soups, or pastas.

Getting the Most for Your Money

In terms of your food budget, there are several factors to consider when shopping for chicken. The more chicken is processed (boned, skinned, cut up), the higher the price. Whole chickens are almost always cheaper than chicken parts, but of course you'll have to do the work yourself if you want individual serving portions: Don't forget to factor in the value of your time. Step-by-step how-tos for cutting up a whole chicken are on page 14. Supermarkets

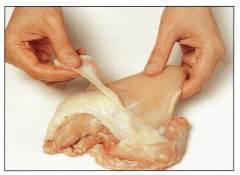

Grasp the skin at the edge of the breast and pull the skin off. Remove any loose pieces of fat.

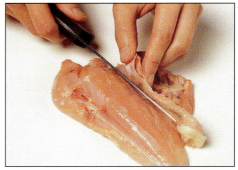

With chicken skinned-side down, start at the thicker side of the breast and work a boning knife between the flesh and the rib bones. Keep the knife pressed against the bones to remove the flesh as cleanly as possible.

Continue cutting along the bones with a slicing motion to free the breast meat in a single piece.

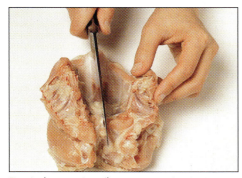

Begin by scoring (but not cutting through) the bony side of the breast with a chef's knife. (This helps when you pop the breastbone out, see below.)

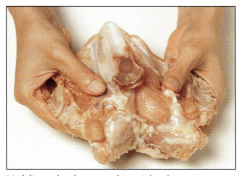

Holding the breast skin-side down, bend the two sides back until the breastbone pops up.

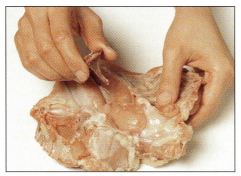

Pull out the breastbone. Note: If you want single-serving breast halves, place the breast skin-side down and cut through it lengthwise.

regularly feature sales on various chicken parts and whole birds; stock up on your favorites when they're well priced and freeze them for future use (see page 13).

SKINLESS, BONELESS VS. BONE-IN WITH SKIN

There are good reasons for buying each of these. With skinless, boneless cuts there is virtually no waste—you get exactly what you pay for. If you're watching your fat intake, you won't want the skin, anyway. And boneless parts cook more quickly. Bone-in cuts with skin cost less, and it's not too tricky to bone them yourself (see techniques, opposite page). Bone-in parts hold their shape better, and the meat is more flavorful when cooked on the bone. Also, the skin keeps the chicken moist while it's cooking.

WHOLE BREASTS VS. BREAST HALVES

Chicken breasts are usually sold split, with each half-breast intended as a portion. However, you can also buy whole, bone-in chicken breasts and split them yourself (see techniques, at left). Let the price—and your time—guide you in your choice.

Safe Handling

As with all meats and seafood, bacteria may be present on raw or undercooked chicken. Several organisms may be present; the one most associated with chicken is *Salmonella enteritidis*, which can cause diarrhea, vomiting, and fever ranging from mild to severe. You can't tell by looking at a chicken whether these bacteria are present. To avoid problems, follow these guidelines:

■ REFRIGERATE OR FREEZE chicken as soon as you bring it home from the store. Remove the store wrapping and rewrap in a zip-seal plastic bag (freezer-proof if freezing). Your refrigerator should be at 40°F. or lower, your freezer at 0°F. (check with a freezer thermometer). Keep chicken refrigerated until you're ready to prepare and cook it. Thaw chicken in the refrigerator or in cold water (see page 13), never on the counter at room temperature.

■ STORE UNCOOKED raw chicken on the bottom shelf of the refrigerator, and be careful not to let its juices touch other foods. If salmonella is present, it can cross-contaminate other foods. The greatest danger from cross-contamination is to foods that will be eaten uncooked, such as fruits and vegetables.

■ KEEP A SEPARATE cutting board for raw meat, poultry, and fish. The best materials are dense ones—either sturdy plastic or a hardwood such as maple. After use, scrub the board with hot soapy water or, if it's not a wooden board, wash it in the dishwasher. (Although a maple or plastic cutting board is preferable for safety, we have photographed all our techniques on white Formica for clarity.)

■ USE A SEPARATE sponge for wiping countertops (apart from the one used for washing dishes). Wash the sponge frequently, preferably in the dishwasher. Replace it often.

- DON'T prepare chicken at the same time you're handling foods to be eaten raw, such as salad greens.

- AFTER PREPARING raw chicken, wash all utensils, your hands, and the counter-top with hot soapy water.

- AFTER CHICKEN is marinated, discard the marinade (unless you are using it for basting, in which case it will get hot enough to be safe). If you want to use the marinade as a sauce, bring it to a full boil and boil for 1 minute.

- DON'T PLACE cooked food on a plate that has held raw chicken. For instance, if you bring raw chicken outside for grilling, bring a second platter to hold the cooked chicken.

- REMOVE ALL the stuffing from a stuffed bird while you're carving. Refrigerate any leftovers separately.

- CHICKEN SHOULD be cooked to an internal temperature of at least 160°F. (see page 19 for more on this).

- THE MAGIC numbers for food safety are 40 and 140. Above 40°F. (refrigerator temperature) or below 140°F. (shortly after cooking), chicken becomes an ideal medium for bacterial growth. Refrigerate leftovers promptly—definitely within two hours, or, in hot weather, immediately.

Selection and Storage

Whether you're shopping for a whole chicken or for parts, use these tips to determine the freshness of your purchase.

- Shop for chicken in a reputable, clean store that has a rapid turnover. The contents of the meat case should look clean and feel cold, and there should be no unpleasant odors present.

- The wrappings of packaged chicken should be well sealed, and not punctured or torn. If the chicken is visible through clear packaging, it should look plump and clean. There should not be an excessive amount of liquid in the package.

- Packaged chicken and chicken products may or may not be marked with a freshness date; it's up to the processor. Sometimes there's a "sell-by" date, which is the last day on which you should purchase the product. You can confidently serve the chicken within two days after the "sell-by" date. Alternatively, the package may have a "use-by" date—the last date on which you should use the product for optimal quality. Buy the package with the latest possible date (these packages are often found *behind* those with more imminent expiration dates), and if you can't use it immediately, freeze it. Freezing "stops the clock" on the expiration date, but use the chicken immediately once you've defrosted it.

- According to the U.S. Department of Agriculture, which regulates the production and sale of poultry, retailers may legally sell fresh or processed poultry products *beyond their expiration date* as long as the product is wholesome. A retailer may also *change* the date on poultry prepared and wrapped in-store, as long as the product is still wholesome. So don't rely totally on what's marked on the package. Take a good look (and sniff) at what you're buying.

- Chicken should always smell fresh—either it should have no aroma at all, or it should have a pleasant "chicken smell." As soon as you get home, unwrap the chicken and sniff. If it smells "off," return it to the store.

- Skin color doesn't indicate the freshness of chicken. Depending on the feed used, chicken skin can vary between shades of white and yellow. However, chicken skin should never look discolored, and the flesh should look pink, not gray.

- If it's a hot day (or you have a long drive home), bring a cooler with you for poultry and other perishables. Never just put bagged groceries in the trunk of a car on a warm day—the temperature in the trunk will be considerably higher than the air outside.

■ Make the meat case your next-to-last stop at the market (frozen food should be last). You want to limit the time that the chicken goes unrefrigerated. Have perishables packed together to help keep the temperature down. When you get home, refrigerate the groceries right away

■ Place packaged fresh chicken in a plastic bag or a shallow dish before refrigerating to contain any leaks.

Thawing Frozen Chicken

Never thaw chicken at room temperature, because of the danger of bacterial growth.

■ If time allows, let chicken thaw in the refrigerator in its original wrappings, allowing 5 hours per pound. A large roaster may take several days to thaw.

■ For speedier thawing, place the wrapped chicken in a sealable plastic bag and place it in a basin of cold water. Change the water every half hour. A whole broiler-fryer will thaw in 2 to 3 hours, a package of boneless breasts in under an hour. You can also thaw frozen chicken in a microwave oven. Follow the directions carefully, and cook the chicken immediately after thawing.

Storing Chicken

Wrap or cover fresh or cooked chicken before refrigerating. When freezing chicken, overwrap with plastic or foil, then label and date the package.

PRODUCT	REFRIGERATED AT 40°F.	FROZEN AT 0°F.
Fresh whole chicken, uncooked	1–2 days	9 months
Fresh chicken parts, uncooked	1–2 days	9 months
Ground chicken, uncooked, and fresh chicken sausage	1–2 days	3–4 months
Liver and giblets	1–2 days	3–4 months
Roast, baked, broiled or grilled chicken, leftover home-cooked	3–4 days	4 months
Cooked chicken in broth or gravy, leftover home-cooked	1–2 days	6 months
Cooked ground chicken (burgers or meatloaf)	3–4 days	2–3 months
Chicken casseroles or soups	3–4 days	4–6 months
Chicken broth or gravy, homemade	1–2 days	6 months
Store-bought roast, barbecued or rotisserie chicken	3–4 days	4 months
Packaged cooked chicken, unopened	5–7 days	3–6 months
Packaged cooked chicken, after opening	1–3 days	4 months
Chicken franks or cold cuts, unopened	2 weeks	1–2 months
Chicken franks or cold cuts, after opening	3–5 days	1–2 months
Cooked chicken sausage	3–4 days	9 months
Chicken salad	3–4 days	not recommended

CUTTING WHOLE CHICKEN INTO SERVING PIECES

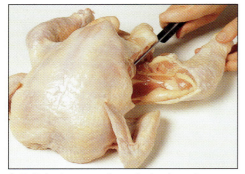

1. Pull the leg away from the body and cut through the skin and flesh with a chef's knife. Bend the thigh back until the joint pops apart, then cut through it.

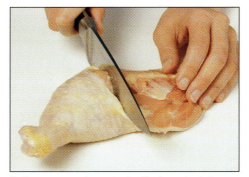

2. Start to cut through the flesh at the joint between the leg and thigh, then bend the two sections together to help you locate the joint. Cut through the joint.

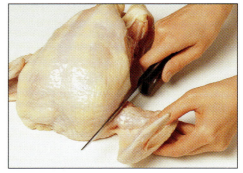

3. Pull the wing away from the body and cut through the skin. Bend the wing back until the joint breaks, then cut through the joint. Cut off the wing tips and discard or save for stock.

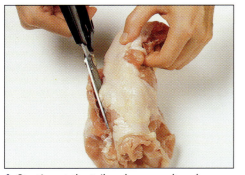

4. Starting at the tail end, use poultry shears to cut through the rib bones along each side of the backbone to separate the breast from the back.

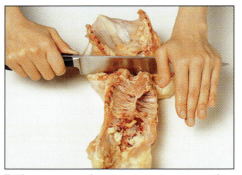

5. Then open up the two pieces to expose the joints at the neck end, and cut through the joints with a chef's knife. Discard the back or save for stock.

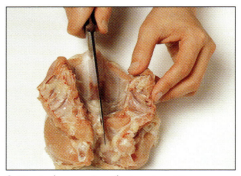

6. Begin by scoring (but not cutting through) the bony side of the breast with a chef's knife. (This helps when you pop the breastbone out, see next step.)

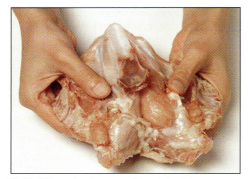

7. Holding the breast skin-side down, bend the two sides back until the breastbone pops up. Pull out the breastbone.

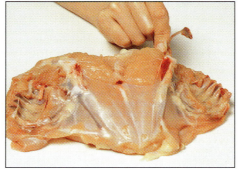

8. Check the flesh at the top of the breast for the wishbone and pull it out. With poultry shears or a chef's knife, cut the breast lengthwise into 2 halves.

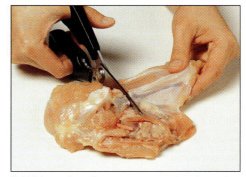

9. With poultry shears, cut crosswise through each breast half to make a total of 4 breast pieces.

Preparing Chicken

Here are some basic techniques for preparing and seasoning chicken before cooking.

CUTTING CHICKEN INTO SERVING PIECES

You can buy a chicken already cut up for cooking, or divide up the bird yourself. To get fairly equal servings of chicken from a whole bird, see the technique photographs on the opposite page. For the recipes in this book, we call for chicken to be cut into 8 serving pieces and occasionally into 10 pieces. The 8 serving pieces are: 2 drumsticks, 2 thighs, and 4 breast quarters. The 10 pieces include the wings (although, because they're largely skin, bone, and fat, wings are not really equivalent to leaner, meatier portions of the bird).

MAKING A CUTLET

Chicken cutlets (also known as scallops) are the quickest-cooking portions for sautéing, and they are also used to roll around fillings. Cutlets are made by pounding skinless, boneless chicken breasts with a meat pounder (or a rolling pin or wooden mallet) until the meat is of an even thickness of ½ or ¼ inch, depending on the recipe (see technique photos, at left). Be gentle: If you're used to pounding veal cutlets for scaloppine, you'll find that chicken is much softer.

CUTTING CHICKEN BREAST FOR STIR-FRY

Ingredients cut into uniform pieces is the secret to a successful stir-fry. Because boneless chicken breasts are tapered in shape, simply cutting across the breast will produce pieces of unequal size. So handle the chicken as follows (see technique photos, at right): Separate the tenderloin and set aside. Then cut the narrow end of the chicken breast crosswise into ½-inch-wide strips until the piece that remains is rectangular. Cut that piece in half lengthwise, then cut each piece crosswise into strips. Finally, cut the tender crosswise into strips.

SEASONING RUBS

Rubbing a mixture of spices, herbs, or other dry flavorings onto chicken skin (or skinless chicken) before cooking serves as the dry equivalent of a marinade. If you're cooking the chicken with the skin on, be sure to rub some of the flavoring mixture under the skin as well. That way, if you remove the skin before eating, the flavor will still be there. If you're particularly fond a certain seasoning combination, mix up a double

Place a boneless chicken breast half on a sheet of plastic wrap on the work surface. Cover with a second sheet of plastic wrap and pound with the flat side of a meat pounder or a rolling pin.

Concentrate on the thicker portion of the breast so that the cutlet is of a uniform thickness. If the cutlet is to be sautéed, it is usually pounded to a ½-inch thickness. If the chicken is to be stuffed and rolled up, it should be pounded to a ¼-inch thickness (as shown above).

Separate the tender from the rest of the boneless breast half. With a sharp knife, cut the narrow end of the chicken breast crosswise into ½-inch-wide strips. Stop as soon as the chicken breast half has been squared off.

Cut the square section of chicken breast lengthwise into 2 pieces (the object here is to cut all pieces uniformly, approximately the width of the chicken tender). Then cut each piece crosswise into ½-inch-wide strips. (Cut the chicken tender crosswise, too.)

or triple batch and store it in a jar, ready for use on short notice.

MARINATING CHICKEN
Letting chicken soak in a marinade is a wonderful way add subtle flavor. There is often something acidic in the marinade, such as wine, vinegar, or citrus juice. Acidic ingredients will penetrate the surface of

TECHNIQUE
STUFFING FLAVORINGS UNDER SKIN

BREASTS Gently loosen the skin from the edge of a bone-in breast half. Slip your fingers under the skin to make a pocket, then place flavorings (such as lemon slices) under the skin. Take care to leave the skin attached in as many spots as possible so the flavoring does not fall out.

WHOLE CHICKEN Place a whole chicken breast-side up with the neck facing away from you. Use your fingers to gently separate the skin from the flesh of the drumsticks and breast, being careful not to tear the skin. Slip in herbs or flavored butter and pat the skin back into place.

the chicken a bit. Most marinades also contain some oil, but this is not a required component. The other ingredients are flavorings—herbs, spices, chilies, citrus zest, ginger, and the like.

When a recipe states that the chicken can be marinated overnight, it's fine to let it sit for up to 24 hours. If the marinade is acidic, however, it can start to break down the chicken and make it mushy: Marinate for no longer than the indicated time. Always place the chicken and marinade in a nonreactive container, such as a glass bowl or baking dish. A heavy-duty sealable plastic bag also works very well, and makes it easy to turn the chicken periodically to coat it with marinade. Place the bag in a dish just in case of leaks. If you're not using a bag, cover the dish. Always marinate chicken in the refrigerator.

STUFFING FLAVORINGS UNDER THE SKIN
Quite a different process from filling a bird with starchy stuffing, this creates a savory layer between the skin and flesh. Even if you remove the skin before you eat the chicken, the flavorful coating will remain. The stuffing can be fresh herbs, lemon slices, or a smooth, creamy mixture that you can spread onto the chicken without tearing the skin. (See technique photos, at left.)

BREADING AND FLOURING
Coating chicken with crumbs, meal, or flour before it is fried, sautéed, or baked creates a tasty crust that may be coarse and crunchy or fine and delicate. These coatings need something to help them adhere to the chicken: This may be beaten eggs or

egg whites, milk, or another liquid. After moistening the chicken, roll it in the coating so that all sides are evenly covered. Gently tap off any excess coating. If you have time, refrigerate the coated chicken pieces for at least 1 hour: This lets the coating set so that it is less likely to come off when the chicken is cooked.

TRUSSING CHICKEN
A roasting chicken is trussed—tied to keep it more compact—primarily to make a nicer presentation (it can also help to keep stuffing from drying out). But forget the

TECHNIQUE
TRUSSING CHICKEN

Bring the "ankles" of the drumsticks together and secure them with a 2-foot length of cotton kitchen string. Tie the string in a double knot.

Twist the wings and tuck the wing tips behind the shoulders of the chicken. This keeps the wing tips from burning and also helps the chicken keep a nicer shape as it roasts.

traditional needle-and-thread technique: Trussing is really very easy. Just hold the ends of the drumsticks together and tie them with a 2-foot length of cotton string. To further enhance the shape of a roast chicken (and to keep the wing tips from scorching), twist the wings and tuck their tips behind the chicken's "shoulders." Snip the string just before carving the chicken.

Cooking Chicken

Versatile as chicken is, you still need to follow some guidelines regarding which parts of the chicken are best for different cooking methods. Cooking techniques are usually divided into "moist heat" methods (stewing, braising, and poaching) and "dry heat" methods (roasting, baking, broiling, and grilling). Stir-frying and sautéing fall somewhere in between the two categories. In general, leaner meats fare better when cooked by moist heat, while juicier, fattier meats will still be moist and juicy after cooking by dry heat. Since chicken is quite lean, these terms are relative: "Leaner" means breast meat, especially skinless breasts; and "fattier" refers to dark meat, such as drumsticks and thighs, especially when cooked with the skin on. The chart on page 18 shows you which cuts are best suited for which methods.

STEWING A stew is chicken and vegetables slow-cooked in a deep pot of broth or other liquid until all the ingredients are tender and the flavors perfectly blended. Some ingredients, such as onions, may be

Poaching Chicken for Salads

CUT	RAW WEIGHT	COOKED WEIGHT (MEAT ONLY)	YIELD (VOLUME) SHREDDED
Breast half, bone-in, skin on	12 oz	6.5 oz	1⅓ cups
Breast half, skinless, boneless	6 oz	4.75 oz	1 cup
Thigh, bone-in, skin on	6 oz	3.75 oz	generous ½ cup
Thigh, skinless, boneless	3.5 oz	2.5 oz	½ cup
Drumstick, skin on	4.75 oz	2 oz	⅓ cup
Whole chicken	3.5 lbs	23 oz	4 cups

Poach chicken breasts (or thighs) in water to cover by at least ½ inch. The poaching water—which can have simple seasonings such as bay leaves or peppercorns—should be at a simmer, not a rolling boil.

After the poached chicken has cooled, shred it, as shown here, by pulling off pieces with your fingers. The shreds will follow the natural grain of the chicken meat. Or, if the recipe calls for it, cut the chicken into chunks.

browned to bring out their flavor, but some recipes omit this step, resulting in a stew with a creamy, delicate color and texture.

BRAISING In this two-stage process, the chicken and other ingredients are browned, then a small amount of liquid is added to the pan. The pan is tightly covered, then the braise simmers on the stovetop or in the oven until the food is tender and the liquid has formed a delicious sauce.

POACHING Most frequently used for skinless breasts, poaching is the gentlest way to cook chicken. The breasts are placed in a shallow pan of simmering liquid (water, broth, or even fruit juice) to which seasonings are usually added. The pan is covered and the chicken cooked at a bare simmer until tender. To poach chicken breasts in quantity for recipes, see above.

SAUTÉING The word sauté means "jump," and when you sauté, you continually shake the pan so that the food "jumps"

Suiting the Method to the Part

Chicken's versatility arises from the fact that almost any cut can be cooked by almost any technique. But some cuts are more suitable for certain methods.

PART	METHODS
Whole broiler-fryer or roaster	Roast, grill (on a spit)
Halves	Roast, bake, broil, grill, braise, stew, oven-fry
Quarters	Bake, broil, grill, oven-fry, braise, stew, fry
Breast halves, bone in	Bake, sauté, broil, grill, oven-fry, braise, poach, fry
Breasts, boneless	Sauté, poach, broil, grill (whole or as kabobs), bake; cook in foil packets; slice for stir-fry; pound for cutlets to sauté or stuff; chop for ground chicken
Legs	Roast, bake, broil, grill, oven-fry, braise, stew, fry
Thighs, bone-in	Bake, broil, grill, oven-fry, braise, stew
Thighs, boneless	Bake, broil, grill, braise, stew, sauté, stir-fry; chop for ground chicken
Drumsticks	Roast, bake, broil, grill, oven-fry, braise, stew, fry
Wings	Bake, broil, grill, braise, fry
Ground chicken	Broil, grill (burgers); bake (meatloaf); simmer (pasta sauce and chili)
Liver	Sauté, broil, grill
Neck and giblets (gizzard, heart)	Sauté and use in stuffing; use in making stock

as it cooks. This constant motion prevents sticking, even when a very small amount of fat is used.

STIR-FRYING This Asian cooking technique is now standard practice in many American kitchens. It's fast, fun, and invites creativity in combining ingredients. You don't need a wok to stir-fry—in fact, on a standard gas or electric stove, a heavy skillet will do a better job. The key factor is to get the wok sizzling hot before adding the oil. The food should be cut into small, uniformly sized pieces (see "Cutting Chicken for Stir-Fry," page 15). Stir and toss the food vigorously until it's just done. Serve stir-fries immediately, while they're steaming hot.

BROILING This dry-heat method evolved from grilling: The food is cooked *under* an open flame (or electrical heating element) rather than *over* an open fire or hot coals. Broiling quickly cooks the flesh of the chicken, and if it's not protected— by its skin, a crumb coating, or a thick, clinging sauce—the chicken will be tough and dry. The recipes in this book direct you to position the oven rack so that the food is 6 to 8 inches below the heat source. If the design of your broiler does not allow you to do this, bake the chicken at a high temperature (450°F.) in the upper third of the oven for approximately the same amount of time (check halfway to be sure it is not overcooking).

GRILLING Cooking chicken parts and burgers over the coals of a barbecue grill adds a delicious smoky flavor. Like broiling, grilling employs a fierce heat that can dry out lean chicken if it's not sauced or basted. Another precaution about grilling: Fatty drippings falling onto the coals can create harmful substances called HCAs, or heterocyclic amines, which are then deposited on the food as the smoke rises. To minimize your exposure to HCAs, don't place the chicken directly over the coals. Instead, push them to the side, leaving a clear space for the drippings to land.

BAKING The difference between "baking" and "roasting" is not entirely clear when you're talking about chicken. But the term "baking" is generally used for cut-up poultry oven-cooked in a shallow pan, covered or uncovered. To help keep the chicken moist, it is often baked with vegetables, or in a sauce.

ROASTING A whole roast chicken, with or without gravy and stuffing, is the essence of home cooking. For this dry-heat method, in which the food is cooked by the circulating hot air in the oven, the chicken should be elevated above the bottom of the pan on a rack (see page 21). Rubbing chicken skin with fat before roasting helps it brown nicely; basting helps, too, but it doesn't keep the chicken moist, because the basting liquid rolls right off the chicken skin. It's important to let a roast chicken stand for about 5 minutes before carving: This allows the juices to redistribute themselves throughout the meat so that it's juicy through and through. For pointers on carving a roast chicken, see page 294. To some people, roast chicken is not complete without a rich pan gravy; see page 202 for how-tos on preparing this simple sauce.

When Is It Done?

■ For the sake of food safety, chicken must be unequivocally done—completely cooked through. Rare poultry is neither palatable nor safe to eat. Chicken should be cooked to an internal temperature of at least 160°F., and the best way to test this is with an instead-read thermometer (see page 21). However, even when cooked to this temperature, chicken may not be "done" in terms of appetizing taste and texture. The meat may still be pink, and the juices may appear cloudy when the flesh is pierced with a knife. You'll want to continue cooking the chicken until the juices run clear, and when, on a whole

chicken, the leg joint will wiggle easily in its socket. At this point, the thermometer will read about 170°F.

■ "Done" does not mean overdone, and chicken (especially when cooked by dry-heat methods such as roasting, baking, or broiling) can easily go from perfectly cooked to dry, tough, and tasteless. Check doneness promptly, and remember that retained heat in roasted and baked chicken will continue to cook the bird a bit after it comes out of the oven.

■ Breast meat, being leaner, cooks more quickly than the dark meat of the legs and thighs. If you want perfectly done chicken when cooking a cut-up bird, check the breast portions first, and remove them when they're done, leaving the dark-meat parts to finish cooking. Keep the breast portions warm until serving time by covering them with foil.

■ Check the chart below for information on cooking times and temperatures.

Poultry Doneness Chart

The doneness tests suggested at below are useful indicators, but for safety's sake, always test chicken with a thermometer. When cooking white- and dark-meat parts together, check the white-meat parts for doneness first. If they are done, remove them and let the dark meat continue cooking until it tests done.

CUT	COOK TO TEMPERATURE	DONENESS TEST
Whole chicken	180°F.	drumstick wiggles easily in socket; juices run clear when chicken is pierced
Whole stuffed chicken	180°F. *(chicken)* 165°F. *(stuffing)*	*chicken:* as above *stuffing:* **must** be checked with a thermometer
Legs, breasts, thighs, drumsticks, or wings, bone-in	170°F.	juices run clear; flesh appears opaque, not translucent, when cut
Breasts or thighs, boneless	160°F.	flesh is opaque when cut
Ground chicken	165°F.	meat appears opaque and is firm to touch; juices run clear
Combination dishes made with *cooked* chicken	165°F.	check with thermometer
Leftovers, reheated	165°F.	check with thermometer

Chicken Nutrition

■ Eating chicken—and substituting it for some of the red meat in your diet—is an excellent way to get your share of protein without consuming a lot of fat. For the most healthful chicken dishes, cook the chicken without the skin, or remove the skin before eating it (see "Fat-Cutting Techniques"). In addition to high-quality protein, chicken is an excellent source of B vitamins, including B_6, B_{12}, and niacin; and of the minerals iron and phosphorus.

■ Most meat and poultry contain roughly the same amount of cholesterol: 20 to 25mg per ounce. Cholesterol is not found in the skin, but in the lean muscle of animal protein. So chicken—even skinless chicken—does not contain markedly less cholesterol than beef or other meats. However, blood cholesterol levels are also affected by saturated fat intake, and skinless chicken is lower in saturated fat than any cut of beef, pork, or lamb.

■ Many health authorities agree that most people would be healthier, suffering less from obesity and certain life-threatening diseases, if the percentage of fat in the American diet were cut to less than 30 percent of total calories. This refers to overall food intake over the course of a day, rather than to the fat content of a single dish or meal. Reducing the amount of red meat eaten daily is one of the primary recommendations for reducing fat intake.

■ The recipes in this book flagged as "Low-Fat" derive 30 percent or less of their calories from fat. The index of Low-Fat recipes (see page 335) guides you to recipes in this "30-percent and under" category.

■ Many recipes in these pages have special tips under the heading "To Reduce the Fat." These suggested ingredient substitutions and alternate techniques can lower the fat content, but not necessarily to the 30-percent level.

■ Some dishes in this book may appear to have a high calorie content, but they are almost always one-dish meals of one sort or another, where accompaniments that would add calories are not necessary. A number of recipes in the Casseroles, One-Dish Meals, and Oven to Table chapters fall into this category: They include vegetables and a starch (such as potatoes, pasta, or grains) along with the chicken.

Fat-Cutting Techniques

■ Removing the skin from chicken lowers the fat content of chicken dramatically (see the chart below). However, studies have shown that if you're cooking by a dry-heat method (roasting, baking, broiling, or grilling), very little of the fat will be

Nutrition Chart

These figures are for 3½-ounce cooked portions (the standard used by the USDA). Actual portion sizes vary. Figures are rounded up to the nearest whole number.

CUT	CALORIES	FAT	SATURATED FAT	CHOLESTEROL
Broiler-fryer, with skin	239	22g	4g	88mg
Broiler-fryer, no skin	190	7g	2g	89mg
Roaster, with skin	223	13g	4g	76mg
Roaster, no skin	167	7g	2g	75mg
Breast, with skin	197	8g	2g	84mg
Breast, no skin	165	4g	1g	85mg
Leg, with skin	232	13g	13g	92mg
Leg, no skin	191	8g	8g	94mg
Thigh, with skin	247	16g	4g	93mg
Thigh, no skin	209	11g	3g	95mg
Drumstick, with skin	216	11g	3g	91mg
Drumstick, no skin	172	6g	1g	93mg
Wing, with skin	290	20g	5g	84mg
Wing, no skin	203	8g	2g	85mg

absorbed by the meat during cooking. So leave the skin on while the chicken cooks, and then remove it before eating.

■ Cooking chicken with the skin on keeps it moist and flavorful, and in most cases the bird looks much more appetizing if brought to the table with its skin on. Note, however, that if you roast or bake skin-on chicken with vegetables, the vegetables—especially starchy ones such as potatoes —will absorb some of the fat.

■ When you sauté skin-on chicken, the fat will end up in the pan; you have the option of pouring it off before continuing with the recipe.

■ When you braise or stew skin-on chicken, however, the fat melts into the cooking liquid and become an integral part of the dish. It's best to remove the skin from chicken parts used in such dishes. Occasionally, in some old-fashioned stews, we have left the skin on, but if you'd prefer, you can remove the skin before cooking.

It's easy to remove the slippery skin from a drumstick if, after peeling the skin halfway back, you grasp it with a paper towel.

■ Pan drippings from roast chicken make delicious sauces and gravies, but they're very fatty. Either chill the drippings and skim off the fat, or pour them into a gravy separator (see below), which will separate the clear juices, leaving the fat behind.

The Right Stuff

The equipment you need to be a proficient chicken cook.

BONING KNIFE A boning knife for chicken should have a blade that is sharp enough to scrape flesh from bones, but also flexible enough to follow the contours of rib bones.

POULTRY SHEARS Stainless-steel scissors with short, sharp blades, and the strength to cut through bones.

CHEF'S KNIFE A knife with a heavy, wedge-shaped blade is a kitchen essential for chopping vegetables and cooked chicken. Choose a size between 8 and 10 inches, depending on your strength and the size of your hands.

MEAT POUNDER Although you can use a wooden mallet to pound chicken, it's easier to keep a metal pounder clean. Most meat pounders come with both flat face and a faceted face (for tenderizing meat); be sure to use the flat side on chicken.

V-RACK This wisely-designed accessory not only elevates a roasting bird out of the fatty juices in the pan (helping it to brown and crisp), it also holds the chicken securely in position so that it doesn't roll or tip.

ROASTING PAN A big, deep roasting pan (about 15 x 11-inch) can handle a big stuffed chicken plus vegetables, and has many other kitchen uses, too. Smaller birds can be roasted in a 9 x 13-inch baking pan. Avoid disposable foil pans, which are dangerously flimsy and can buckle as you take them from the oven.

BULB BASTER Easier to use than a spoon, a bulb baster sucks up juices from the pan so that you can squeeze them over the chicken, focusing on particular parts of the bird, if necessary.

INSTANT-READ THERMOMETER A pocket-size device about the size of a fountain pen, this is the professional's favorite thermometer. Rather than leaving it in the roast (which allows precious juices to escape), the shaft of the thermometer is inserted briefly; the temperature will register within 5 to 10 seconds.

GRAVY SEPARATOR An ingenious gadget for defatting pan juices from roast or pan-cooked chicken. Pour the juices into the cup, and the fat rises to the top, allowing you to pour off the defatted juices through the spout.

Appetizers & First Courses

Meant to stimulate the appetite for what follows—or to spark a thirst for ice-cold drinks—these tasty bites include sit-down starters as well as festive fingerfoods. Here's where fun foods, such as Buffalo wings, Chinese dumplings, mini-meatballs, and single-serving pizzas take center stage.

Little Chicken Salad Rolls

To make this Asian-inspired first course, chicken is poached in a ginger broth, then shredded and tossed with a soy-vinegar dressing, shredded carrot, and slivered bell pepper. The salad is rolled up in buttery-soft Boston lettuce leaves and served with roasted peanuts and a sweet-and-sour dipping sauce.

4	tablespoons soy sauce
4	tablespoons rice vinegar
1	teaspoon sugar
1	cup chicken broth, canned or homemade (page 45)
2	slices (¼ inch thick) fresh ginger
¾	pound skinless, boneless chicken breasts or thighs
1	carrot, shredded
1	red bell pepper, slivered
16	Boston lettuce leaves
16	fresh mint leaves
3	tablespoons finely chopped dry-roasted peanuts

1. In small saucepan, stir together 3 tablespoons of soy sauce, 1 tablespoon of vinegar, and the sugar. Stir over low heat until sugar has dissolved. Set dipping sauce aside to cool.

2. In large skillet, bring broth and ginger to a boil over medium heat. Add chicken, reduce to a simmer, cover, and cook 12 minutes or until chicken is cooked through, turning chicken over midway through cooking. Remove chicken from broth (discard broth). When cool enough to handle, shred chicken.

3. In medium bowl, stir together remaining 3 tablespoons vinegar and 1 tablespoon soy sauce. Add shredded chicken, carrot, and bell pepper, and toss to combine.

4. Place lettuce leaves, hollow-side up, on work surface. Place a mint leaf in each. Dividing evenly, spoon chicken mixture into lettuce leaves and sprinkle peanuts on top. Roll leaves up and serve with dipping sauce.

FROM THE FRIDGE

Use 1¾ cups shredded cooked chicken breasts or thighs. Omit step 2. In step 3, add 1 teaspoon finely grated fresh ginger to chicken mixture.

LOW FAT

Prep Time: 40 minutes
Cooking Time: 15 minutes
Makes 8 servings

NUTRITION INFORMATION
Per Serving
Calories 84
Total Fat 2g
Saturated Fat 0.5g
Cholesterol 25mg
Sodium 592mg
Protein 12g
Carbohydrates 4g

Chicken & Goat Cheese Quesadillas

The quesadilla, whose name derives from the Spanish word for cheese, is great with almost any cheese. Try sharp Cheddar, tangy feta, or creamy Fontina. Even cream cheese would work.

4	ounces mild goat cheese
8	flour tortillas (6-inch diameter)
1	cup shredded cooked chicken breasts or thighs—leftover or poached (page 17)
½	cup mild bottled salsa
1	pickled jalapeño pepper, finely chopped with seeds
2	tablespoons olive oil

1. Spread goat cheese on 4 tortillas. Sprinkle chicken on top. Spoon salsa (2 tablespoons per tortilla) over chicken and sprinkle with jalapeño. Top with remaining 4 tortillas.

2. In small nonstick skillet, heat 1½ teaspoons of oil over medium heat. Add 1 quesadilla and cook 1 minute or until bottom tortilla is crisp and golden brown. Turn quesadilla over and cook 1 minute or until crisp and golden brown on second side. Repeat using 1½ teaspoons of oil for each quesadilla. Cut each quesadilla into 4 wedges. Serve hot or warm.

TO REDUCE THE FAT

Reduce oil to 1 tablespoon and use it to brush outsides of quesadillas. Place them on baking sheet and bake in preheated 400°F. oven 5 minutes or until tortillas are crisped and cheese is melted. Cut into wedges as directed.
Calories 82, Total Fat 4g, Saturated Fat 2g, Cholesterol 13mg, Sodium 184mg, Protein 5g, Carbohydrates 6g

QUICK TO FIX
LEFTOVERS

Prep Time: 15 minutes
Cooking Time: 10 minutes
Makes 16 wedges

NUTRITION INFORMATION
Per Wedge
Calories 90
Total Fat 5g
Saturated Fat 2g
Cholesterol 13mg
Sodium 184mg
Protein 5g
Carbohydrates 6g

LITTLE CHICKEN SALAD ROLLS

CHICKEN & BROCCOLI QUICHE

Prep Time: 15 minutes
Cooking Time: 1 hour 10 minutes
Makes 6 servings

NUTRITION INFORMATION
Per Serving
Calories 448
Total Fat 32g
Saturated Fat 17g
Cholesterol 234mg
Sodium 582mg
Protein 20g
Carbohydrates 20g

Chicken & Broccoli Quiche

The good news is that quiche has made a comeback after slipping from sight for a while. This savory custard pie is tasty warm or cold, and slender wedges of quiche make attractive appetizers. For a light meal, serve a larger portion with a vinaigrette-dressed salad on the side.

- 1 store-bought pie crust (9-inch diameter), thawed if frozen
- 1½ cups broccoli florets
- ½ cup milk
- ¾ cup heavy or whipping cream
- 4 large eggs
- ½ teaspoon salt
- ¼ teaspoon cayenne pepper
- 1 cup shredded sharp Cheddar cheese (4 ounces)
- 1 cup shredded cooked chicken breasts or thighs—leftover or poached (page 17)

1. Preheat oven to 375°F. Line a 9-inch pie plate with pie crust. With fork, prick bottom of pie crust. Line pie shell with aluminum foil and fill with pie weights or dried beans. Bake for 15 minutes. Remove foil and weights; bake for 10 minutes or until crust is cooked through. Set aside. Leave oven on.

2. Meanwhile, bring medium saucepan of water to a boil. Add broccoli, cover, and cook 5 minutes or until tender. Drain well. (Or steam broccoli for 5 minutes.)

3. In medium bowl, whisk together milk, cream, eggs, salt, and cayenne. Stir in Cheddar. Scatter broccoli and chicken in baked shell. Place shell on a baking sheet and pour in custard mixture. Bake 35 to 40 minutes or until custard is set. Cool 30 minutes before cutting.

CHICKEN & ASPARAGUS QUICHE Substitute 1 cup asparagus pieces (½-inch lengths) for broccoli. Substitute Gruyère for Cheddar. In step 3, add 3 thinly sliced scallions and ⅓ cup minced fresh dill to custard mixture.
Calories 447, Total Fat 32g, Saturated Fat 16g, Cholesterol 235mg, Sodium 517mg, Protein 20g, Carbohydrates 19g

Prep Time: 25 minutes
Cooking Time: 15 minutes
Makes 24 fritters

NUTRITION INFORMATION
Per Fritter
Calories 60
Total Fat 4g
Saturated Fat 1g
Cholesterol 19mg
Sodium 79mg
Protein 4g
Carbohydrates 3g

Chicken Fritters

Old-fashioned fritters are deep-fried, but these herbed chicken patties are briefly sautéed, and then baked—a far healthier idea. Use a nonstick pan to protect the delicate crumb coating. Serve the fritters with a bowl of salsa, or arrange them on a platter with broiled halved plum tomatoes.

- 1½ cups finely chopped cooked chicken breasts or thighs—leftover or poached (page 17)
- ⅓ cup grated Parmesan cheese
- ¼ cup chopped fresh basil leaves
- 1 large egg
- 2 tablespoons heavy or whipping cream
- 1 teaspoon grated lemon zest
- 1 tablespoon fresh lemon juice
- ¼ teaspoon salt
- ¼ teaspoon freshly ground black pepper
- 4 slices firm-textured white bread (4 ounces)
- ¼ cup olive oil
- 8 lemon wedges

1. Preheat oven to 250°F. In large bowl, combine chicken, Parmesan, basil, egg, cream, lemon zest, lemon juice, salt, and pepper, and mix well. Shape into 24 small oval patties.

2. In food processor, process bread until finely crumbled. Transfer to large plate or sheet of waxed paper. Dip patties into bread crumbs, coating each side.

3. In large nonstick skillet, heat 2 tablespoons of oil over medium heat. Add as many fritters as will fit comfortably without crowding, and sauté 5 minutes or until golden brown on both sides. Transfer to large baking sheet. Repeat with remaining 2 tablespoons oil and patties. Bake patties 5 minutes or until piping hot. Serve with lemon wedges.

Buffalo Chicken Wings
with Blue Cheese Sauce

This modern classic juxtaposes spicy (wings), creamy (blue cheese sauce), and crunchy (celery) to perfection. How hot you make the wings is up to you—increase or decrease the hot pepper sauce to taste.

Prep Time: 10 minutes
Cooking Time: 40 minutes
Makes 8 servings

WINGS:

- ½ cup hot pepper sauce (red)
- 2 tablespoons olive oil
- 1½ teaspoons salt
- 1 teaspoon freshly ground black pepper
- 16 chicken wings (about 3 pounds), wing tips removed, or 32 drumettes
- 6 stalks celery, cut into 3 x ¼-inch matchsticks

BLUE CHEESE SAUCE:

- 1 cup reduced-fat sour cream
- ¼ cup reduced-fat mayonnaise
- 1 teaspoon Worcestershire sauce
- 4 ounces blue cheese, crumbled
- 2 scallions, minced

1. Preheat oven to 450°F. Prepare Wings: In large bowl, whisk together hot pepper sauce, oil, salt, and pepper. Cut wings in half at joint. Add to bowl and toss well to coat. Place chicken wings on jelly-roll pan. Pour any remaining marinade over chicken. Bake for 35 to 40 minutes, turning wings occasionally, until skin is browned and lightly crisp.

2. Meanwhile, prepare Blue Cheese Sauce: In medium bowl, stir together sour cream, mayonnaise, and Worcestershire. Stir in blue cheese and scallions. Cover and refrigerate until serving time. Serve hot wings with celery sticks and Blue Cheese Sauce.

IN A HURRY?

Use bottled blue cheese salad dressing instead of making Blue Cheese Sauce.

NUTRITION INFORMATION
Per Serving
Calories 348
Total Fat 26g
Saturated Fat 9g
Cholesterol 75mg
Sodium 1189mg
Protein 23g
Carbohydrates 6g

Spicy-Sweet Chicken Wings

Don't discard the wing tips you've cut off: Save them for making chicken stock.

Prep Time: 25 minutes plus
     marinating time
Cooking Time: 40 minutes
Makes 48 pieces

- ¾ cup fresh lime juice (about 9 limes)
- ⅓ cup packed light brown sugar
- 3 tablespoons olive oil
- 1½ teaspoons salt
- 1½ teaspoons cayenne pepper
- 1½ teaspoons ground ginger
- ¾ teaspoon freshly ground black pepper
- ¼ teaspoon ground allspice
- ¼ teaspoon ground nutmeg
- 24 chicken wings (about 4½ pounds), wing tips removed

1. In large bowl, whisk together lime juice, brown sugar, oil, salt, cayenne, ginger, black pepper, allspice, and nutmeg. Measure out 3 tablespoons of lime mixture and set aside to use as a basting mixture.

2. Cut wings in half at joint and remove skin from drumette (meatier portion of wing with only 1 bone). Add all the chicken to lime mixture in large bowl, and toss to coat. Cover and refrigerate at least 1 hour or up to 4 hours.

3. Preheat oven to 400°F. Lift wings from marinade (discard any marinade left in large bowl). Arrange wings on jelly-roll pan. Bake for 40 minutes, turning wings occasionally, until chicken is cooked through. Brush chicken with reserved basting mixture 10 minutes before end of cooking time.

CHILI-HONEY GLAZED DRUMETTES In step 1, reduce lime juice to 3 tablespoons; substitute 2 tablespoons honey for brown sugar; omit ginger, allspice, and nutmeg, and add 1 tablespoon chili powder. Substitute 48 drumettes for chicken wings and remove skin. Marinate and bake as directed.
Calories 37, Total Fat 1.5g, Saturated Fat 0.5g, Cholesterol 16mg, Sodium 66mg, Protein 5g, Carbohydrates 1g

NUTRITION INFORMATION
Per Piece
Calories 51
Total Fat 3g
Saturated Fat 1g
Cholesterol 14mg
Sodium 63mg
Protein 5g
Carbohydrates 1g

BUFFALO CHICKEN WINGS WITH BLUE CHEESE SAUCE

Curried Chicken Turnovers

These two-bite triangular turnovers are reminiscent of samosas—little Indian snacks filled with vegetables or meat. Though small in size, the phyllo-wrapped turnovers pack a lot of flavor, thanks to curry powder, ground ginger, and mango chutney. Serve them with additional chutney for dipping.

    2 teaspoons olive oil
    1 small onion, minced
    2 cloves garlic, minced
 1½ teaspoons curry powder
   ¾ teaspoon ground ginger
    1 all-purpose potato (4 ounces), peeled
       and cut into ¼-inch dice
   ½ cup chicken broth
   ½ teaspoon salt
    2 cups diced (½ inch) cooked chicken breasts
       or thighs—leftover or poached (page 17)
    3 tablespoons mango chutney, finely chopped
  10 sheets (11 x 17-inch) phyllo dough
    6 tablespoons butter, melted

1. In large nonstick skillet, heat oil over medium heat. Add onion and garlic, and cook, stirring frequently, 7 minutes or until onion is tender. Stir in curry powder and ginger, and cook until fragrant, about 1 minute.

2. Stir in potato, ¼ cup of water, the broth, and salt, and bring to a boil. Reduce to a simmer, cover, and cook 7 minutes or until potato is tender. Remove from heat. Transfer potato mixture to medium bowl and stir in chicken and chutney. Let filling cool to room temperature.

3. Preheat oven to 400°F. Work with 2 sheets of phyllo at a time and keep remainder covered with plastic wrap. Lay 1 sheet of phyllo on work surface with long side facing you. Brush with some of the melted butter. Place second sheet on top and brush with butter. Cut crosswise into 8 strips.

4. Place a generous teaspoon of filling onto top corner of each strip. Fold up flag-fashion (see technique photos, at right). As they are made, place turnovers on lightly greased baking sheet and brush their tops with some butter. Repeat with remaining dough and filling. Bake for 10 minutes. Flip turnovers over and bake for 5 minutes or until golden brown. Serve hot.

CURRIED CHICKEN CRESCENTS Prepare filling as directed. Substitute one 8-ounce package plus one 4-ounce package of refrigerator crescent roll dough (a total of 12 crescent rolls) for phyllo. Omit melted butter. Unroll 1 triangle of crescent roll dough at a time. Spoon generous 3 tablespoons filling onto wide end of a triangle and roll up toward pointed end. Turn ends down and slightly under to form crescent. Bake at 400°F. for 15 minutes or until golden brown and piping hot. Makes 12 large turnovers.
Per turnover: Calories 172, Total Fat 7g, Saturated Fat 2g, Cholesterol 20mg, Sodium 415mg, Protein 10g, Carbohydrates 17g

LEFTOVERS

Prep Time: 45 minutes
Cooking Time: 30 minutes
Makes 40 turnovers

NUTRITION INFORMATION
Per Turnover
Calories 51
Total Fat 2.5g
Saturated Fat 1g
Cholesterol 11mg
Sodium 101mg
Protein 3g
Carbohydrates 4g

TECHNIQUE

MAKING A FLAG FOLD

After cutting phyllo into strips, place filling on top corner and fold short end diagonally over filling so it meets the long side. Flip the triangle downward.

Flip the triangle downward again, this time along the diagonal. Continue folding in this fashion (like folding a flag) until you reach the end of the strip.

CURRIED CHICKEN TURNOVERS

CHICKEN & RED PEPPER SKEWERS WITH ASIAN PEANUT SAUCE

Prep Time: 20 minutes
Cooking Time: 5 minutes
Makes 4 servings

NUTRITION INFORMATION
Per Serving
Calories 176
Total Fat 9.5g
Saturated Fat 2g
Cholesterol 47mg
Sodium 556mg
Protein 16g
Carbohydrates 8g

Chicken & Red Pepper Skewers with Asian Peanut Sauce

The tangy cilantro-laced peanut sauce is great with grilled beef kabobs, too. When you slip the chicken and pepper pieces onto the skewers, don't pack them too tightly, or they won't cook evenly.

PEANUT SAUCE:

- 3 tablespoons peanut butter
- 1 tablespoon rice vinegar
- 1 tablespoon lower-sodium soy sauce
- 2 teaspoons sugar
- 1 clove garlic, crushed and peeled
- ¼ cup finely chopped cilantro

CHICKEN & PEPPERS:

- 2 tablespoons lower-sodium soy sauce
- 1 teaspoon sugar
- 1 teaspoon sesame oil
- ½ teaspoon ground ginger
- 1 clove garlic, crushed and peeled
- ½ pound skinless, boneless chicken thighs, cut into 36 pieces
- 1 red bell pepper, cut into 24 chunks

1. Make Peanut Sauce: In food processor or blender, combine peanut butter, vinegar, soy sauce, sugar, garlic, and ¼ cup of water. Process until smooth. Transfer peanut mixture to bowl and stir in cilantro.

2. Prepare Chicken: In medium bowl, stir together soy sauce, sugar, sesame oil, ginger, and garlic. Add chicken and toss to coat.

3. Preheat broiler. Alternating chicken and bell pepper, thread 3 pieces of chicken and 2 pieces of bell pepper on each of 12 skewers (6 to 8 inches long). Broil skewers 6 inches from heat, turning skewers midway, for 5 minutes or until chicken is cooked through. Serve with Peanut Sauce.

TO REDUCE THE FAT

Use chicken breasts instead of thighs and use reduced-fat peanut butter in peanut sauce.

Calories 171, Total Fat 6.5g, Saturated Fat 1g, Cholesterol 33mg, Sodium 540mg, Protein 17g, Carbohydrates 12g

Prep Time: 15 minutes
Cooking Time: 30 minutes
Makes 24 pieces

NUTRITION INFORMATION
Per Piece
Calories 31
Total Fat 1g
Saturated Fat 0g
Cholesterol 16mg
Sodium 76mg
Protein 4g
Carbohydrates 0g

Thai Cilantro Drumettes

Cilantro, also sold as coriander or Chinese parsley, is sometimes sold with its roots still attached. If you can buy it this way, don't chop off the roots, which are a signature ingredient in Thai cooking. Rinse the roots well before using them, and then enjoy the authentic Thai flavor.

- ¾ cup cilantro sprigs, with roots if possible
- 2 cloves garlic, crushed and peeled
- 1 tablespoon chopped fresh ginger
- ¼ cup fresh lime juice (about 3 limes)
- 1 tablespoon olive oil
- 1 pickled jalapeño pepper, with seeds
- ½ teaspoon salt
- 24 chicken drumettes (about 2 pounds), skin removed

1. Preheat oven to 425°F. In food processor or blender, combine cilantro, garlic, ginger, lime juice, oil, jalapeño, and salt. Process until combined. Add 3 tablespoons of water and process to a smooth paste. Transfer cilantro mixture to a shallow glass baking dish.

2. Add drumettes to baking dish with cilantro mixture and rub mixture into them. Bake drumettes for 30 minutes or until skin is golden brown and chicken is cooked through.

Chicken Dumplings with Sesame Dipping Sauce

Imagine how impressed your guests will be when you serve this Chinese-restaurant specialty at home! The dumplings are easy to make using store-bought wonton wrappers, which are sold in many supermarkets and in Asian grocery stores.

CHICKEN DUMPLINGS:

- ½ pound ground chicken
- ¼ cup thinly sliced scallions
- ¼ cup minced canned water chestnuts
- ¼ cup chopped cilantro
- 4 teaspoons lower-sodium soy sauce
- ½ teaspoon ground ginger
- ½ teaspoon salt
- ¼ teaspoon freshly ground black pepper
- 24 wonton wrappers (3-inch square)

SESAME DIPPING SAUCE:

- ¼ cup lower-sodium soy sauce
- 1 tablespoon sesame oil
- 2 teaspoons rice vinegar
- ½ teaspoon sugar
- ¼ cup thinly sliced scallions

1. Prepare the Chicken Dumplings: In medium bowl, combine chicken, scallions, water chestnuts, cilantro, soy sauce, ginger, salt, and pepper. Mix well.

2. Working with several wonton wrappers at a time and keeping remainder loosely covered with dampened cloth, start filling wontons: With point of a wrapper facing you, place generous teaspoonful of filling on bottom half of wrapper. With moistened finger or pastry brush, moisten two sides of wonton (see technique photo, top right). Fold two moistened sides over filling and press to seal and form a triangle (bottom photo). Repeat with remaining wonton wrappers and filling.

3. Make the Sesame Dipping Sauce: In small bowl, whisk together soy sauce, sesame oil, vinegar, sugar, and scallions.

4. Bring a large pot of water to a boil. Add dumplings and cook 4 minutes or until dumplings float to surface and chicken is cooked through (filling will be firm to the touch). Drain. Serve with Sesame Dipping Sauce.

WONTON SOUP Prepare dumplings as directed. In medium saucepan, bring 3 cups chicken broth and 3 cups water to a boil over medium heat. Add dumplings and cook as directed. Stir Sesame Dipping Sauce ingredients directly into broth. Makes 6 servings.

Calories 201, Total Fat 7g, Saturated Fat 1.5g, Cholesterol 34mg, Sodium 1467mg, Protein 11g, Carbohydrates 22g

LOW FAT

Prep Time: 30 minutes
Cooking Time: 15 minutes
Makes 24 dumplings

NUTRITION INFORMATION
Per Dumpling
Calories 47
Total Fat 1.5g
Saturated Fat 0.5g
Cholesterol 9mg
Sodium 235mg
Protein 3g
Carbohydrates 5g

TECHNIQUE

MAKING DUMPLINGS

Place filling on one half of wonton wrapper, then use your finger dipped into water to moisten two sides.

Fold wonton wrapper over filling and press the dough together from the edges all the way up to the filling. This seals the dumpling and ensures that it will not fall apart when it's boiled.

CHICKEN DUMPLINGS WITH SESAME DIPPING SAUCE

COCONUT-PEANUT NUGGETS WITH CURRY DIPPING SAUCE

Prep Time: 20 minutes
Cooking Time: 15 minutes
Makes 6 servings

NUTRITION INFORMATION
Per Serving
Calories 471
Total Fat 21g
Saturated Fat 8g
Cholesterol 90mg
Sodium 892mg
Protein 45g
Carbohydrates 27g

Coconut-Peanut Nuggets with Curry Dipping Sauce

The creamy dipping sauce offers a pleasing contrast to the crunchy-crusted chicken nuggets, with their delectable coating of spices, flaked coconut, and chopped peanuts.

2½	teaspoons ground cumin
1½	teaspoons ground coriander
1	teaspoon salt
1	teaspoon curry powder
½	teaspoon freshly ground black pepper
2	pounds chicken tenders or 1-inch chunks of skinless, boneless breast or thigh
1½	cups flaked coconut
1	cup peanuts, finely chopped
2	egg whites
1	cup plain low-fat yogurt
¼	cup mango chutney, finely chopped
4	teaspoons fresh lemon juice

1. Preheat oven to 425°F. In large bowl, stir together cumin, coriander, salt, curry powder, and pepper. Measure out 2 teaspoons of spice mixture and set aside. Add chicken tenders and mix to coat. In shallow dish or pie plate, combine coconut and peanuts. In another shallow dish, beat egg whites with 1 tablespoon of water. Dip chicken into egg white mixture, then into coconut mixture, pressing it into chicken.

2. Place coated chicken on greased jelly-roll pan and bake for 15 minutes or until cooked through.

3. Meanwhile, in medium bowl, stir together yogurt, chutney, lemon juice, and reserved spice mixture. Serve hot nuggets with cool dipping sauce.

LOW FAT

QUICK TO FIX

Prep Time: 5 minutes
Cooking Time: 15 minutes
Makes 6 servings

NUTRITION INFORMATION
Per Serving
Calories 353
Total Fat 12g
Saturated Fat 2g
Cholesterol 88mg
Sodium 820mg
Protein 37g
Carbohydrates 18g

Honey-Mustard Chicken Tenders

Chicken tenders, cut from the underside of the breast, are (as their name implies) choice morsels. They're also among the most expensive cuts, so you may want to substitute breast or thigh meat that you cut up yourself. Either way, the herbed honey-mustard coating turns the chicken into a treat.

6	tablespoons spicy brown mustard
4	teaspoons honey
1½	teaspoons dried tarragon
1	teaspoon salt
½	teaspoon cayenne pepper
2	pounds chicken tenders or 1-inch chunks of skinless, boneless breast or thigh
6	slices firm-textured white bread (6 ounces)
¼	cup olive oil

1. Preheat oven to 425°F. In large bowl, whisk together mustard, honey, tarragon, salt, and cayenne. Add chicken tenders, turning to coat.

2. In food processor, process bread to fine crumbs. Transfer crumbs to plate or sheet of waxed paper. Dip chicken in crumbs, pressing to coat. Transfer to a lightly greased baking sheet. Drizzle oil over chicken and bake for 15 minutes or until crust is golden brown and set and chicken is cooked through.

Chicken Liver Mousse

If your bank account doesn't permit you to serve foie gras as a first course, try this light, velvety mousse instead. Rich with butter and cream, and boasting an unexpected shot of whiskey, the mousse is delicious on slightly salty crackers or triangles of crisp toast.

  3 tablespoons unsalted butter
  1 large onion, thinly sliced
  1 large McIntosh apple, peeled and thinly sliced
1½ pounds chicken livers, trimmed
  1 teaspoon salt
  ½ teaspoon freshly ground black pepper
  ¼ cup Scotch or Bourbon
  3 tablespoons heavy or whipping cream
     Parsley leaves, for garnish

1. In large skillet, heat 2 tablespoons of butter over medium-low heat. Add onion and cook, stirring frequently, 10 minutes or until tender and lightly golden. Add apple and cook 5 minutes or until tender. Transfer mixture to food processor.

2. Add remaining 1 tablespoon butter to pan and melt over medium heat. Add chicken livers, sprinkle with ½ teaspoon of salt and the pepper, and cook, stirring frequently, 5 minutes or until livers are cooked through.

3. Remove pan from heat. Stir in Scotch, return to heat, and cook 2 minutes. With slotted spoon, transfer livers to food processor. Return skillet to heat and reduce liquid to ½ cup. Pour reduced liquid into processor. Add cream and remaining ½ teaspoon salt, and process until very smooth.

4. Pour mousse mixture into 5-cup serving bowl or ramekin. Smooth top with rubber spatula. Place sheet of plastic wrap directly on surface of mousse. Cover and refrigerate several hours or until set. Arrange parsley leaves on top before serving.

Prep Time: 20 minutes plus chilling time
Cooking Time: 25 minutes
Makes 16 servings

NUTRITION INFORMATION
Per Serving
Calories 93
Total Fat 5g
Saturated Fat 2.5g
Cholesterol 197mg
Sodium 181mg
Protein 8g
Carbohydrates 4g

Mini Chicken Meatballs

These diminutive meatballs are not strongly flavored, so they go well with all sorts of dips: salsa, blue cheese sauce (see page 28), peanut sauce (page 33), or sesame sauce (page 34). You can also simmer the meatballs in pasta sauce and serve them over small portions of spaghetti.

  2 teaspoons plus 2 tablespoons olive oil
  1 small onion, minced
  2 cloves garlic, minced
  2 slices firm-textured white bread, crumbled
  2 tablespoons milk
  1 pound ground chicken
  1 large egg
  ⅓ cup chopped parsley
  ¼ cup grated Parmesan cheese
  ½ teaspoon salt
  ¼ cup flour
  1 cup chicken broth, canned or homemade (page 45)

1. In small skillet, heat 2 teaspoons of oil over medium-low heat. Add onion and garlic, and cook, stirring frequently, 7 minutes or until onion is tender. Transfer to large bowl.

2. Add bread and milk to sautéed onion, and stir until bread is thoroughly moistened. Add chicken, egg, parsley, Parmesan, and salt; mix until well combined. Shape into 36 walnut-size meatballs. Dredge meatballs in flour, shaking off excess.

3. In large skillet, heat 1 tablespoon of oil over medium heat. Add half of meatballs to skillet and sauté 5 minutes or until golden brown; transfer meatballs to plate. Add remaining 1 tablespoon oil and meatballs to skillet, and sauté 5 minutes.

4. Return all meatballs to skillet. Add broth, reduce heat to medium-low, cover, and simmer 5 minutes or until meatballs are cooked through. With slotted spoon, transfer meatballs to serving bowl.

Prep Time: 20 minutes
Cooking Time: 25 minutes
Makes 36 meatballs

NUTRITION INFORMATION
Per Meatball
Calories 43
Total Fat 2.5g
Saturated Fat 0.5g
Cholesterol 17mg
Sodium 93mg
Protein 3g
Carbohydrates 2g

Prep Time: *35 minutes*
Cooking Time: *45 minutes*
Makes *24 mushrooms*

NUTRITION INFORMATION
Per Mushroom
Calories 52
Total Fat 3g
Saturated Fat 0.5g
Cholesterol 11mg
Sodium 135mg
Protein 3g
Carbohydrates 3g

Chicken & Ham-Stuffed Mushrooms

Some markets sell jumbo mushroom caps labeled "stuffers." Those are the ones to use for this recipe.

24 jumbo mushrooms (about 2½ pounds)
3 tablespoons olive oil
1 small onion, finely chopped
2 cloves garlic, minced
½ pound ground chicken
¼ pound ham, finely chopped
⅓ cup chopped parsley
2 tablespoons spicy brown mustard
½ teaspoon salt
½ teaspoon dried marjoram or oregano

1. Separate mushroom caps and stems. Trim the very ends of 12 stems and coarsely chop; discard remaining stems.

2. Preheat oven to 425°F. In large skillet, heat 1 tablespoon of oil over low heat. Add onion and garlic, and cook 5 minutes or until tender. Add chopped mushroom stems and cook, stirring frequently, for 15 minutes or until tender and liquid has evaporated. Transfer onion-mushroom mixture to large bowl; cool to room temperature.

3. Add chicken, ham, parsley, mustard, salt, and marjoram, and mix well. In large bowl, toss mushroom caps with remaining 2 tablespoons olive oil.

4. Place mushroom caps gill-side down on baking sheet and bake 12 minutes or until mushrooms are firm-tender (but not collapsed). Turn mushroom caps gill-side up and cool to room temperature on baking sheet. Leave oven on.

5. Fill each mushroom cap with ground chicken mixture. Bake 15 minutes or until chicken is cooked through. Serve hot.

SAUSAGE-STUFFED MUSHROOMS Prepare mushrooms as directed. In step 2, when sautéing mushroom stems, add ¼ cup dry red wine and cook until evaporated. In step 3, reduce ground chicken to 6 ounces; omit ham and add 6 ounces finely chopped, fully-cooked chicken sausage. Stuff and bake mushrooms as directed.
Calories 53, Total Fat 3g, Saturated Fat 0.5g, Cholesterol 11mg, Sodium 120mg, Protein 4g, Carbohydrates 3g

CHICKEN & HAM-STUFFED MUSHROOMS

INDIVIDUAL SAUSAGE, MUSHROOM & RED ONION PIZZAS

Prep Time: 20 minutes
Cooking Time: 25 minutes
Makes 4 servings

NUTRITION INFORMATION

Per Serving

Calories 743

Total Fat 26g

Saturated Fat 8g

Cholesterol 100mg

Sodium 2772mg

Protein 51g

Carbohydrates 80g

HINTS & TIPS

➤ Part-skim mozzarella
behaves very much like
whole-milk cheese when
you melt it on pizza. But
don't substitute fat-free
mozzarella—it won't give
you that deliciously stringy,
oozy, dairy-rich, authentic
mozzarella experience.

➤ You'll find ready-to-use
white bread dough or pizza
dough in the freezer case
at your supermarket. You'll
need to thaw the dough for
about 4 hours at room
temperature before using it.
Some pizzerias will also sell
you a portion of their own
fresh pizza dough.

Individual Sausage, Mushroom & Red Onion Pizzas

With the boldly beckoning aroma of these sausage-topped pizzas baking in your oven, you'll have a hard time keeping guests out of the kitchen. Ready-to-bake pizza dough and white bread dough, either of which is fine for this recipe, are widely available at supermarkets.

1	tablespoon olive oil
2	cloves garlic, minced
1	pound mushrooms, thinly sliced
¼	teaspoon salt
1¼	pounds store-bought pizza or bread dough
1	cup bottled marinara sauce
8	ounces part-skim mozzarella cheese, shredded
¾	pound fully cooked chicken sausages, thinly sliced
1	small red onion, halved and thinly sliced

1. Preheat oven to 450°F. In large skillet, heat oil over low heat. Add garlic and cook 1 minute. Add mushrooms, sprinkle with salt, and cook, stirring frequently, 5 minutes or until tender. Drain off mushroom liquid.

2. Divide pizza dough into 4 pieces. On lightly floured work surface, roll each piece to 7-inch round. Place on 2 lightly greased baking sheets. Roll sides of dough up slightly to form raised edges. Spread marinara sauce over dough rounds. Sprinkle with mozzarella, then mushrooms, then sausages, then onion.

3. Bake for 15 minutes or until bottoms are crusty and cheese is bubbly. If both baking sheets are in the oven at the same time, switch their positions in the oven halfway through baking so the pizzas brown evenly.

FROM THE FRIDGE

Use 1¾ cups shredded cooked chicken thighs in place of the chicken sausage.

CHICKEN, OLIVE & ARTICHOKE PIZZAS Omit

mushrooms, sausages, and red onion. In step 1, add 1 pound skinless, boneless chicken breast cut into 1-inch chunks when sautéing garlic. Cook chicken 4 minutes or until almost cooked through. Shape dough and top with marinara sauce and mozzarella as directed. Top with 1 cup Calamata olives (pitted and coarsely chopped), 2 jars (6 ounces each) drained marinated artichoke hearts, and chicken. Bake pizzas 25 minutes or until bottoms are crusty and cheese is bubbly.

Calories 859, Total Fat 36g, Saturated Fat 9g, Cholesterol 99mg, Sodium 3338mg, Protein 56g, Carbohydrates 83g

Soups, Salads & Sandwiches

Chicken soup, chicken salad, and chicken sandwiches will never be the same. Chicken soup can be a creamy curried puree or a Tuscan vegetable chowder. Salad? A quick-to-fix pasta tossed with asparagus, or a Chinese-style salad fragrant with sesame. And the sandwiches include such new-fashioned favorites as wraps, stuffed pitas, and sandwiches made with thick, herb-flavored focaccia.

BEST HOMEMADE CHICKEN SOUP

Prep Time: 20 minutes
Cooking Time: 1 hour 40 minutes
Makes 8 servings

NUTRITION INFORMATION
Per Serving
Calories 291
Total Fat 7g
Saturated Fat 1.5g
Cholesterol 76mg
Sodium 704mg
Protein 27g
Carbohydrates 28g

Best Homemade Chicken Soup

Instead of a whole chicken, you could use a 3-pound package of chicken parts.

1 whole chicken (about 3½ pounds), neck and giblets reserved, liver discarded
1 large onion, peeled and halved
2 cloves garlic, peeled
1 bay leaf
2 teaspoons salt
½ teaspoon dried rosemary
¼ teaspoon freshly ground black pepper
2 tablespoons olive oil
3 carrots, cut into matchsticks
2 stalks celery, thinly sliced
2 leeks, cut into matchsticks
1 red bell pepper, cut into thin strips
1 parsnip, peeled and cut into matchsticks
1 white turnip, peeled and cut into matchsticks
6 ounces linguine
⅔ cup chopped fresh dill

1. In 8-quart Dutch oven or soup pot, combine chicken, neck, giblets (excluding liver), and water to cover by 1 inch (about 11 cups). Bring mixture to a boil, skimming any foam that rises to the surface. Add onion, garlic, bay leaf, 1 teaspoon of salt, the rosemary, and black pepper and return to a boil. Reduce to a simmer and cook 1 hour or until chicken is cooked through. Discard giblets and neck. Cool chicken in broth. When chicken is cool enough to handle, remove and discard skin. Remove chicken meat from bones and discard bones. Shred chicken and set aside.

2. Strain broth through colander and discard solids. Skim any fat from surface. Rinse Dutch oven and return strained broth to pot.

3. In large skillet or saucepan, heat oil over medium heat. Add carrots, celery, leeks, bell pepper, parsnip, and turnip, and stir to coat. Cover and cook, stirring occasionally, 20 minutes or until vegetables are crisp-tender. Uncover and cook 10 minutes or until vegetables are tender and lightly browned.

4. Meanwhile, bring broth in Dutch oven to a boil, covered. When vegetables are 10 minutes from being cooked, add pasta to broth and cook according to package directions. Add sautéed vegetables, chicken pieces, remaining 1 teaspoon salt, and fresh dill to broth. Return to a boil, then serve.

Prep Time: 10 minutes
Cooking Time: 2 hours 30 minutes
Makes 9 cups

NUTRITION INFORMATION
Per Cup
Calories 35
Total Fat 0g
Saturated Fat 0g
Cholesterol 0mg
Sodium 132mg
Protein 7g
Carbohydrates 1g

Homemade Chicken Broth

Freeze the broth in one-cup portions and it's ready for use in recipes or as single servings.

1 whole chicken (about 3½ pounds), cut up
2 carrots, cut into large chunks
1 large onion, skin on, quartered
1 stalk celery, cut into large chunks
1 tomato, halved
2 cloves garlic, unpeeled
¼ teaspoon salt
¼ teaspoon dried rosemary, crumbled
¼ teaspoon dried thyme

1. In 8-quart Dutch oven or soup pot, combine chicken and water to cover by 2 inches (about 10 cups). Bring the mixture to a boil over high heat, skimming any foam that rises to surface.

2. Add carrots, onion, celery, tomato, garlic, salt, rosemary, and thyme. Return to a boil, reduce to a simmer, and cook 2½ hours or until rich and flavorful. Strain (discarding solids, including chicken) and use for soup or store in refrigerator or freezer for later use. Defat before using.

RAVIOLI IN BRODO For 4 servings, use 6 cups of Homemade Chicken Broth. Bring broth to a boil, add ¾ teaspoon salt and ½ teaspoon freshly ground black pepper. Add 1 package (9 ounces) frozen ravioli (spinach or cheese) and return broth to a boil. Cook until ravioli are al dente. Sprinkle each serving with 2 teaspoons chopped fresh basil, 1 tablespoon chopped parsley, and 1 tablespoon grated Parmesan.
Calories 225, Total Fat 3.5g, Saturated Fat 2g, Cholesterol 11mg, Sodium 869mg, Protein 20g, Carbohydrates 26g

Hot & Sour Soup

A classic offering at Chinese restaurants, this Szechuan soup is very tasty when made with strips of chicken instead of pork. Rice vinegar is an Asian product; it's milder than other vinegars.

LOW FAT

Prep Time: 30 minutes plus mushroom soaking time
Cooking Time: 10 minutes
Makes 4 servings

1	cup dried shiitake mushrooms (1 ounce)
1½	cups boiling water
2	cups chicken broth, canned or homemade (page 45)
¼	cup rice vinegar
1	teaspoon sugar
1	teaspoon freshly ground black pepper
½	teaspoon salt
2	cups shredded Napa cabbage
¾	pound skinless, boneless chicken breasts, cut crosswise into ¼-inch-wide strips
2	ounces Canadian bacon, cut into matchsticks
2	tablespoons cornstarch blended with ¼ cup water
2	scallions, thinly sliced
2	teaspoons sesame oil

1. In small bowl, combine mushrooms and boiling water. Let stand 20 minutes or until mushrooms have softened. With your fingers, lift mushrooms from liquid. Rinse mushrooms under warm water. Cut off tough stems. Thinly slice mushroom caps. Strain mushroom soaking liquid through paper towel-lined sieve.

2. In large saucepan, combine broth, vinegar, sugar, pepper, salt, 2 cups of water, mushrooms, and mushroom soaking liquid. Bring to a boil over medium heat. Reduce to a simmer. Add Napa cabbage, chicken, and Canadian bacon, and cook 2 minutes or until chicken is cooked through. Return to a boil, stir in cornstarch mixture, and cook, stirring gently, 1 minute or until thickened. Remove from heat and stir in scallions and sesame oil.

NUTRITION INFORMATION
Per Serving
Calories 199
Total Fat 5g
Saturated Fat 1g
Cholesterol 56mg
Sodium 1076mg
Protein 24g
Carbohydrates 13g

Mexican Chicken Soup

Fresh cilantro, chilies, and lime juice bring authentic Mexican flavor to this warming soup, perfect for a chilly evening. The sautéed tortilla strips float like crunchy "noodles" atop each bowl.

Prep Time: 20 minutes
Cooking Time: 25 minutes
Makes 4 servings

3	tablespoons olive oil
6	corn tortillas (6-inch diameter), halved and each half cut crosswise into ½-inch-wide strips
1	small onion, minced
2	cloves garlic, minced
1	cup chopped canned tomatoes
1	can (4½ ounces) chopped mild green chilies
1	pickled jalapeño pepper, minced with seeds
1½	cups chicken broth, canned or homemade (page 45)
½	teaspoon chili powder
½	teaspoon salt
1¼	pounds skinless, boneless chicken thighs, cut into ½-inch chunks
⅓	cup chopped cilantro
3	tablespoons fresh lime juice (about 2 limes)

1. In Dutch oven or 5-quart saucepan, heat 1 tablespoon of oil over medium heat. Add half of tortilla strips and sauté 3 minutes or until lightly crisped. Remove with slotted spoon and drain on paper towels. Repeat with 1 tablespoon of oil and remaining tortilla strips.

2. Add remaining 1 tablespoon oil, onion, and garlic to pan and cook 5 minutes or until tender. Add tomatoes, mild green chilies, pickled jalapeño, broth, chili powder, salt, and 1½ cups of water, and bring to a boil. Reduce to a simmer, cover, and cook 5 minutes.

3. Add chicken, cover, and simmer 5 minutes or until chicken is cooked through. Stir in cilantro and lime juice. Garnish with tortilla strips.

TO REDUCE THE FAT

Omit oil in step 1. Spray tortilla strips with nonstick cooking spray and toast in 350°F. oven for 5 minutes or until slightly crisped. Substitute skinless, boneless chicken breasts for thighs.

Calories 327, Total Fat 11g, Saturated Fat 2g, Cholesterol 118mg, Sodium 1124mg, Protein 32g, Carbohydrates 26g

NUTRITION INFORMATION
Per Serving
Calories 387
Total Fat 17g
Saturated Fat 3g
Cholesterol 118mg
Sodium 1124mg
Protein 32g
Carbohydrates 26g

MEXICAN CHICKEN SOUP

Quick Chicken & Corn Chowder

Here's a real "pantry shelf" soup—one you can make from ingredients you have on hand. If there's no heavy cream in the fridge, you can use evaporated milk (you'll save calories, too—see below).

- 2 tablespoons olive oil
- 4 scallions, thinly sliced
- 1 green bell pepper, cut into ½-inch squares
- ½ pound red-skinned potatoes, unpeeled, cut into ¼-inch dice
- 3 tablespoons flour
- 1 cup chicken broth, canned or homemade (page 45)
- ½ teaspoon salt
- ¼ teaspoon cayenne pepper
- ¼ teaspoon dried thyme
- 1 can (14¾ ounces) creamed corn
- 1½ cups diced cooked chicken breasts or thighs— leftover or poached (page 17)
- ½ cup heavy or whipping cream

1. In large saucepan, heat oil over medium heat. Add scallions, bell pepper, and potatoes, and cook 5 minutes or until bell pepper is crisp-tender. Add flour, stirring to coat.

2. Stir in broth, salt, cayenne, thyme, and 1 cup of water, and bring to a boil. Reduce to simmer, cover, and cook 5 minutes or until potato is tender. Stir in creamed corn, chicken, and cream; bring to a boil, then serve.

TO REDUCE THE FAT

In step 1, reduce oil to 1 tablespoon, but use nonstick saucepan. In step 2, use evaporated milk in place of heavy cream.

Calories 318, Total Fat 8.5g, Saturated Fat 2.5g, Cholesterol 54mg, Sodium 930mg, Protein 23g, Carbohydrates 39g

QUICK TO FIX
LEFTOVERS

Prep Time: 15 minutes
Cooking Time: 15 minutes
Makes 4 servings

NUTRITION INFORMATION
Per Serving
Calories 408
Total Fat 21g
Saturated Fat 8.5g
Cholesterol 85mg
Sodium 907mg
Protein 21g
Carbohydrates 37g

Asian Noodle Soup

A few tasty additions turn plain chicken broth into a fragrant Chinese-style soup. The fresh ginger, hot pepper sauce, and watercress each adds its own brand of "heat" to this recipe.

- 2 teaspoons peanut or vegetable oil
- 2 cloves garlic, minced
- 1 piece (1 inch) fresh ginger, peeled and minced
- 1½ cups chicken broth, canned or homemade (page 45)
- ½ teaspoon salt
- ¼ teaspoon hot pepper sauce (red)
- 1 pound skinless, boneless chicken breasts
- 2 carrots, thinly sliced
- 4 ounces vermicelli, angel hair pasta, or thin egg noodles
- 1 bunch watercress, tough stems trimmed
- 2 scallions, white and tender green parts, cut into 2-inch matchsticks
- 1 tablespoon sesame oil

1. In large saucepan, heat peanut oil over low heat. Add garlic and ginger, and cook, stirring frequently, 1 minute or until fragrant.

2. Add broth, salt, hot pepper sauce, and 3 cups of water, and bring to a boil. Add chicken, reduce to a simmer, cover, and cook 15 minutes or until chicken is cooked through. With a slotted spoon, transfer chicken to plate. When cool enough to handle, shred chicken.

3. Return broth to a boil. Add carrots and cook 2 minutes. Add vermicelli and cook 5 minutes or until pasta is almost tender. Add watercress, scallions, sesame oil, and chicken, and cook 2 minutes or until watercress has wilted and chicken is heated through.

FROM THE FRIDGE

Use 3 cups shredded cooked chicken breasts or thighs instead of uncooked chicken. Add chicken in step 3 when adding watercress. In step 2, increase chicken broth to 3 cups and add only 1½ cups of water.

LOW FAT

Prep Time: 20 minutes
Cooking Time: 25 minutes
Makes 4 servings

NUTRITION INFORMATION
Per Serving
Calories 315
Total Fat 8g
Saturated Fat 1.5g
Cholesterol 66mg
Sodium 795mg
Protein 32g
Carbohydrates 27g

QUICK CHICKEN & CORN CHOWDER

CHICKEN, VEGETABLE & GARBANZO SOUP WITH CHIPOTLE PEPPERS

Prep Time: 20 minutes
Cooking Time: 45 minutes
Makes 4 servings

NUTRITION INFORMATION
Per Serving
Calories 220
Total Fat 7.5g
Saturated Fat 1g
Cholesterol 40mg
Sodium 857mg
Protein 15g
Carbohydrates 24g

HINTS & TIPS

➤ You can cook the chicken ahead of time and refrigerate it and the strained broth separately. When you're ready to continue with the recipe, skim any fat, then add the broth as directed in step 3. Add the chicken to the soup along with the broth to give it extra time to reheat.

➤ If you're unable to find chipotles in adobo at your market, substitute 1 pickled jalapeño for the chipotle and 2 teaspoons chili powder for the adobo sauce.

Chicken, Vegetable & Garbanzo Soup with Chipotle Peppers

Chipotle peppers, which are smoke-dried jalapeños, add a deep, rich flavor to Mexican and Tex-Mex dishes. In addition to the whole dried chilies, you can also buy canned chipotles packed in adobo, a thick, brick-red tomato sauce. Chipotles in adobo are sold in the Mexican foods section of many supermarkets, and in Latin-American grocery stores.

- ¾ pound bone-in chicken thighs, skin removed
- 1 tablespoon olive oil
- 1 small onion, minced
- 3 cloves garlic, minced
- 2 carrots, halved lengthwise and thinly sliced crosswise
- 1 red bell pepper, slivered
- 1 green bell pepper, slivered
- ¼ pound mushrooms, thinly sliced
- 1 canned chipotle pepper in adobo, minced with seeds
- 1 can (15½ ounces) garbanzos (chick-peas), rinsed and drained
- 2 tablespoons tomato paste
- ½ teaspoon adobo sauce (from can)
- 1 teaspoon salt
- ½ teaspoon dried rosemary

1. In medium saucepan, bring chicken and 4 cups of water to a boil over medium heat. Reduce to a simmer, partially cover, and cook 30 minutes or until chicken is tender. Remove chicken; strain and reserve broth. When cool enough to handle, cut chicken from bone and cut into bite-size pieces.

2. Meanwhile, in large saucepan, heat oil over low heat. Add onion and garlic, and cook 7 minutes or until onion is tender. Add carrots and cook 2 minutes. Add bell peppers and cook, stirring frequently, 7 minutes or until peppers are crisp-tender. Add mushrooms and chipotle pepper, and cook 5 minutes or until mushrooms are tender.

3. Add strained chicken broth to vegetables in saucepan. Stir in garbanzos, tomato paste, adobo sauce, salt, and rosemary, and bring to a boil. Reduce to a simmer, cover, and cook 10 minutes to develop flavors. Stir in chicken and cook 2 minutes or until heated through.

TO REDUCE THE FAT

Use skinless chicken breasts instead of thighs. In step 2, omit oil and cook onion, garlic, and other vegetables in 1 cup of broth.

Calories 212, Total Fat 4g, Saturated Fat 0.5g, Cholesterol 1mg, Sodium 857mg, Protein 21g, Carbohydrates 24g

Peanut-Chicken Soup

This dish is based on a traditional West-African stew made with a cut-up chicken; for this rendition, chicken thigh meat is shredded. There's no need for chicken broth here because in cooking the chicken thighs (along with ginger and garlic), you create all the broth you need.

- ¾ pound bone-in chicken thighs, skin removed
- 1 tablespoon ground ginger
- 2 cloves garlic, minced
- 2 teaspoons olive oil
- 1 small onion, minced
- ½ cup canned crushed tomatoes
- 2 tablespoons tomato paste
- ½ cup creamy peanut butter
- 1 teaspoon salt
- ¼ teaspoon cayenne pepper
- ⅓ cup chopped cilantro

1. In medium saucepan, combine chicken, ginger, garlic, and water to cover by 1 inch. Bring to a boil over medium heat, reduce to a simmer, partially cover, and cook 30 minutes or until chicken is cooked through. Remove chicken; strain and reserve broth. Discard garlic. When cool enough to handle, shred chicken.

2. Meanwhile, in large saucepan, heat oil over low heat. Add onion and cook, stirring occasionally, 5 minutes or until tender. Stir in tomatoes and tomato paste, and cook until slightly thickened, about 5 minutes.

3. Whisk in peanut butter, salt, cayenne, and 3 cups of reserved broth. Bring to a boil, reduce to a simmer, and add chicken to pan. Simmer 5 minutes to blend flavors. Stir in cilantro.

FROM THE FRIDGE

Substitute 1½ cups shredded cooked chicken breasts or thighs for uncooked chicken. In step 1, combine 3 cups chicken broth with ginger and garlic, and simmer, covered, for 15 minutes. Strain broth and use as directed in step 3. Add cooked chicken to soup in step 3.

Prep Time: 15 minutes
Cooking Time: 50 minutes
Makes 4 servings

NUTRITION INFORMATION
Per Serving
Calories 299
Total Fat 21g
Saturated Fat 3.5g
Cholesterol 40mg
Sodium 891mg
Protein 20g
Carbohydrates 12g

Creamy Curried Chicken Soup

In India, home of some of the world's greatest curries, the spices are always sautéed before liquid is added. This ensures that the spices will contribute their full richness to the recipe.

- 1 tablespoon olive oil
- 3 scallions, thinly sliced
- 1 clove garlic, minced
- 2 teaspoons mild curry powder
- ¾ teaspoon ground ginger
- 2 tablespoons flour
- 1½ cups chicken broth, canned or homemade (page 45)
- 1 cup milk
- ½ teaspoon salt
- 1 cup cubed cooked chicken breast or thighs—leftover or poached (page 17)
- ½ cup frozen peas
- ⅓ cup chopped cilantro (optional)

1. In medium saucepan, heat oil over low heat. Add scallions and garlic, and cook, stirring frequently, 2 minutes or until scallions have wilted. Stir in curry powder and ginger, and cook 1 minute. Stir in flour.

2. Add broth and 1½ cups of water, and whisk over medium heat until mixture comes to a boil. Stir in milk and salt. Add chicken and peas, and cook 2 minutes or just until heated through. Stir in cilantro.

CREAMY CHICKEN SOUP WITH ASPARAGUS In step

1, when sautéing scallions and garlic, add 1 teaspoon dried tarragon and ½ teaspoon oregano; omit curry powder and ginger. In step 2, when adding broth and water, add 3 cups of cut asparagus and omit peas. Substitute ¼ cup chopped parsley and 2 tablespoons snipped chives for cilantro.
Calories 177, Total Fat 7.5g, Saturated Fat 2.5g, Cholesterol 38mg, Sodium 743mg, Protein 17g, Carbohydrates 11g

QUICK TO FIX
LEFTOVERS

Prep Time: 15 minutes
Cooking Time: 10 minutes
Makes 4 servings

NUTRITION INFORMATION
Per Serving
Calories 173
Total Fat 7.5g
Saturated Fat 2.5g
Cholesterol 38mg
Sodium 762mg
Protein 15g
Carbohydrates 11g

CREAMY CURRIED CHICKEN SOUP

SMOKED CHICKEN & MUSHROOM SOUP WITH BARLEY

Prep Time: 15 minutes
Cooking Time: 1 hour
Makes 4 servings

NUTRITION INFORMATION

Per Serving

Calories 267

Total Fat 9g

Saturated Fat 2g

Cholesterol 84mg

Sodium 959mg

Protein 24g

Carbohydrates 23g

Smoked Chicken & Mushroom Soup with Barley

In this hearty soup, chunks of smoked chicken stand in for the sausage often used to flavor such dishes. Serve the soup with thick slices of sourdough or whole-wheat peasant bread and sweet butter.

1 tablespoon olive oil

1 large onion, minced

3 cloves garlic, minced

2 carrots, thinly sliced

½ pound mushrooms, thickly sliced

¼ cup pearl barley

½ cup canned tomatoes, chopped with their juice

¾ pound skinless, boneless chicken thighs

1¼ teaspoons salt

¾ teaspoon freshly ground black pepper

3 ounces smoked chicken,
    cut into ½-inch chunks

1. In large saucepan, heat oil over medium heat. Add onion and garlic, and cook, stirring frequently, 7 minutes or until tender. Add carrots and cook 2 minutes. Add mushrooms and cook 2 to 3 minutes. Stir in barley.

2. Add tomatoes, chicken, salt, pepper, and 5 cups of water. Bring to a boil, reduce to a simmer, cover, and cook 40 minutes or until barley is tender and chicken is cooked through.

3. With slotted spoon, lift chicken from pot. Skim any fat from soup. When cool enough to handle, shred chicken and return to soup along with smoked chicken. Cook 2 minutes or until heated through.

Prep Time: 25 minutes
Cooking Time: 40 minutes
Makes 4 servings

NUTRITION INFORMATION

Per Serving

Calories 291

Total Fat 9g

Saturated Fat 1g

Cholesterol 54mg

Sodium 1210mg

Protein 17g

Carbohydrates 37g

Winter Vegetable Soup with Chicken

Although brimming with sturdy root vegetables—carrots, parsnips, turnips, and sweet potatoes—this is a light-tasting soup. A squeeze of fresh lemon juice, stirred in just before serving, adds sprightly flavor.

1 pound bone-in chicken thighs, skin removed

1 tablespoon olive oil

1 medium onion, minced

3 cloves garlic, minced

2 carrots, thinly sliced

1 large parsnip (8 ounces), thinly sliced

1 large white turnip (8 ounces), peeled and
    cut into ½-inch chunks

1 sweet potato (8 ounces), peeled and
    cut into ½-inch chunks

⅓ cup oil-packed sun-dried tomatoes,
    drained and coarsely chopped

1¾ teaspoons salt

¾ teaspoon ground ginger

½ teaspoon freshly ground black pepper

1 tablespoon fresh lemon juice

1. In medium saucepan, combine chicken and 4 cups of water. Bring to a boil over medium heat, reduce to a simmer, partially cover, and cook 30 minutes or until chicken is cooked through. Remove chicken and skim any foam from broth. When cool enough to handle, remove chicken from bone and shred.

2. Meanwhile, in large saucepan, heat oil over low heat. Add onion and garlic, and cook 7 minutes or until onion is tender. Add carrots, parsnip, turnip, sweet potato, sun-dried tomatoes, salt, ginger, and pepper, and stir to coat. Add 1 cup of water, cover, and cook 10 minutes or until vegetables are firm-tender.

3. Add reserved broth and chicken, and return to a boil. Reduce to a simmer, cover, and cook 10 minutes or until vegetables are tender and soup is flavorful. Stir in lemon juice.

FROM THE FRIDGE

Omit step 1 and use 1½ cups shredded cooked chicken instead of uncooked thighs. Add cooked chicken in step 3 along with 2 cups of canned chicken broth and 2 cups of water.

AVGOLEMONO SOUP WITH GREEK MEATBALLS

Tuscan Bread Soup

Prep Time: 30 minutes
Cooking Time: 50 minutes
Makes 4 servings

NUTRITION INFORMATION

Per Serving
Calories 386
Total Fat 16g
Saturated Fat 4.5g
Cholesterol 78mg
Sodium 1260mg
Protein 27g
Carbohydrates 33g

Rather than serving bread or crackers on the side, try this old-country idea: Slices of pan-toasted bread go into the pot before the soup is added, and more bread goes on top, sprinkled with Parmesan.

- 2 tablespoons olive oil
- 1 medium onion, minced
- 3 cloves garlic, minced
- 1 carrot, halved lengthwise and thinly sliced
- 1 stalk celery, halved lengthwise and thinly sliced
- ¾ pound skinless, boneless chicken thighs, cut into bite-size pieces
- 1 cup dry white wine
- 8 slices (1 inch thick) country-style bread, crusts removed
- 1½ cups chicken broth, canned or homemade (page 45)
- ½ teaspoon salt
- ½ teaspoon freshly ground black pepper
- ½ cup grated Parmesan cheese

1. In large saucepan, heat 1 tablespoon of oil over medium heat. Add onion and garlic, and cook, stirring frequently, 7 minutes or until onion is tender. Add carrot and celery, and cook, stirring frequently, 5 minutes or until tender. Add chicken and stir to coat. Add wine, increase heat to high, and cook 2 minutes.

2. Preheat oven to 350°F. In large nonstick skillet, heat 1½ teaspoons of oil. Add 4 bread slices and cook until golden brown on both sides. Repeat with remaining 1½ teaspoons oil and 4 slices of bread.

3. Transfer 4 bread slices to casserole or Dutch oven. Spoon chicken-vegetable mixture over bread. Top with remaining bread. Stir together broth, 2 cups of water, salt, and pepper, and pour on top. Sprinkle with Parmesan. Cover and bake for 35 minutes or until chicken is cooked through, soup is piping hot, and bread is soft.

Avgolemono Soup with Greek Meatballs

Prep Time: 25 minutes
Cooking Time: 15 minutes
Makes 4 servings

NUTRITION INFORMATION

Per Serving
Calories 304
Total Fat 11g
Saturated Fat 3g
Cholesterol 207mg
Sodium 1305mg
Protein 20g
Carbohydrates 30g

Avgolemono means "egg-lemon" in Greek, and this variation of the classic soup is fortified with little chicken meatballs for a heartier dish. Orzo is a pasta shaped like long grains of rice.

- ½ pound ground chicken
- 3 large eggs
- 3 slices firm-textured white bread (3 ounces), crumbled
- 2 cloves garlic, minced
- ½ cup snipped fresh dill
- ⅓ cup fresh mint leaves, finely chopped
- ¾ teaspoon salt
- ½ teaspoon grated lemon zest
- 2½ cups chicken broth, canned or homemade (page 45)
- ½ cup orzo
- ¼ cup fresh lemon juice (about 2 lemons)

1. In medium bowl, combine chicken, 1 egg, bread, garlic, ¼ cup of dill, the mint, ½ teaspoon of salt, and the lemon zest. Mix until well combined. Shape mixture into 24 meatballs.

2. In Dutch oven or soup pot, bring broth, remaining ¼ teaspoon salt, and 2½ cups of water to a boil over medium heat. Add orzo and cook 7 minutes.

3. Reduce broth to a simmer. Gently drop meatballs into broth and cook 5 minutes or until meatballs are cooked through and orzo is tender.

4. In small bowl, whisk lemon juice and remaining 2 eggs to combine. Slowly stir some of the hot soup broth into egg mixture. Stir egg mixture back into soup, simmer 30 seconds, and remove from heat. Stir in remaining ¼ cup dill. Serve immediately; do not reheat.

Chopped Chicken Salad with Olives

If you've been packing tuna-salad sandwiches into the family's lunch bags for as long as you can remember, maybe it's time for a change of pace. This vibrant chicken salad with its lemony dressing, roasted peppers, and sassy green olives, is great on a roll or whole-wheat bread.

- 1   red bell pepper, cut lengthwise into flat panels
- 1   teaspoon grated lemon zest
- ¼   cup fresh lemon juice (about 2 lemons)
- 3   tablespoons mayonnaise
- 2   tablespoons olive oil
- ¼   teaspoon salt
- ½   cup pimiento-stuffed olives, coarsely chopped
- 2   stalks celery, thinly sliced
- 3   cups chopped cooked chicken breasts or thighs—leftover or poached (page 17)

1. Preheat broiler. Place pepper pieces, skin-side up, on broiler rack and broil 4 inches from heat for 10 minutes or until skin is blackened. When peppers are cool enough to handle, peel them and cut into bite-size pieces.

2. In large bowl, whisk together lemon zest, lemon juice, mayonnaise, oil, and salt. Add olives and celery, and toss. Add chicken and roasted pepper, and toss to coat.

Prep Time: 15 minutes
Cooking Time: 10 minutes
Makes 4 servings

NUTRITION INFORMATION
Per Serving
Calories 339
Total Fat 21g
Saturated Fat 3.5g
Cholesterol 95mg
Sodium 705mg
Protein 33g
Carbohydrates 4g

Chicken-Potato Salad with Basil Dressing

Take that staple "side order," potato salad, add poached chicken breast and blanched green beans, and you've got yourself an appealing warm-weather main dish. The chicken and vegetables are tossed with a basil-garlic dressing and served on a bed of fresh spinach (arugula is good, too).

- ½   pound green beans
- 1   pound all-purpose potatoes, peeled and cut into 1-inch chunks
- 1   cup chicken broth, canned or homemade (page 45)
- 3   cloves garlic, crushed and peeled
- 1½   pounds skinless, boneless chicken breasts
- 1   cup packed fresh basil leaves
- 2   tablespoons mayonnaise
- ½   teaspoon grated lemon zest
- 1   tablespoon fresh lemon juice
- ½   teaspoon salt
- 6   cups spinach leaves, rinsed and dried

1. In large pot of boiling salted water, cook green beans 4 minutes or until crisp-tender (timing will vary depending upon thickness of beans). With slotted spoon, transfer beans to large bowl. Add potatoes to boiling water, reduce to a gentle boil, and cook 15 minutes or until tender. Drain and add to bowl with green beans.

2. Meanwhile, in large skillet, combine broth, garlic, and 1 cup of water. Bring to a boil and add chicken. Reduce to a simmer, cover, and cook 15 minutes, turning chicken over midway, until chicken is cooked through. Remove chicken and garlic from broth and set aside. Measure out ⅓ cup of broth and set aside. When cool enough to handle, cut chicken into 1-inch chunks. Add to bowl with beans and potatoes.

3. In food processor or blender, combine reserved garlic, basil, mayonnaise, lemon zest, lemon juice, reserved ⅓ cup broth, and salt. Process until smooth. Pour dressing over chicken mixture and toss well to coat. Serve salad on bed of spinach leaves.

FROM THE FRIDGE

Use 3 cups cooked chicken chunks (1-inch) instead of uncooked chicken breasts. In step 2, in small saucepan, cook garlic in ½ cup chicken broth (omit water) for 3 minutes. Complete recipe as directed.

Prep Time: 25 minutes
Cooking Time: 20 minutes
Makes 4 servings

NUTRITION INFORMATION
Per Serving
Calories 362
Total Fat 8.5g
Saturated Fat 1.5g
Cholesterol 103mg
Sodium 779mg
Protein 46g
Carbohydrates 26g

NUTRITION INFORMATION

Per Serving
Calories 398
Total Fat 29g
Saturated Fat 8g
Cholesterol 138mg
Sodium 519mg
Protein 27g
Carbohydrates 8g

Cobb Salad

California, home of so many famous salads, is the home to the Cobb salad, which originated at the Brown Derby restaurant in Hollywood. Liven up the lettuce, if you like, with other greens, such as romaine, curly endive, scallions, or watercress.

6 slices bacon (about 4 ounces)

8 cups chopped iceberg lettuce

2 generous cups shredded cooked chicken breasts or thighs—leftover or poached (page 17)

1 large tomato, diced

4 ounces blue cheese, crumbled

2 hard-cooked eggs, coarsely chopped

1 avocado, cut into ½-inch cubes

⅓ cup olive oil

3 tablespoons red wine vinegar

¼ teaspoon salt

1. In large skillet, cook bacon over medium-low heat 7 minutes or until crisp and cooked through. Drain on paper towels; crumble.

2. Place lettuce, chicken, tomato, blue cheese, chopped egg, avocado, and crumbled bacon in a large bowl.

3. In small bowl, whisk together oil, vinegar, and salt. Pour dressing over ingredients in large bowl and toss gently to coat with dressing.

COBB SALAD

Chicken Salad with Citrus

Enjoy the bright taste of summer in midwinter when you serve this salad made with orange and grapefruit segments. Red onion and piquant Greek olives offer the perfect contrast to the citrus.

QUICK TO FIX
LEFTOVERS

Prep Time: 30 minutes
Makes 4 servings

- 3 navel oranges
- 2 ruby red grapefruits
- 3 tablespoons olive oil
- 1 tablespoon balsamic vinegar
- 2 teaspoons Dijon mustard
- ½ teaspoon salt
- 2 generous cups shredded cooked chicken breasts or thighs—leftover or poached (page 17)
- ½ cup Calamata olives, pitted and sliced
- ½ cup slivered red onion
- 2 bunches arugula, tough stems trimmed (about 6 cups)

1. With paring knife, cut off and discard skin, white pith, and outer membrane of oranges and grapefruits. Working over a bowl to catch juices, section oranges and grapefruits: Use paring knife to cut along both sides of each dividing membrane to release segments, transferring them to smaller bowl. Squeeze any juice left in membranes into bowl. Measure out 3 tablespoons of citrus juice and transfer to large salad bowl (reserve any extra juice for another use).

2. Whisk oil, vinegar, mustard, and salt into citrus juice in salad bowl. Add chicken, olives, onion, arugula, and orange and grapefruit sections, and toss well.

TO REDUCE THE FAT

Substitute ½ cup bottled nonfat or low-fat balsamic vinaigrette for citrus dressing. Stir 2 teaspoons Dijon mustard into storebought dressing.

Calories 306, Total Fat 8g, Saturated Fat 1.5g, Cholesterol 72mg, Sodium 818mg, Protein 29g, Carbohydrates 29g

NUTRITION INFORMATION
Per Serving
Calories 384
Total Fat 18g
Saturated Fat 3g
Cholesterol 72mg
Sodium 728mg
Protein 29g
Carbohydrates 27g

Sweet Potato & Apple Salad with Chicken

To save time, microwave the sweet potatoes: Pierce them in several places, then cook according your oven manufacturer's instructions (usually about 12 minutes for 4 medium sweet potatoes).

Prep Time: 20 minutes
Cooking Time: 50 minutes
Makes 4 servings

- 1½ pounds bone-in chicken thighs, skin removed
- ¾ teaspoon salt
- 1 pound sweet potatoes
- 3 tablespoons mayonnaise
- 3 tablespoons cider vinegar
- ½ teaspoon chili powder
- ½ teaspoon ground cumin
- ½ teaspoon sugar
- 2 McIntosh apples, cut into ½-inch chunks
- 1 Granny Smith apple, cut into ½-inch chunks
- 1 stalk celery, thinly sliced

1. Preheat oven to 425°F. Place chicken thighs in baking pan and sprinkle with ¼ teaspoon of salt. Place sweet potatoes in separate baking pan. Place both pans in oven and bake chicken for 30 minutes or until cooked through; bake sweet potatoes for 50 minutes or until tender but not falling apart (timing will vary depending on size).

2. In large bowl, whisk together mayonnaise, vinegar, chili powder, cumin, sugar, and remaining ½ teaspoon salt. Add apples and celery, and toss to combine.

3. When chicken is cool enough to handle, cut meat off bone and cut into ½-inch chunks. When sweet potatoes are cool enough to handle, peel and cut into 1-inch cubes.

4. Add chicken and sweet potatoes to salad and toss gently to combine. Serve at room temperature or chilled.

TO REDUCE THE FAT

Use chicken breasts instead of thighs and use reduced-fat mayonnaise instead of full-fat version.

Calories 306, Total Fat 4.5g, Saturated Fat 1g, Cholesterol 65mg, Sodium 621mg, Protein 27g, Carbohydrates 40g

NUTRITION INFORMATION
Per Serving
Calories 344
Total Fat 13g
Saturated Fat 2.5g
Cholesterol 87mg
Sodium 602mg
Protein 21g
Carbohydrates 38g

CHICKEN SALAD WITH CITRUS

Penne Salad
with Chicken & Asparagus

Fresh asparagus deserves delicate treatment—you don't want to "clobber" it with a heavy sauce.
A pasta salad with chicken and slivers of colorful bell pepper turns this springtime treat into a meal.

LOW FAT
QUICK TO FIX
LEFTOVERS

Prep Time: 15 minutes
Cooking Time: 15 minutes
Makes 4 servings

- 2 cloves garlic, peeled
- 8 ounces penne or other tube pasta
- 1 pound asparagus, cut into 2-inch lengths
- ¼ cup Dijon mustard
- 3 tablespoons olive oil
- 3 tablespoons rice vinegar
- ¾ teaspoon salt
- 3 cups diced cooked chicken breasts or thighs— leftover or poached (page 17)
- 2 orange or red bell peppers, slivered
- 6 cups salad greens, such as frisée

1. Bring a large pot of water to a boil. Add garlic and cook 1 minute; remove with slotted spoon. Add penne to boiling water and cook according to package directions. Add asparagus to cooking water 3 minutes before pasta is done. Drain well.

2. Meanwhile, in large bowl, whisk together mustard, oil, vinegar, and salt. Mince blanched garlic and add to bowl along with chicken and bell peppers. Add drained pasta and asparagus, and toss well. Cool to room temperature. Serve on bed of salad greens.

PASTA SALAD WITH CHICKEN, CHERRY TOMATOES & BROCCOLI Substitute 3 stalks broccoli for asparagus. Peel broccoli stems and cut into ¼-inch-thick slices. Cut broccoli tops into small florets. Add to pasta cooking water 3 minutes before pasta is done. In step 2, substitute white wine vinegar for rice vinegar. Substitute 2 cups halved cherry tomatoes for bell peppers.
Calories 535, Total Fat 15g, Saturated Fat 2.5g, Cholesterol 89mg, Sodium 909mg, Protein 43g, Carbohydrates 52g

NUTRITION INFORMATION
Per Serving
Calories 540
Total Fat 15g
Saturated Fat 2.5g
Cholesterol 89mg
Sodium 888mg
Protein 45g
Carbohydrates 52g

Chicken Taco Salad

This salad is a taco turned inside-out—a bed of iceberg lettuce topped with crunchy tortilla chips,
salsa-sauced chicken, shredded Monterey Jack (or Cheddar, if you like), and diced avocado.

LOW FAT
QUICK TO FIX
LEFTOVERS

Prep Time: 20 minutes
Cooking Time: 10 minutes
Makes 4 servings

- 4 corn tortillas (6-inch diameter), cut into 8 wedges each
- 3 tablespoons fresh lime juice
- ½ teaspoon salt
- ½ teaspoon chili powder
- 1½ cups mild or medium-hot bottled tomato salsa
- ⅓ cup chopped cilantro
- 2 cups shredded cooked chicken breasts or thighs—leftover or poached (page 17)
- 1 can (10 ounces) black beans, rinsed and drained
- 6 cups shredded iceberg lettuce
- ¼ cup shredded Monterey Jack cheese (1 ounce)
- ½ cup diced avocado

1. Preheat oven to 425°F. Place tortilla wedges on a baking sheet. Spray with nonstick cooking spray. Sprinkle with 2 tablespoons of lime juice. Sprinkle with salt and chili powder. Bake for 7 minutes or until crisp.

2. In large bowl, toss together salsa, cilantro, and remaining 1 tablespoon lime juice. Add chicken and beans, and toss to combine. Line plates with lettuce. Top with tortilla chips, chicken mixture, Monterey Jack, and avocado.

CHICKEN GAZPACHO SALAD Omit tortillas, lime juice, salt, and chili powder. Cut chicken into bite-size pieces and toss with salsa and cilantro. Add 1 large peeled, seeded, and diced (½-inch) cucumber; 1 diced green bell pepper; and ¼ cup finely chopped red onion. Spoon chicken mixture over lettuce. Omit cheese. Top with avocado as directed.
Calories 249, Total Fat 6g, Saturated Fat 1g, Cholesterol 60mg, Sodium 1142mg, Protein 27g, Carbohydrates 21g

NUTRITION INFORMATION
Per Serving
Calories 316
Total Fat 8.5g
Saturated Fat 2.5g
Cholesterol 67mg
Sodium 1507mg
Protein 29g
Carbohydrates 30g

PENNE SALAD WITH CHICKEN & ASPARAGUS

CARIBBEAN CHICKEN SALAD WITH TROPICAL FRUITS

Prep Time: 25 minutes

Makes 4 servings

NUTRITION INFORMATION

Per Serving

Calories 314

Total Fat 4.5g

Saturated Fat 1g

Cholesterol 89mg

Sodium 590mg

Protein 35g

Carbohydrates 36g

TECHNIQUE

HOW TO CUBE A MANGO

Cut one half of mango off the pit. Repeat on the other side. With a sharp knife, score each mango half into squares, cutting to, but not through, the skin.

Turn the mango half inside out to pop the cut pieces outward. Cut the pieces away from the skin.

Caribbean Chicken Salad with Tropical Fruits

The kiss of sweetness and the bite of spice—that's a perfect snapshot of Caribbean cuisine. Here, lush ripe mango and papaya get a sassy kick of hot pepper sauce and fresh ginger. When tropical fruits are not available, make the salad with cantaloupe and honeydew.

1 piece (2 inches) fresh ginger

¼ cup ketchup

3 tablespoons fresh lime juice (about 2 limes)

1 tablespoon plus 1 teaspoon honey

1 teaspoon hot pepper sauce (red)

½ teaspoon salt

1 small red onion, halved and thinly sliced

1 large tomato, cut into 16 wedges

3 cups shredded cooked chicken breasts or thighs—leftover or poached (page 17)

1 mango (15 ounces), peeled and cut into 1-inch cubes

1 papaya (15 ounces), peeled and cut into 1-inch cubes

1. With a box grater set over bowl, grate ginger. With your fingers, squeeze ginger to extract as much juice as possible. Measure out 1 tablespoon of ginger juice and transfer to large bowl.

2. Whisk ketchup, lime juice, honey, hot pepper sauce, and salt into ginger juice until well combined. Add onion and tomato, and toss to combine.

3. Add chicken, mango, and papaya, and toss gently to combine. Serve salad immediately. If not serving immediately, toss all of the ingredients except papaya together. Then, just before serving, add papaya.

PINEAPPLE CHICKEN SALAD Drain 1 can (20 ounces) of juice-packed pineapple chunks, reserving ¼ cup of juice. Omit ginger. In step 2, substitute chili sauce for ketchup; omit hot pepper sauce; add pineapple juice to dressing. Substitute pineapple chunks for mango and papaya. Sprinkle salad with ¼ cup slivered almonds, toasted.

Calories 374, Total Fat 8.5g, Saturated Fat 1.5g, Cholesterol 89mg, Sodium 606mg, Protein 36g, Carbohydrates 40g

HINTS & TIPS

➤ Papaya contains enzymes that soften meat (meat tenderizer is made from papayas), so if this fruit is combined with the chicken too far ahead of time, it will turn the chicken mushy. If you want to assemble the salad in advance, combine everything except the papaya, which you can toss in just before serving.

Chicken & Spinach Salad with Bacon Dressing

The "wilted" salad—in which greens are wilted by tossing them with a warm dressing made with vinegar and bacon drippings—is a classic of French country cooking. This version, a cross between that French recipe and the popular American spinach salad, is a light but satisfying lunch. Serve the salad as soon as you toss it so that the spinach still retains a little of its crispness.

LOW FAT
QUICK TO FIX
LEFTOVERS

Prep Time: 15 minutes
Cooking Time: 10 minutes
Makes 4 servings

- 8 cups spinach leaves, washed and dried
- 2 cups shredded cooked chicken breasts or thighs—leftover or poached (page 17)
- ¼ pound mushrooms, thinly sliced
- ½ cup thinly sliced red onion
- 6 slices bacon (about 4 ounces)
- 2 tablespoons flour
- ½ cup cider vinegar
- ½ cup chicken broth
- 1 teaspoon sugar
- ½ teaspoon salt
- ½ teaspoon freshly ground black pepper

1. In large bowl, toss together spinach (torn into smaller pieces, if desired), chicken, mushrooms, and onion.

2. In medium skillet, cook bacon over medium-low heat 7 minutes or until crisp. With slotted spoon, transfer bacon to paper towels to drain; reserve fat in skillet. When cool enough to handle, crumble bacon and scatter over spinach.

3. Return skillet to medium heat. Whisk in flour and cook 1 minute. Whisk in vinegar, broth, sugar, salt, and pepper. Cook 1 minute until slightly thickened. Pour hot dressing over spinach and toss to combine. Serve immediately.

NUTRITION INFORMATION
Per Serving
Calories 227
Total Fat 7g
Saturated Fat 2g
Cholesterol 66mg
Sodium 691mg
Protein 29g
Carbohydrates 13g

Chicken & Wild Rice Salad with Lemon Vinaigrette

The robust, chewy texture and nutlike flavor of wild rice make it a good choice for a salad. Here, the rice is cooked "pilaf-style" by first sautéing it and then simmering it in broth. Note that wild rice takes longer to cook than either white or brown rice—almost an hour.

LEFTOVERS

Prep Time: 25 minutes
Cooking Time: 1 hour
Makes 4 servings

- 3 teaspoons plus 1 tablespoon olive oil
- 3 scallions, thinly sliced
- 2 cloves garlic, finely chopped
- 1 cup wild rice
- 2 cups chicken broth, canned or homemade (page 45)
- 1 teaspoon grated lemon zest
- ½ teaspoon salt
- ⅓ cup fresh lemon juice (about 3 lemons)
- 1 red bell pepper, cut into ¼-inch dice
- ⅓ cup Calamata olives, pitted and halved
- ¼ cup pine nuts or pecans, toasted
- 3 cups shredded cooked chicken breasts or thighs—leftover or poached (page 17)

1. In large saucepan, heat 1 teaspoon of oil over low heat. Add scallions and garlic, and cook, stirring frequently, 1 minute or until scallions are soft. Add wild rice and stir to coat. Add broth, lemon zest, salt, and 1 cup of water, and bring to a boil. Reduce to a simmer, cover, and cook 55 minutes or until wild rice is tender.

2. Meanwhile, in large bowl, whisk together lemon juice and remaining 2 teaspoons plus 1 tablespoon oil. When wild rice has cooked, drain off any remaining liquid. Spoon hot cooked rice into bowl with lemon vinaigrette. Toss gently with fork.

3. Add bell pepper, olives, pine nuts, and chicken, and toss well. Serve warm, at room temperature, or chilled.

NUTRITION INFORMATION
Per Serving
Calories 484
Total Fat 19g
Saturated Fat 3.5g
Cholesterol 89mg
Sodium 1099mg
Protein 42g
Carbohydrates 38g

CHICKEN & WILD RICE SALAD WITH LEMON VINAIGRETTE

SESAME CHICKEN SALAD

Prep Time: 20 minutes
Cooking Time: 2 minutes
Makes 4 servings

NUTRITION INFORMATION
Per Serving
Calories 263
Total Fat 13g
Saturated Fat 2g
Cholesterol 60mg
Sodium 508mg
Protein 25g
Carbohydrates 12g

Sesame Chicken Salad

The perfect summer entrée, this Chinese-style chicken and vegetable salad offers the cool crunch of cucumber, bell pepper, and snow peas along with shredded chicken in a velvety sesame dressing.

2 cloves garlic, peeled
½ pound snow peas, strings removed
1 red bell pepper, cut into 2-inch-long matchsticks
1 piece (2 inches) fresh ginger, peeled and thickly sliced
3 tablespoons sesame oil
3 tablespoons lower-sodium soy sauce
2½ teaspoons sugar
2½ teaspoons rice vinegar
¼ teaspoon crushed red pepper flakes
1 cucumber, peeled, halved lengthwise, seeded, and cut into 2-inch-long matchsticks
2 cups shredded cooked chicken breasts or thighs—leftover or poached (page 17)

1. In large pot of boiling water, blanch garlic 1 minute; remove with slotted spoon. Add snow peas and bell pepper, and blanch 15 seconds; drain well.

2. In food processor, combine blanched garlic, ginger, sesame oil, soy sauce, sugar, vinegar, and red pepper flakes, and process until smooth.

3. Transfer dressing to large bowl. Add snow peas, bell pepper, cucumber, and chicken, and toss to combine. Serve at room temperature or chilled.

ASIAN NOODLE SALAD WITH CHICKEN Cook
8 ounces of linguine according to package directions. Rinse and drain. In step 1, substitute 2 carrots cut into thin matchsticks for snow peas; blanch with bell pepper. In step 2, omit sesame oil and add ¼ cup peanut butter and ½ cup chicken broth; increase soy sauce to ⅓ cup; increase sugar and vinegar to 1 tablespoon each. Omit cucumbers. Toss vegetables, linguine, and dressing together.

Calories 473, Total Fat 12g, Saturated Fat 2.5g, Cholesterol 60mg, Sodium 1068mg, Protein 36g, Carbohydrates 56g

Prep Time: 15 minutes
Cooking Time: 15 minutes
Makes 4 servings

NUTRITION INFORMATION
Per Serving
Calories 511
Total Fat 23g
Saturated Fat 4.5g
Cholesterol 111mg
Sodium 1156mg
Protein 47g
Carbohydrates 27g

Chicken Caesar Salad

The Caesar is one salad that's popular with children. They really go for the sweet romaine, tangy Parmesan dressing, and crisp croutons. They'll love the spice-rubbed sautéed chicken, too.

1 tablespoon chili powder
¾ teaspoon ground cumin
¾ teaspoon salt
½ teaspoon sugar
4 cups French bread cubes (½-inch)
2 tablespoons olive oil
1½ pounds skinless, boneless chicken breasts
¼ cup mayonnaise
¼ cup grated Parmesan cheese
2 tablespoons fresh lemon juice
1 tablespoon drained capers
1 teaspoon anchovy paste
8 cups torn romaine lettuce

1. Preheat oven to 400°F. In small bowl, stir together chili powder, cumin, salt, and sugar. Transfer 1 tablespoon of mixture to large bowl. Add bread cubes and 1 tablespoon of oil, and toss to coat. Transfer bread to baking sheet and bake for 10 minutes or until crisp and golden, tossing bread cubes midway through.

2. Meanwhile, rub remaining spice mixture onto both sides of chicken. In medium nonstick skillet, heat remaining 1 tablespoon oil over medium heat. Add chicken and cook, turning occasionally, 15 minutes or until cooked through. Remove chicken from pan, reserving any pan juices. When cool enough to handle, slice chicken on diagonal.

3. In large bowl, whisk together mayonnaise, Parmesan, lemon juice, capers, anchovy paste, and any pan juices. Add lettuce and croutons, and toss well. Divide salad among 4 serving plates and top with sliced chicken.

CHICKEN & VEGETABLE WRAPS

*Prep Time: 10 minutes plus
  marinating time*
Cooking Time: 1 hour
Makes 4 servings

NUTRITION INFORMATION

Per Serving
Calories 445
Total Fat 11g
Saturated Fat 3g
Cholesterol 188mg
Sodium 1330mg
Protein 50g
Carbohydrates 34g

BBQ Chicken on a Bun

*Marinated and baked, then shredded and doused with chili sauce, this chicken on a bun bears a
close resemblance to the "pulled pork" of Southern barbecue fame. If you prefer white meat to dark
(or want to reduce the fat content of the dish), substitute boneless chicken breasts for thighs. If you
do this, you will need to marinate the chicken for only 2 hours.*

1   small onion, sliced
3   cloves garlic, peeled
3   tablespoons distilled white vinegar
¾   teaspoon salt
½   teaspoon freshly ground black pepper
¼   teaspoon dried thyme
¼   teaspoon dried oregano
2   pounds skinless, boneless chicken thighs
½   cup chili sauce
4   hamburger buns, toasted

1. In food processor, combine onion, garlic, vinegar, salt,
pepper, thyme, oregano, and ⅓ cup of water. Process to paste.
Transfer marinade to zip-seal plastic bag. Add chicken and toss
to coat. Refrigerate at least 4 hours or up to overnight.

2. Preheat oven to 300°F. Place chicken and its marinade in
baking dish large enough to hold it in a single layer. Cover and
bake for 1 hour or until chicken is very tender.

3. When cool enough to handle, shred chicken. Transfer
chicken to bowl and toss with chili sauce. Serve chicken
mixture on toasted buns.

CHICKEN BURRITOS Complete recipe as directed, but
omit buns. Preheat oven to 350°F. Dividing evenly, spread
BBQ Chicken down middle of 8 flour tortillas (8-inch diameter). Sprinkle with ½ pound shredded pepperjack cheese,
2 thinly sliced scallions, and ¼ cup chopped cilantro. Roll
tortillas up, place on a lightly greased baking sheet, and bake
for 5 minutes or until cheese has melted.
*Calories 460, Total Fat 24g, Saturated Fat 11g, Cholesterol 60mg,
Sodium 716mg, Protein 20g, Carbohydrates 41g*

---

*Prep Time: 25 minutes plus
  chilling time*
Cooking Time: 10 minutes
Makes 4 servings

NUTRITION INFORMATION

Per Serving
Calories 617
Total Fat 33g
Saturated Fat 16g
Cholesterol 100mg
Sodium 953mg
Protein 25g
Carbohydrates 54g

Chicken & Vegetable Wraps

*Your kids will be the envy of their classmates when they bring these rolled "sandwiches" for
lunch. The lahvash (a soft Armenian flatbread) is filled with a spiral of colorful fillings: basil
cheese spread, smoked chicken, roasted red peppers, and sautéed summer squash.*

2   tablespoons olive oil
3   cloves garlic, minced
2   small yellow squash (6 ounces each), halved
    crosswise and thinly sliced lengthwise
¼   teaspoon salt
1   package (8 ounces) cream cheese,
    at room temperature
½   cup fresh basil leaves
3   tablespoons grated Parmesan cheese
4   rectangular lahvash breads (11 x 9-inch)
½   pound thinly sliced smoked chicken
1   jar (12 ounces) roasted red pepper, drained
    and cut into wide strips

1. In large skillet, heat oil over medium-low heat. Add garlic
and cook 1 minute. Add squash, sprinkle with salt, and cook,
tossing occasionally, 5 minutes or until very soft. Set squash
mixture aside to cool slightly.

2. In food processor, combine cream cheese, basil, and
Parmesan, and process until smooth. Dividing evenly, spread
cream-cheese mixture over lahvash, leaving ½-inch border
all around.

3. Layer chicken over cream cheese. Top with roasted
pepper and squash. Tightly roll lahvash, starting from a short
end. Wrap in foil and refrigerate at least 1 hour or up to
8 hours. To serve, unwrap and cut each lahvash in half
on the diagonal.

Chicken Club Sandwich

Leftover roast chicken is perfect for these triple-decker fork-and-knife sandwiches. Use good firm bread; make the sandwiches with whole wheat if you prefer it. To keep the sandwiches from toppling as you take them to the table, spear them with wooden skewers or frill-topped toothpicks.

- 8 slices bacon (about 6 ounces)
- 12 slices firm-textured white bread (12 ounces), toasted
- 8 teaspoons mayonnaise
- 3 cups mesclun or other mixed salad greens
- 2 cooked skinless, boneless chicken breast halves, thinly sliced crosswise—leftover or poached (page 17)
- 1 large tomato, cut into 8 slices
- 4 teaspoons Dijon mustard

1. In large skillet, cook bacon over medium-low heat 7 minutes or until crisp. Drain on paper towels.

2. Brush one side of each of 8 slices of toast with 1 teaspoon mayonnaise. Top each with salad greens. Divide chicken evenly among lettuce-topped toast slices. Place slice of tomato on each chicken-topped slice of toast. Top each with slice of bacon.

3. Assemble sandwiches: Stack 2 chicken-topped slices of toast on top of one another, chicken-side up. Spread 1 teaspoon mustard on 1 side of remaining 4 slices of toast. Place mustard-side down on top of sandwiches. Cut each sandwich in half on diagonal.

CHICKEN CROISSANTS Omit bacon and bread. Substitute reduced-fat mayonnaise for full-fat version and combine it with 2 tablespoons chopped mango chutney and 1 teaspoon Dijon mustard. Coarsely chop chicken and toss with mayonnaise mixture. Dice tomato and toss with ½ teaspoon salt. Split 4 croissants horizontally. Place ½ cup of mesclun on each bottom half; omit mustard. Top with chicken mixture and diced tomato. Replace top of croissant.
Calories 400, Total Fat 15g, Saturated Fat 7g, Cholesterol 49mg, Sodium 972mg, Protein 25g, Carbohydrates 39g

QUICK TO FIX
LEFTOVERS

Prep Time: 20 minutes
Cooking Time: 10 minutes
Makes 4 servings

NUTRITION INFORMATION
Per Serving
Calories 484
Total Fat 17g
Saturated Fat 4g
Cholesterol 66mg
Sodium 890mg
Protein 31g
Carbohydrates 47g

Open-Face Chicken, Avocado & Tomato Sandwiches

The pairing of velvety avocado with springy sprouts on whole-grain toast is very California, very "sixties"—and very satisfying. The toast is spread with a simplified Russian dressing, and sliced chicken and tomatoes make up the sandwich's magnificent middle.

- 2 tablespoons mayonnaise
- 1 tablespoon ketchup
- 3 teaspoons fresh lemon juice
- 4 slices whole-grain bread, toasted
- 2 cooked skinless, boneless chicken breast halves, thinly sliced crosswise—leftover or poached (page 17)
- 1 avocado, cut into ½-inch chunks
- 1 large tomato, cut into ½-inch chunks
- ½ teaspoon salt
- 1 cup alfalfa sprouts

1. In small bowl, stir together mayonnaise, ketchup, and 1 teaspoon of lemon juice.

2. Brush mixture onto one side of toast. Divide chicken slices evenly among 4 slices of toast, placing it on top of mayonnaise mixture.

3. Toss avocado with remaining 2 teaspoons lemon juice. Add tomato and salt, and toss to combine. Place on top of the chicken and top with alfalfa sprouts.

QUICK TO FIX
LEFTOVERS

Prep Time: 15 minutes
Makes 4 servings

NUTRITION INFORMATION
Per Serving
Calories 308
Total Fat 15g
Saturated Fat 2.5g
Cholesterol 53mg
Sodium 566mg
Protein 24g
Carbohydrates 20g

CHICKEN CLUB SANDWICH

LEMON-BASIL CHICKEN IN PITA POCKETS

Prep Time: 25 minutes
Makes 4 servings

NUTRITION INFORMATION
Per Serving
Calories 478
Total Fat 18g
Saturated Fat 3g
Cholesterol 89mg
Sodium 914mg
Protein 39g
Carbohydrates 38g

Lemon-Basil Chicken in Pita Pockets

Pita, Middle-Eastern pocket bread, is a convenient container for meals on the run. For a refreshing change from mayonnaise-dressed salads, try this mix of diced chicken and fresh herbs in a basil-scented lemon dressing. Wrap the pitas in foil, leaving the open side at the top, and off you go!

1 teaspoon grated lemon zest
¼ cup olive oil
3 tablespoons fresh lemon juice
1 teaspoon Dijon mustard
½ teaspoon salt
¼ teaspoon freshly ground black pepper
¾ cup packed fresh basil leaves, finely chopped
¼ cup finely chopped parsley
3 scallions, thinly sliced
2 tablespoons capers
3 cups diced (¼-inch) cooked chicken breasts or thighs—leftover or poached (page 17)
4 sandwich-size pita breads (6-inch diameter)

1. In large bowl, whisk together lemon zest, oil, lemon juice, mustard, salt, and pepper. Add basil, parsley, scallions, and capers, and stir to combine. Add chicken and toss to coat.

2. Make a cut in one side of each pita bread and spoon chicken salad into bread. Serve immediately.

AVOCADO STUFFED WITH CHICKEN SALAD Prepare chicken salad as directed. Halve and pit 2 large avocados. Scoop about 2 tablespoons of flesh from each avocado half and stir into chicken salad. Spoon chicken salad into avocado halves. Omit pita breads.
Calories 515, Total Fat 37g, Saturated Fat 6g, Cholesterol 89mg, Sodium 604mg, Protein 36g, Carbohydrates 13g

Prep Time: 15 minutes
Makes 4 servings

NUTRITION INFORMATION
Per Serving
Calories 559
Total Fat 26g
Saturated Fat 2.5g
Cholesterol 100mg
Sodium 856mg
Protein 34g
Carbohydrates 44g

Chicken, Apple & Brie on a Roll

Brie is a soft-ripened cheese with a downy white rind and a cream-colored interior; when the cheese is at its peak, it practically melts at room temperature. If you haven't bought Brie before, ask for help in selecting a piece that's ready to eat. The wedge of cheese should look plump (not shrunken) and should yield when you poke it. At home, refrigerate the cheese, but serve it at room temperature.

¼ cup mayonnaise
2 tablespoons mango chutney, finely chopped
2 teaspoons Dijon mustard
4 Kaiser rolls, split
2 cooked skinless, boneless chicken breast halves, thinly sliced crosswise—leftover or poached (page 17)
6 ounces Brie, cut into 4 slices
1 large McIntosh apple, cut into thin wedges

1. In small bowl, stir together mayonnaise, chutney, and mustard. Spread mixture over bottom halves of rolls.

2. Divide chicken evenly among 4 rolls. Top chicken with Brie and apple wedges. Cover with roll tops.

Chicken Muffaletta with Pickled Vegetables

The pride of New Orleans, the muffaletta is a family-size sandwich made from a great big round loaf of crusty bread. The loaf is split like a gargantuan hamburger bun and filled with generous portions of ham, salami, Provolone, and a unique condiment known as "olive salad."

- 1 large round loaf (8-inch diameter, 16 ounces) country bread, halved horizontally
- 1 clove garlic, peeled and halved
- 3 tablespoons olive oil
- 1 cup pimiento-stuffed olives, coarsely chopped
- 1 stalk celery, quartered lengthwise and thinly sliced
- 1 red bell pepper, finely chopped
- 2 cooked skinless, boneless chicken breast halves, thinly sliced crosswise—leftover or poached (page 17)
- ¼ pound thinly sliced Provolone cheese
- 6 ounces thinly sliced smoked chicken
- ¼ pound thinly sliced Virginia ham
- 1 jar (12 ounces) pickled garden vegetables, drained and coarsely chopped

1. With your fingers, starting ½ inch from edge of loaf, remove and discard 1 inch of bread dough from bottom half of loaf. Rub inside of bottom half with cut garlic clove. Discard garlic.

2. Brush inside of loaf with oil. In medium bowl, stir together olives, celery, and bell pepper. Spoon onto bottom of loaf. Layer chicken breast, Provolone, smoked chicken, and ham on top. Spoon garden vegetables on top of meats. Replace top of loaf.

3. Wrap loaf in foil. Place on jelly-roll pan or large plate and place heavy weight on top. Refrigerate at least 6 hours or up to overnight. To serve, unwrap and cut muffaletta into 8 wedges.

LEFTOVERS

Prep Time: 30 minutes plus chilling time
Makes 8 servings

NUTRITION INFORMATION
Per Serving
Calories 357
Total Fat 16g
Saturated Fat 5g
Cholesterol 56mg
Sodium 1437mg
Protein 25g
Carbohydrates 27g

Broiled Chicken & Fontina Sandwiches with Tomato

The grilled-cheese-and-tomato sandwich—standard coffee-shop fare—could use a slight update. Try this heartier interpretation made with oregano-grilled chicken and Fontina on semolina bread.

- 1 teaspoon dried oregano
- ½ teaspoon salt
- ½ teaspoon freshly ground black pepper
- ½ teaspoon sugar
- ¾ pound skinless, boneless chicken breasts or thighs
- 1 tablespoon olive oil
- 1 loaf semolina bread (10 inches long, 9 ounces), cut crosswise into 4 pieces
- 1 clove garlic, peeled and halved
- ½ pound Italian Fontina cheese, thinly sliced
- 1 large tomato, cut into 8 slices

1. Preheat broiler. In small bowl, combine oregano, salt, pepper, and sugar. Rub mixture into chicken. Place chicken on broiler rack and drizzle with oil. Broil 6 inches from heat for 5 minutes per side or until golden brown and cooked through. Slice chicken on the diagonal. Leave broiler on.

2. Slice each piece of bread horizontally, but not all the way through, so that it opens like a book. Rub bread with cut garlic. Dividing evenly, place chicken on one side of each open piece of bread. Top chicken and other side of bread with cheese.

3. Broil sandwiches 6 inches from heat for 1 minute or until cheese melts. Place tomato slices over chicken-side of sandwich and close up halves.

QUICK TO FIX

Prep Time: 15 minutes
Cooking Time: 15 minutes
Makes 4 servings

NUTRITION INFORMATION
Per Serving
Calories 508
Total Fat 22g
Saturated Fat 12g
Cholesterol 115mg
Sodium 1120mg
Protein 41g
Carbohydrates 34g

CHICKEN MUFFALETTA WITH PICKLED VEGETABLES

Grilled Stilton & Chicken Sandwich

The king of English cheeses, Stilton has a firm, ivory-colored "body" evenly laced with blue-green veins. Stilton is milder than Roquefort or Gorgonzola, but stronger than some of the Scandinavian blues, such as Saga and Danablu, or the widely available American blue cheeses. Use your favorite.

½ cup red currant jelly

1 tablespoon plus 1 teaspoon fresh lemon juice

1 tablespoon olive oil

½ teaspoon salt

½ teaspoon freshly ground black pepper

4 Kaiser rolls, split

1 pound skinless, boneless chicken breasts or thighs

6 ounces Stilton or other blue cheese, crumbled

1 Bartlett pear, peeled and cut into ¼-inch dice

1 small red onion, halved and thinly sliced

1. Preheat broiler. In small bowl, stir together jelly, lemon juice, oil, salt, and pepper. Brush 1½ teaspoons of jelly mixture on each cut side of the rolls.

2. Place chicken breasts on broiler rack. Brush remainder of jelly mixture on chicken. Broil 6 inches from heat for 5 minutes per side or until cooked through. Leave broiler on. When chicken is cool enough to handle, slice on the diagonal.

3. Place chicken slices on bottom halves of split rolls. In small bowl, combine Stilton and pear. Spoon over chicken and place bottom halves (with chicken and cheese mixture) on broiler rack. Broil for 1 minute or until cheese starts to melt. Remove and cover with onion slices and roll tops.

GRILLED CHEDDAR & CHICKEN SANDWICH Substitute white Cheddar for Stilton, apple jelly for red currant jelly, and a crisp green apple for pear. Use a cracked-wheat or other whole-grain bread instead of Kaiser rolls.

Calories 593, Total Fat 21g, Saturated Fat 10g, Cholesterol 110mg, Sodium 897mg, Protein 43g, Carbohydrates 60g

LOW FAT

QUICK TO FIX

Prep Time: 10 minutes
Cooking Time: 10 minutes
Makes 4 servings

NUTRITION INFORMATION
Per Serving
Calories 613
Total Fat 20g
Saturated Fat 9g
Cholesterol 98mg
Sodium 1283mg
Protein 42g
Carbohydrates 67g

Pesto Chicken on Focaccia

The thick, chewy round (or rectangle) of bread called focaccia, which resembles a pizza crust, is traditionally baked with minimal toppings—herbs, coarse salt, or just a sprinkling of good olive oil. In Italy, a slice of focaccia is a popular snack. But thick slabs of this rustic bread make wonderfully hearty sandwiches. Look for focaccia at your supermarket or at an Italian bakery.

1 clove garlic, peeled

½ cup packed fresh basil leaves

3 tablespoons grated Parmesan cheese

1 tablespoon plus 2 teaspoons olive oil

2 tablespoons slivered almonds

¼ teaspoon salt

1 round focaccia (10-inch diameter, 8 ounces)

2 cups mixed greens

2 cooked skinless, boneless chicken breast halves, thinly sliced crosswise on the diagonal—leftover or poached (page 17)

½ cup bottled roasted red peppers, cut into thin strips

1. Preheat oven to 400°F. To make the pesto: In small pan of boiling water, blanch garlic 1 minute. Drain and transfer to food processor. Add basil, Parmesan, oil, almonds, salt, and 2 tablespoons of water, and process until smooth.

2. Bake focaccia for 10 minutes. When cool enough to handle, slice in half horizontally. Spread the pesto onto both focaccia halves. Top with mixed greens. Place chicken and then roasted peppers on top of greens. Cover with focaccia top. To serve, cut into 4 wedges.

QUICK TO FIX

LEFTOVERS

Prep Time: 15 minutes
Cooking Time: 15 minutes
Makes 4 servings

NUTRITION INFORMATION
Per Serving
Calories 356
Total Fat 13g
Saturated Fat 3g
Cholesterol 55mg
Sodium 599mg
Protein 30g
Carbohydrates 30g

PESTO CHICKEN ON FOCACCIA

HOMEMADE SAUSAGE & PEPPER HEROES

Prep Time: 25 minutes
Cooking Time: 30 minutes
Makes 4 servings

NUTRITION INFORMATION
Per Serving
Calories 573
Total Fat 25g
Saturated Fat 5g
Cholesterol 98mg
Sodium 1445mg
Protein 32g
Carbohydrates 56g

Homemade Sausage & Pepper Heroes

The compelling fragrance of Italian sausage, peppers, onions, and garlic will draw the family to the kitchen. Sample a sandwich and you'll be transported to Little Italy.

1	pound ground chicken
½	cup chopped parsley
½	cup oil-packed sun-dried tomatoes, minced
¼	cup grated Parmesan cheese
1	slice firm-textured white bread, crumbled
1	teaspoon fennel seeds
1¼	teaspoons salt
¼	teaspoon freshly ground black pepper
2	tablespoons olive oil
1	large Spanish onion, thickly sliced
3	cloves garlic, slivered
2	green bell peppers, cut into matchsticks
1	red bell pepper, cut into matchsticks
2	tablespoons red wine vinegar
4	hoagie rolls, split

1. In large bowl, stir together chicken, parsley, sun-dried tomatoes, Parmesan, bread, fennel seeds, ¾ teaspoon of salt, and the black pepper. With moistened hands, shape mixture into 8 cigar-shaped sausages.

2. In large skillet, heat 1 tablespoon of oil over medium heat. Add onion and garlic, and cook, stirring frequently, 10 minutes or until onion is golden brown and tender. Add bell peppers and cook, stirring frequently, 7 minutes or until tender. Sprinkle vinegar and remaining ½ teaspoon salt over pepper mixture and cook 1 minute; set aside.

3. In large skillet, heat remaining 1 tablespoon oil over medium heat. Add sausages and cook, turning them frequently, for 10 minutes or until cooked through. Spoon pepper mixture and sausages over cut rolls.

LOW FAT
QUICK TO FIX
LEFTOVERS

Prep Time: 20 minutes
Cooking Time: 10 minutes
Makes 4 servings

NUTRITION INFORMATION
Per Serving
Calories 415
Total Fat 10g
Saturated Fat 3g
Cholesterol 93mg
Sodium 1012mg
Protein 39g
Carbohydrates 38g

Cajun Chicken Sandwiches

It's much easier to roast a bell pepper when it's cut into flat panels: Slice off the top and bottom, then seed the pepper and cut it vertically into four to six sections (depending on the natural shape of the pepper). When the charred pepper pieces are cool, the skin will lift off easily.

1	red bell pepper, cut lengthwise into flat panels
1	green bell pepper, cut lengthwise into flat panels
¼	cup reduced-fat mayonnaise
3	tablespoons reduced-fat sour cream
¾	teaspoon freshly ground black pepper
¾	teaspoon salt
½	teaspoon garlic powder
¼	teaspoon dried oregano
¼	teaspoon dried thyme
¼	teaspoon cayenne pepper
3	cups chunks (½-inch) cooked chicken breasts— leftover or poached (page 17)
1	stalk celery, quartered lengthwise and thinly sliced
4	hoagie rolls, split and toasted

1. Preheat broiler. Broil bell pepper pieces, skin-side up, 4 inches from heat for 10 minutes or until skin is blackened. When peppers are cool enough to handle, peel them and cut into ½-inch squares.

2. In large bowl, whisk together mayonnaise, sour cream, black pepper, salt, garlic powder, oregano, thyme, and cayenne. Add roasted peppers, chicken, and celery, and toss to coat. Serve on toasted rolls.

Casseroles, Stews & One-Dish Meals

What a comfort it is to know that the Dutch oven simmering away in the oven (or on the stove)

holds a complete dinner dish, replete with vegetables and rice, noodles, or potatoes. Choose from

recipes that are all-American, Mexican, Italian, Asian, and many more.

Chicken Pot Pie

This beloved American way with leftover chicken is even better when made with freshly cooked chunks of chicken breast. In place of the usual flaky crust, this pot pie is topped with a round of puff pastry. And for an invitingly smoky flavor, a few strips of bacon are crumbled into the filling.

Prep Time: 20 minutes
Cooking Time: 50 minutes
Makes 4 servings

NUTRITION INFORMATION
Per Serving
Calories 774
Total Fat 47g
Saturated Fat 13g
Cholesterol 141mg
Sodium 983mg
Protein 36g
Carbohydrates 51g

6 slices bacon (about 4 ounces), cut crosswise into 1-inch pieces

3 carrots, thinly sliced

3 tablespoons flour

2⅓ cups milk

¾ teaspoon salt

¼ teaspoon freshly ground black pepper

¾ pound skinless, boneless chicken breast, cut into 1-inch chunks

1 cup frozen peas

1 sheet (10 x 9-inch) store-bought puff pastry

1 large egg, lightly beaten with 1 teaspoon water

1. In large saucepan, cook bacon over medium-low heat 7 minutes or until crisp. Transfer bacon to paper towels to drain. Add carrots to pan and cook, stirring frequently, 7 minutes or until crisp-tender. Sprinkle flour over carrots and stir until well coated.

2. Gradually whisk milk into pan. Stir in salt and pepper, and cook until lightly thickened. Stir in chicken and peas, and cook 10 minutes or until chicken is cooked through. Add crumbled bacon and stir to combine.

3. Preheat oven to 400°F. Spoon chicken mixture into 9-inch deep-dish pie plate. Cool to room temperature.

4. Using a pie plate as a template, cut puff pastry into 9-inch round. With sharp paring knife, cut scallops into edge of round (see technique photo, at right). Place pastry round on top of chicken mixture. Brush with egg mixture (being careful not to let any drip down sides of puff pastry.) Place pie plate on a baking sheet and for bake 30 minutes or until piping hot and puff pastry has risen.

FROM THE FRIDGE

Use 1½ cups cooked chicken chunks, preferably thigh meat, in place of uncooked chicken. Do not cook chicken in step 2; simply stir it into pan after white sauce has cooked, and remove from heat.

CREAMY CHICKEN & VEGETABLE BAKE WITH CRESCENT ROLL CRUST
Prepare filling as directed, spooning it into 7 x 11-inch baking dish. Use 6 refrigerator crescent rolls (from 8-ounce package). Unroll each crescent and use to top casserole. Bake 25 minutes or until piping hot and golden brown.

Calories 579, Total Fat 32g, Saturated Fat 12g, Cholesterol 141mg, Sodium 1152mg, Protein 34g, Carbohydrates 38g

---

HINTS & TIPS

➤ You'll find ready-to-use puff pastry in the freezer case of your supermarket. It comes in a box, usually with two sheets of pastry per package. They're separated with a sheet of paper so that you can remove one portion of pastry without thawing both.

➤ Whenever you use an egg glaze (as in this recipe) to give puff pastry an attractive sheen, be careful not to let any of the glaze drip down the cut edges of the uncooked puff pastry dough. Any egg glaze on the dough will prevent it from puffing up to its full height when it bakes.

TECHNIQUE

PUFF PASTRY PIE TOP

Using a pie plate as a template, cut the puff pastry into a 9-inch round. With a sharp paring knife, cut scallops into the edge of the pastry round.

CHICKEN POT PIE

Carolina Chicken Stew

Buttery cornmeal dumplings flecked with scallions top this Carolina barbecue-style stew.

CHICKEN:

- 1 cup ketchup
- ¼ cup cider vinegar
- 2 tablespoons butter, melted
- 4 teaspoons honey
- 1½ teaspoons Worcestershire sauce
- ¾ teaspoon dry mustard
- ½ teaspoon salt
- ½ teaspoon freshly ground black pepper
- 1 whole chicken (about 3½ pounds), cut into 8 serving pieces (page 14), skin removed

SCALLION DUMPLINGS:

- 1 cup flour
- ½ cup yellow cornmeal
- 2½ teaspoons baking powder
- ½ teaspoon salt
- ⅓ cup cold butter, cut up
- 3 scallions, thinly sliced
- ½ cup plus 2 tablespoons milk

1. Prepare Chicken: Preheat oven to 375°F. In 3-quart nonreactive casserole, combine ketchup, vinegar, butter, honey, Worcestershire, dry mustard, salt, pepper, and ⅓ cup of water. Add chicken and toss to coat. Bake, uncovered, for 20 minutes.

2. Meanwhile, make Scallion Dumplings: In medium bowl, stir together flour, cornmeal, baking powder, and salt. With pastry blender or two knives, cut in cold butter until mixture resembles coarse meal. Stir in scallions. Make well in center and stir in milk until mixture is dampened and just combined.

3. With large spoon, spoon 8 dumplings around edge of baking dish onto hot chicken and sauce. Return to oven and bake for 30 minutes or until piping hot and cooked through.

Prep Time: 25 minutes
Cooking Time: 55 minutes
Makes 4 servings

NUTRITION INFORMATION
Per Serving
Calories 707
Total Fat 29g
Saturated Fat 15g
Cholesterol 195mg
Sodium 1998mg
Protein 48g
Carbohydrates 64g

Three-Cheese Macaroni

- 2 stalks broccoli, cut into bite-size pieces
- 10 ounces elbow macaroni
- 3 tablespoons butter
- 2 tablespoons flour
- 3 cups milk
- ¾ teaspoon salt
- ¼ teaspoon cayenne pepper
- ¼ pound Fontina cheese, shredded (1 cup)
- ¼ pound Gruyère cheese, shredded (1 cup)
- ½ cup grated Parmesan cheese
- 4 cups diced cooked chicken breasts or thighs—leftover or poached (page 17)
- 2 slices firm-textured white bread, crumbled

1. Preheat oven to 350°F. In large pot of boiling water, cook broccoli 3 minutes. Remove broccoli, add macaroni, and cook according to package directions. Drain and add to broccoli.

2. In large saucepan, melt 2 tablespoons of butter over low heat. Whisk in flour until well combined. Gradually whisk in milk. Stir in salt and cayenne; simmer 5 minutes or until slightly thickened. Remove from heat and add Fontina, Gruyère, and ¼ cup of Parmesan, stirring until melted.

3. Pour cheese sauce over broccoli and pasta in large bowl and stir in chicken. Spoon mixture into 9 x 13-inch glass baking dish. Cover with foil and bake for 25 minutes.

4. Meanwhile, in small saucepan, melt remaining 1 tablespoon butter. Uncover baking dish, sprinkle with bread crumbs and remaining ¼ cup Parmesan, and drizzle with melted butter. Bake for 10 to 15 minutes or until piping hot and crusty.

MACARONI & CHEDDAR WITH SUN-DRIED TOMATOES Substitute 3 cups cauliflower florets for broccoli. In step 2, add 1 teaspoon dry mustard when adding cayenne; increase cayenne to ½ teaspoon. Substitute ½ pound sharp Cheddar, shredded, for Fontina and Gruyère; omit Parmesan from sauce (but use ¼ cup on top of casserole). Add ½ cup chopped sun-dried tomatoes to sauce. Bake as directed.
Calories 730, Total Fat 31g, Saturated Fat 16g, Cholesterol 154mg, Sodium 1090mg, Protein 55g, Carbohydrates 58g

LEFTOVERS

Prep Time: 15 minutes
Cooking Time: 1 hour
Makes 6 servings

NUTRITION INFORMATION
Per Serving
Calories 684
Total Fat 28g
Saturated Fat 16g
Cholesterol 160mg
Sodium 1044mg
Protein 55g
Carbohydrates 51g

CAROLINA CHICKEN STEW

CHICKEN & EGGPLANT LASAGNA

NUTRITION INFORMATION

Per Serving

Calories 960

Total Fat 46g

Saturated Fat 18g

Cholesterol 168mg

Sodium 1713mg

Protein 53g

Carbohydrates 85g

HINTS & TIPS

➤ Add some oil to the water in which you cook the lasagna, and the noodles will be less likely to stick together after you drain them.

➤ If you have to transport the lasagna—say, to a potluck supper—assemble it in a heavy-duty foil baking pan. Place the pan on a cookie sheet or jelly-roll pan for easier (and safer) handling.

➤ You can make your own ground chicken at home: Cut a pound of skinless, boneless chicken breasts into chunks and process until the chicken is ground as you like it. Be sure to use pulsing (on-and-off) motions so the chicken retains some texture and does not turn into a paste.

Chicken & Eggplant Lasagna

Lasagna is universally popular, and lasagna fans will welcome this hearty variation. It's a combination of "red" lasagna and "white" lasagna: There are tomatoes in the chicken-and-eggplant filling, but the sauce is a creamy "balsamella," or Italian white sauce.

9 lasagna noodles

4 tablespoons olive oil

1 onion, finely chopped

3 cloves garlic, minced

2 eggplants (1½ pounds total), peeled and cut into ½-inch chunks

1 can (35 ounces) tomatoes packed in puree, chopped with puree

1 pound ground chicken

1¼ teaspoons salt

2 tablespoons butter

3 tablespoons flour

2½ cups milk

½ pound part-skim mozzarella cheese, shredded

¼ cup grated Parmesan cheese

1. In large pot of boiling water, cook lasagna noodles according to package directions; drain.

2. Meanwhile, in large skillet, heat 1 tablespoon of oil over medium-low heat. Add onion and garlic, and cook, stirring frequently, 7 minutes or until onion is tender.

3. Add remaining 3 tablespoons oil to pan, increase heat to medium, add eggplant, and cook 5 minutes or until eggplant is firm-tender. Add tomatoes; bring to a boil, reduce to a simmer, and cook 5 minutes. Stir in chicken and ¾ teaspoon of salt, and cook 7 minutes or until chicken is cooked through.

4. In medium saucepan, melt butter over low heat. Whisk in flour and stir until well combined. Gradually whisk in milk. Add remaining ½ teaspoon salt and cook, stirring frequently, 5 minutes or until sauce is slightly thickened and coats back of spoon.

5. Spoon ½ cup of eggplant mixture into bottom of 9 x 13-inch glass baking dish. Lay 3 noodles in bottom of pan, overlapping slightly. Spoon half of eggplant mixture over noodles. Spoon one-third of white sauce and one-third of mozzarella on top. Top with 3 noodles, remaining eggplant mixture, half remaining white sauce, and half remaining mozzarella. Top with remaining 3 lasagna noodles, remaining white sauce, Parmesan, and mozzarella.

6. Cover loosely with foil and bake for 30 minutes. Uncover and bake for 5 minutes or until sauce is bubbly and cheese has melted.

FROM THE FRIDGE

Substitute 3 cups finely chopped leftover chicken breast or thigh in place of ground chicken. Stir into eggplant-tomato mixture at end of step 3 and remove from heat (do not cook for 7 minutes).

CHICKEN & PORTOBELLO LASAGNA Cook noodles as directed. In step 2, increase garlic to 4 cloves and sauté with onion as directed. In step 3, substitute 1½ pounds thinly sliced portobello mushrooms for eggplant and decrease oil used to cook mushrooms to 2 tablespoons. After cooking mushrooms, drain off excess liquid from skillet. Add tomatoes to skillet and cook as directed, adding ½ teaspoon dried rosemary, crumbled, to tomato mixture. Make white sauce, layer, and bake as directed.

Calories 938, Total Fat 43g, Saturated Fat 18g, Cholesterol 168mg, Sodium 1714mg, Protein 55g, Carbohydrates 84g

Braised Chicken
with Leeks & Cream

To really reduce the fat in this luscious braise, substitute evaporated milk (or even evaporated skimmed milk) for the heavy cream.

- 2   tablespoons olive oil
- 4   bone-in chicken breast halves (about 2½ pounds), skin removed
- ¼   cup flour
- 3   cloves garlic, slivered
- 6   leeks, halved lengthwise, cut into 1-inch slices
- 1   pound all-purpose potatoes, peeled and cut into ½-inch chunks
- 6   carrots, halved lengthwise and cut into 1-inch lengths
- 1   cup chicken broth, canned or homemade (page 45)
- 1   teaspoon salt
- ½   cup heavy or whipping cream

1. Preheat oven to 350°F. In Dutch oven, heat oil over medium heat. Dredge chicken in flour, shaking off excess. Add chicken to pan and sauté 4 minutes per side or until golden brown. With slotted spoon, transfer chicken to plate.

2. Add garlic and leeks to pan and cook, stirring frequently, 5 minutes. Add potatoes and carrots, cover, and cook, stirring occasionally, 5 minutes or until carrots are crisp-tender. Add broth and salt, and bring to a boil. Return chicken breasts to pan, burying them slightly in leek mixture.

3. Cover, place in oven, and bake for 30 minutes or until chicken is cooked through and vegetables are tender. On stove-top, add cream to Dutch oven and bring to a boil over high heat. Serve hot.

LOW FAT

Prep Time: 25 minutes
Cooking Time: 50 minutes
Makes 4 servings

NUTRITION INFORMATION
Per Serving
Calories 621
Total Fat 21g
Saturated Fat 8.5g
Cholesterol 148mg
Sodium 1054mg
Protein 50g
Carbohydrates 58g

Mediterranean Chicken
with Two Beans & Fennel

Fennel is a celery-like vegetable; the edible part is the bulbous base, rather than the stalks. Fennel is most abundant in the fall. If you can't find it, substitute celery and a pinch of crushed fennel seeds.

- ½   pound green beans, cut into 2-inch lengths
- 2   tablespoons olive oil
- 1   whole chicken (about 3½ pounds), cut into 8 serving pieces (page 14), skin removed
- ¼   cup flour
- 1   bulb fennel (1½ pounds), trimmed and sliced lengthwise into ½-inch-wide pieces
- 4   cloves garlic, slivered
- 1   cup chicken broth, canned or homemade (page 45)
- 2   tablespoons fresh lemon juice
- ½   teaspoon salt
- ¼   teaspoon dried rosemary, crumbled
- ¼   teaspoon dried thyme
- ¼   teaspoon freshly ground black pepper
- 1   can (19 ounces) white kidney beans (cannellini), rinsed and drained

1. Preheat oven to 350°F. In large pot of boiling water, blanch green beans 3 minutes; drain and set aside.

2. In Dutch oven, heat oil over medium-high heat. Dredge chicken in flour, shaking off excess. Add chicken to pan and sauté 4 minutes per side or until golden brown. With slotted spoon, transfer chicken to plate.

3. Add fennel to pan, reduce heat to medium, and cook, stirring frequently, 7 minutes or until fennel is lightly golden. Add garlic and cook 1 minute. Add broth, lemon juice, salt, rosemary, thyme, and pepper, and bring to a boil. Return chicken to pan and bring to a boil. Cover, place in oven, and bake for 35 minutes or until chicken is cooked through.

4. Stir in white kidney beans and green beans, return to oven, and cook 5 minutes or until heated through.

LOW FAT

Prep Time: 20 minutes
Cooking Time: 1 hour
Makes 4 servings

NUTRITION INFORMATION
Per Serving
Calories 464
Total Fat 14g
Saturated Fat 2.5g
Cholesterol 133mg
Sodium 1007mg
Protein 52g
Carbohydrates 31g

MEDITERRANEAN CHICKEN WITH TWO BEANS & FENNEL

Chicken Gratin with Yukon Gold Potatoes, Carrots & Gruyère

Yukon Gold potatoes have deep yellow flesh, and the color almost fools you into thinking that they have a buttery flavor. If you can't get Yukon Golds, substitute red-skinned potatoes.

- 1 clove garlic, peeled and halved
- 1 pound Yukon Gold potatoes, peeled and thinly sliced
- 3 carrots, thinly sliced
- 3 tablespoons olive oil
- 2 tablespoons flour
- 2 cups milk
- 2 teaspoons Dijon mustard
- ¾ teaspoon salt
- ¾ teaspoon freshly ground black pepper
- 6 ounces Gruyère cheese, shredded (1½ cups)
- 4 skinless, boneless chicken breast halves (about 1½ pounds)

1. Preheat oven to 375°F. Rub bottom of 7 x 11-inch glass baking dish with garlic; discard. In large bowl, toss together potatoes, carrots, and 2 tablespoons of oil. Transfer to prepared dish and bake for 20 minutes.

2. Meanwhile, in medium saucepan, heat remaining 1 tablespoon oil. Whisk in flour and stir until well combined with oil. Gradually add milk and cook 5 minutes or until slightly thickened. Stir in mustard and ½ teaspoon each of salt and pepper. Remove from heat; stir in Gruyère.

3. Pour half of cheese sauce over potato-carrot mixture. Lay chicken on top and sprinkle with remaining ¼ teaspoon each salt and pepper. Spoon remaining cheese sauce on top. Bake for 35 minutes or until chicken is cooked through and potatoes and carrots are tender.

Prep Time: 25 minutes
Cooking Time: 55 minutes
Makes 4 servings

NUTRITION INFORMATION
Per Serving
Calories 636
Total Fat 30g
Saturated Fat 13g
Cholesterol 163mg
Sodium 834mg
Protein 59g
Carbohydrates 30g

Basil Chicken with Squash & Tomatoes

Any kind of summer squash (zucchini, pattypan, crookneck) can be used in this basil-scented casserole. For a change, serve it over rice instead of pasta, or use a different pasta shape.

- 3 tablespoons olive oil
- 4 bone-in chicken breast halves (about 2½ pounds), skin removed, halved crosswise
- 2 tablespoons flour
- 1 leek, halved lengthwise, cut crosswise into ½-inch-wide strips
- 3 cloves garlic, minced
- 2 yellow squash (6 ounces each), halved lengthwise and cut crosswise into 1-inch lengths
- 1 zucchini (6 ounces), halved lengthwise and cut crosswise into 1-inch lengths
- 1 can (28 ounces) tomatoes, drained and chopped
- ¾ cup chopped fresh basil leaves
- ¾ teaspoon salt
- 10 ounces penne or ziti

1. Preheat oven to 350°F. In Dutch oven, heat 2 tablespoons of oil over medium heat. Dredge chicken in flour, shaking off excess. Add chicken to pan and sauté 4 minutes per side or until golden brown. With slotted spoon, transfer chicken to plate.

2. Add leek, garlic, and remaining 1 tablespoon oil to pan and cook, stirring occasionally, 5 minutes or until leek is tender. Add yellow squash and zucchini, and sauté 5 to 7 minutes or until crisp-tender. Add tomatoes, ½ cup of basil, and salt, and bring to a boil. Return chicken to pan and bring to a boil. Cover, place pan in oven, and bake for 25 minutes or until chicken is cooked through. Stir in remaining ¼ cup basil.

3. Meanwhile, in large pot of boiling water, cook pasta according to package directions. Drain. Serve sauce and chicken over pasta.

LOW FAT

Prep Time: 15 minutes
Cooking Time: 45 minutes
Makes 4 servings

NUTRITION INFORMATION
Per Serving
Calories 657
Total Fat 14g
Saturated Fat 2.5g
Cholesterol 107mg
Sodium 1137mg
Protein 56g
Carbohydrates 75g

Prep Time: 30 minutes
Cooking Time: 25 minutes
Makes 4 servings

NUTRITION INFORMATION
Per Serving
Calories 579
Total Fat 19g
Saturated Fat 7g
Cholesterol 121mg
Sodium 1240mg
Protein 51g
Carbohydrates 55g

Chicken Chipotle Casserole with Pear Salsa

Manchego is a full-flavored Spanish cheese, excellent for melting. If you can't get it, use Provolone.

- 1 can (28 ounces) tomatoes, chopped, with juice
- 1 chipotle pepper in adobo, minced with seeds
- 2 tablespoons olive oil
- 1½ teaspoons ground cumin
- 1 teaspoon salt
- 6 corn tortillas (6-inch diameter)
- 1½ pounds skinless, boneless chicken breasts, cut into 1-inch chunks
- 1 cup frozen corn kernels
- ⅔ cup grated Manchego cheese (3 ounces)
- 2 firm-ripe pears, cut into ½-inch cubes
- 1 red bell pepper, cut into ½-inch squares
- ¼ cup minced red onion
- 2 tablespoons fresh lime juice
- 1 tablespoon honey

1. Preheat oven to 450°F. In large bowl, stir together tomatoes, chipotle pepper, oil, 1 teaspoon of cumin, and ½ teaspoon of salt.

2. Lightly grease bottom of 7 x 11-inch glass baking dish. Place 2 tortillas, slightly overlapping, in baking dish. Spoon one-third of tomato mixture on top, top with half of chicken, half of corn, and half of cheese. Place another 2 tortillas on top. Spoon half of remaining tomato mixture and all of remaining chicken, corn, and cheese on top. Top with remaining 2 tortillas and remaining tomato mixture. Bake for 25 minutes or until chicken is cooked through.

3. Meanwhile, in medium bowl, stir together pears, bell pepper, onion, lime juice, honey, remaining ½ teaspoon cumin, and ½ teaspoon salt. Refrigerate until serving time. Serve casserole with salsa.

CHICKEN CHIPOTLE CASSEROLE WITH PEAR SALSA

WINTER CHICKEN STEW

Prep Time: 25 minutes plus
  mushroom soaking time
Cooking Time: 1 hour
Makes 4 servings

NUTRITION INFORMATION
Per Serving
Calories 646
Total Fat 14g
Saturated Fat 2.5g
Cholesterol 133mg
Sodium 739mg
Protein 54g
Carbohydrates 72g

Chicken Cacciatore with Spaghetti

Cacciatore means "hunter style"; mushrooms are a signature ingredient of dishes with this name.

½ cup dried porcini mushrooms
½ cup boiling water
2 tablespoons olive oil
1 whole chicken (about 3½ pounds), cut into 8 serving pieces (page 14), skin removed
¼ cup flour
1 onion, finely chopped
3 cloves garlic, minced
½ pound mushrooms, trimmed and quartered
1½ cups canned tomatoes, drained and chopped
¾ teaspoon salt
¼ teaspoon freshly ground black pepper
3 strips (3 x ½-inch) orange zest
10 ounces spaghetti

1. In small bowl, combine dried porcini and boiling water. Let stand 20 minutes or until softened. With fingers, lift porcini from water. Coarsely chop. Strain soaking liquid through a paper towel-lined sieve; reserve.

2. Preheat oven to 350°F. In Dutch oven, heat oil over medium-high heat. Dredge chicken in flour, shaking off excess. Add chicken to pan and sauté 4 minutes per side or until golden brown. Transfer chicken to plate.

3. Reduce heat to medium-low, add onion and garlic to pan, and sauté 7 minutes or until onion is tender. Add fresh mushrooms to pan and cook 5 minutes or until mushrooms begin to give off liquid. Add reserved mushroom soaking liquid and soaked mushrooms; increase heat to high and cook 2 minutes. Add tomatoes, salt, pepper, and orange zest. Return chicken to pan and bring to a boil. Cover, place in oven, and bake for 35 minutes or until chicken is cooked through.

4. Meanwhile, in large pot of boiling water, cook spaghetti according to package directions; drain. Top spaghetti with sauce and chicken.

Prep Time: 25 minutes
Cooking Time: 1 hour 5 minutes
Makes 4 servings

NUTRITION INFORMATION
Per Serving
Calories 474
Total Fat 14g
Saturated Fat 2.5g
Cholesterol 133mg
Sodium 735mg
Protein 48g
Carbohydrates 40g

Winter Chicken Stew

Cold-weather appetites call for sustaining meals made with hearty ingredients, such as winter vegetables. Here, red potatoes, Brussels sprouts, and carrots are oven-braised with chicken.

2 tablespoons olive oil
1 whole chicken (about 3½ pounds), cut into 8 serving pieces (page 14), skin removed
¼ cup flour
3 carrots, cut into 2-inch lengths
8 cloves garlic, peeled
1 pound small red-skinned potatoes, quartered
1 package (10 ounces) frozen Brussels sprouts
1 cup chicken broth, canned or homemade (page 45)
½ teaspoon salt
½ teaspoon dried sage

1. In Dutch oven, heat oil over medium heat. Dredge chicken in flour; reserve excess. Add chicken to pan and sauté 4 minutes per side or until golden. Transfer chicken to plate.

2. Preheat oven to 350°F. Add carrots and garlic to pan and cook 5 minutes or until garlic is lightly colored. Add potatoes, Brussels sprouts, broth, salt, and sage, and bring to a boil. Return chicken to pan and bring to a boil. Cover, place pan in oven, and bake for 45 minutes or until chicken is cooked through and potatoes are tender.

3. Remove pan from oven. With slotted spoon, transfer chicken to platter. In small bowl, blend reserved dredging flour and ½ cup of cooking liquid from casserole. Stir mixture into stew and bring to a boil. Cook 1 minute or until slightly thickened. Spoon over chicken.

CHICKEN STEW WITH SPRING VEGETABLES

Substitute 4 skinless, boneless chicken breast halves (about 1½ pounds) for whole chicken. In step 1, use nonstick Dutch oven and reduce oil to 1 tablespoon. In step 2, sauté 6 scallions, cut into 1-inch lengths, along with garlic and carrots. Omit Brussels sprouts; decrease broth to ¾ cup; substitute rosemary for sage; and add 1 cup frozen peas. Complete as directed.
Calories 409, Total Fat 6.5g, Saturated Fat 1g, Cholesterol 99mg, Sodium 670mg, Protein 46g, Carbohydrates 41g

Chicken Stew with Cider & Apples

There's an old-world feeling to this dish, which is made with apples, cabbage, and potatoes. When fresh cider is out of season, you can use apple juice—or hard cider—instead.

LOW FAT

Prep Time: 25 minutes
Cooking Time: 1 hour 10 minutes
Makes 4 servings

- 2 tablespoons unsalted butter
- 1 whole chicken (about 3½ pounds), cut into 8 serving pieces (page 14), skin removed
- ¼ cup flour
- 1 small onion, finely chopped
- 1½ pounds all-purpose potatoes, peeled and thickly sliced
- 1 small green cabbage (1 pound), halved and cut into 1-inch wedges
- 2 Granny Smith apples, peeled and cut into ½-inch chunks
- ½ cup apple cider
- ¾ teaspoon salt
- ½ teaspoon freshly ground black pepper

1. Preheat oven to 350°F. In Dutch oven, melt butter over medium heat. Dredge chicken in flour, shaking off excess. Add chicken to pan and sauté 4 minutes per side or until golden brown. With slotted spoon, transfer chicken to plate.

2. Add onion to pan, reduce heat to low, and cook, stirring frequently, 5 minutes or until soft. Add potatoes, cabbage, and apples. Cover and cook, stirring occasionally, 10 minutes or until cabbage has wilted. Add cider, salt, and pepper; increase heat to high and cook 2 minutes or until slightly reduced.

3. Return chicken to pan and bring to a boil. Cover, place pan in oven, and bake for 50 minutes or until chicken is cooked through.

NUTRITION INFORMATION
Per Serving
Calories 497
Total Fat 12g
Saturated Fat 5g
Cholesterol 149mg
Sodium 614mg
Protein 46g
Carbohydrates 51g

CHICKEN STEW WITH PEARL ONIONS & PEARS
Sauté chicken as directed in step 1. In step 2, substitute 2 cups frozen pearl onions for onion. Sprinkle with 1 tablespoon sugar and sauté 5 minutes or until onions are golden brown. Omit potatoes and cabbage. Substitute 2 firm-ripe pears, peeled and sliced, for apples. Sauté 5 minutes or until pears are crisp-tender. Omit cider. Add ¾ cup chicken broth, ¼ cup balsamic vinegar, ½ teaspoon salt, ½ teaspoon black pepper, and ½ teaspoon dried tarragon, and bring to a boil. Cover, place pan in oven, and bake for 50 minutes or until chicken is cooked through. On stovetop, add ¼ cup heavy cream and cook over high heat until cream is slightly reduced. Stir in ¼ cup chopped parsley. Spoon sauce over chicken.
Calories 419, Total Fat 15g, Saturated Fat 7g, Cholesterol 162mg, Sodium 646mg, Protein 43g, Carbohydrates 27g

Latin American Chicken

Turmeric—in place of costly saffron—tints the rice a rich golden yellow in this adaptation of arroz con pollo. Serve with a tomato salad for a bright, festive dinner.

LOW FAT

Prep Time: 20 minutes
Cooking Time: 50 minutes
Makes 4 servings

- 2 tablespoons olive oil
- 1 whole chicken (about 3½ pounds), cut into 8 serving pieces (page 14), skin removed
- ¼ cup flour
- 3 scallions, thinly sliced
- 1 cup rice
- ½ teaspoon turmeric
- 1¼ cups chicken broth, canned or homemade (page 45)
- 1 can (19 ounces) black beans, rinsed and drained
- 1 teaspoon grated lemon zest
- ½ teaspoon salt

1. Preheat oven to 350°F. In Dutch oven, heat oil over medium-high heat. Dredge chicken in flour, shaking off excess. Add chicken to pan and sauté 4 minutes per side or until golden brown. With slotted spoon, transfer chicken to plate.

2. Stir scallions into pan and cook 1 minute or until softened. Stir in rice, turmeric, broth, beans, lemon zest, salt, and ¾ cup of water. Bring to a boil. Add chicken and return to a boil. Cover, place in oven, and bake for 40 minutes or until chicken and rice are tender.

NUTRITION INFORMATION
Per Serving
Calories 571
Total Fat 14g
Saturated Fat 2.5g
Cholesterol 133mg
Sodium 986mg
Protein 50g
Carbohydrates 57g

CHICKEN STEW WITH CIDER & APPLES

Chicken Braised in Herbed Cream Sauce

All you need to round out this simple but elegant meal is a tossed green salad with a lemon vinaigrette. If you buy fresh tarragon for the chicken dish, mince some to toss into the salad. A light fruit dessert would be best after a cream-based entrée. Try pears poached in white wine.

LOW FAT

Prep Time: 20 minutes
Cooking Time: 55 minutes
Makes 4 servings

NUTRITION INFORMATION
Per Serving
Calories 641
Total Fat 21g
Saturated Fat 6.5g
Cholesterol 208mg
Sodium 776mg
Protein 53g
Carbohydrates 58g

- 2 tablespoons olive oil
- 1 whole chicken (about 3½ pounds), cut into 8 serving pieces (page 14), skin removed
- ¼ cup flour
- 1 large onion, finely chopped
- 3 cloves garlic, minced
- ½ cup dry vermouth or white wine
- ½ cup chicken broth
- 2 tablespoons snipped chives
- ¾ teaspoon salt
- 8 ounces broad egg noodles
- 1 cup frozen peas
- ¼ cup heavy or whipping cream
- 2 tablespoons chopped fresh tarragon or 1 teaspoon dried

1. Preheat oven to 350°F. In Dutch oven, heat oil over medium heat. Dredge chicken in flour, shaking off excess. Add chicken to pan and sauté 4 minutes per side or until golden brown. With slotted spoon, transfer chicken to plate.

2. Reduce heat to low. Add onion and garlic to pan, and sauté 5 minutes or until soft. Add vermouth to pan, increase heat to high, and cook 2 minutes. Add broth, chives, and salt, and bring to a boil. Return chicken to pan and bring to a boil. Cover, place pan in oven, and bake for 35 minutes or until chicken is cooked through.

3. Meanwhile, in large pot of boiling water, cook noodles according to package directions. Drain and place in large serving bowl.

4. When chicken is done, transfer to serving bowl. Add peas, cream, and tarragon to Dutch oven and cook over high heat until sauce is slightly reduced and peas are heated through. Spoon sauce over chicken and noodles.

CHICKEN PAPRIKASH In step 1, increase oil for sautéing chicken to 3 tablespoons. In step 2, stir 2 tablespoons paprika into pan once onion is tender and cook 2 minutes. Add vermouth and cook as directed. Add broth; substitute ½ teaspoon caraway seeds for chives; increase salt to 1 teaspoon. Bake chicken and cook noodles as directed. In small bowl, stir together ½ cup reduced-fat sour cream and 1 tablespoon flour. In step 4, omit cream and tarragon. Stir sour-cream mixture into pan and cook over low heat 2 minutes or until no floury taste remains. Stir in peas. Spoon sauce over chicken and noodles.
Calories 686, Total Fat 23g, Saturated Fat 5.5g, Cholesterol 197mg, Sodium 934mg, Protein 55g, Carbohydrates 63g

HINTS & TIPS

➤ If you're not a martini fan, you may not know that vermouth is a fortified white wine subtly flavored with herbs and spices. Use dry (white) vermouth for this recipe, not a sweet (red) vermouth.

➤ Some—but not all—of the alcohol will evaporate when you simmer the sauce. If you don't want *any* alcohol in the dish, substitute broth for the vermouth or wine.

➤ Note that the recipe says "snipped chives" rather than "chopped." That's because scissors are really the best tool for the job (use them for dill, too).

CHICKEN BRAISED IN HERBED CREAM SAUCE

CHICKEN WITH PEAS & CILANTRO

Prep Time: 15 minutes plus
   mushroom soaking time
Cooking Time: 1 hour 10 minutes
Makes 4 servings

NUTRITION INFORMATION

Per Serving

Calories 494

Total Fat 14g

Saturated Fat 2.5g

Cholesterol 130mg

Sodium 620mg

Protein 40g

Carbohydrates 52g

Chicken in Porcini & Red Wine Sauce

Porcini is the Italian name for a wild mushroom prized throughout Europe. Intensely savory, dried porcini are used as a seasoning. They're the least expensive (and no less flavorful) when sold in broken pieces.

1   package (.35 ounce) dried porcini mushrooms

½   cup boiling water

2   tablespoons olive oil

4   whole chicken legs (about 2½ pounds), split into drumsticks and thighs (page 14), skin removed

¼   cup flour

1   small red onion, finely chopped

4   carrots, thinly sliced

½   pound fresh shiitake mushrooms, stems trimmed and caps thinly sliced

3   cloves garlic, minced

1   cup dry red wine

¾   teaspoon salt

½   teaspoon dried rosemary, crumbled

¼   teaspoon crushed red pepper flakes

1½   pounds small red-skinned potatoes, quartered

1. In small bowl, combine dried porcini and boiling water. Let stand 20 minutes or until softened. With your fingers, lift porcini from water and rinse under warm water. Coarsely chop. Strain soaking liquid through paper towel-lined sieve; reserve.

2. Preheat oven to 350°F. In Dutch oven, heat oil over medium-high heat. Dredge chicken in flour, shaking off excess. Add chicken to pan and sauté 4 minutes per side or until golden brown. With slotted spoon, transfer chicken to plate.

3. Add onion and carrots to pan, and cook, stirring frequently, 7 minutes or until onion is tender. Stir in fresh shiitakes, garlic, and porcini, and cook, stirring frequently, 5 minutes or until fresh mushrooms are tender.

4. Stir in wine, increase heat to high, and cook 3 minutes. Add salt, rosemary, red pepper flakes, and reserved mushroom soaking liquid. Bring to a boil, stir in potatoes and chicken, and return to a boil. Cover, place in oven, and bake for 45 minutes or until chicken and potatoes are tender.

Prep Time: 15 minutes
Cooking Time: 50 minutes
Makes 4 servings

NUTRITION INFORMATION

Per Serving

Calories 543

Total Fat 13g

Saturated Fat 7g

Cholesterol 133mg

Sodium 1407mg

Protein 50g

Carbohydrates 56g

Chicken with Peas & Cilantro

There's more than a hint of Southeast Asian cuisine here; but in spite of its exotic roots, this rich and fragrant stew qualifies as first-class "comfort food."

¾   cup canned crushed tomatoes

½   cup coconut milk

½   cup chopped cilantro

2   tablespoons fresh lime juice

2   tablespoons soy sauce

1   tablespoon light brown sugar

3   scallions, thinly sliced

3   cloves garlic, minced

1   tablespoon minced fresh ginger

1   teaspoon salt

1   whole chicken (about 3½ pounds), cut into 8 serving pieces (page 14), skin removed

1   cup rice

1   package (10 ounces) frozen peas

1. Preheat oven to 350°F. In Dutch oven, combine tomatoes, coconut milk, ¼ cup of cilantro, the lime juice, soy sauce, brown sugar, scallions, garlic, ginger, and ½ teaspoon of salt.

2. Add chicken to Dutch oven, turning to coat. Bring mixture to a boil over medium heat. Cover, place in oven, and bake for 40 minutes or until chicken is cooked through.

3. Meanwhile, in medium covered saucepan, bring 2¼ cups water to a boil. Add rice and remaining ½ teaspoon salt. Reduce heat to a simmer, cover, and cook 17 minutes or until rice is tender.

4. Stir peas into Dutch oven and cook 5 minutes or until heated through. Stir in remaining ¼ cup cilantro. Serve sauce and chicken over rice.

Spicy Asian Chicken Braised with Mushrooms

Hoisin sauce, sold in jars in the Asian foods section of the supermarket, is made from soybeans, garlic, chilies, and other seasonings. It's a potent and popular flavoring for Chinese dishes.

LOW FAT

Prep Time: 15 minutes
Cooking Time: 40 minutes
Makes 4 servings

NUTRITION INFORMATION
Per Serving
Calories 490
Total Fat 9.5g
Saturated Fat 2g
Cholesterol 118mg
Sodium 1561mg
Protein 39g
Carbohydrates 58g

- 3 scallions, thinly sliced
- 3 cloves garlic, crushed and peeled
- 3 slices (¼-inch-thick) fresh ginger
- ¼ cup lower-sodium soy sauce
- ¼ cup hoisin sauce
- ¼ cup chicken broth
- 1 tablespoon sesame oil
- 1 teaspoon crushed red pepper flakes
- 1 teaspoon sugar
- ¾ teaspoon salt
- 8 chicken drumsticks (about 2½ pounds), skin removed
- 1 pound mushrooms, quartered
- 1 large green bell pepper, cut into ½-inch pieces
- 1½ teaspoons cornstarch blended with 1 tablespoon water
- 1 cup rice

1. In Dutch oven, stir together scallions, garlic, ginger, soy sauce, hoisin sauce, broth, sesame oil, red pepper flakes, sugar, and ¼ teaspoon of salt. Stir in chicken, mushrooms, and bell pepper.

2. Bring to a boil over medium heat. Reduce heat to a simmer, cover, and cook 35 minutes or until chicken is cooked through and vegetables are tender. Stir in cornstarch mixture and cook, stirring constantly, for 1 minute or until slightly thickened.

3. Meanwhile, in medium covered saucepan, bring 2¼ cups of water to a boil. Add rice and remaining ½ teaspoon salt. Reduce heat to a simmer, cover, and cook 17 minutes or until rice is tender. Serve sauce and chicken with rice.

Chicken, Butternut Squash & Lentil Stew

To cut up the butternut squash, you'll need a large, sturdy chef's knife. To make the procedure easier, first cut off the "neck" of the squash, and then halve the thicker bottom part.

LOW FAT

Prep Time: 15 minutes
Cooking Time: 55 minutes
Makes 4 servings

NUTRITION INFORMATION
Per Serving
Calories 433
Total Fat 14g
Saturated Fat 2.5g
Cholesterol 141mg
Sodium 556mg
Protein 43g
Carbohydrates 35g

- 2 tablespoons olive oil
- 1 onion, finely chopped
- 3 cloves garlic, minced
- ½ cup lentils, rinsed and picked over
- 1 small butternut squash (1¼ pounds), peeled, halved, seeded, and cut into ½-inch chunks
- 1 cup canned tomatoes, chopped with their juice
- 2 teaspoons chili powder
- 1 teaspoon ground coriander
- ½ teaspoon salt
- ⅛ teaspoon ground cloves
- 1½ pounds skinless, boneless chicken thighs, cut into 1-inch chunks

1. Preheat oven to 350°F. In Dutch oven, heat oil over medium heat. Add onion and garlic, and cook, stirring frequently, 7 minutes or until onion is golden and tender.

2. Stir in lentils, squash, tomatoes, chili powder, coriander, salt, cloves, and ½ of cup water; bring to a boil. Add chicken. Cover, place in oven, and bake for 45 minutes or until chicken and lentils are cooked through and squash is tender.

FROM THE FRIDGE

Use 3 cups shredded cooked chicken thighs instead of uncooked chicken. Stir chicken into stew for last 15 minutes of cooking.

SPICY ASIAN CHICKEN BRAISED WITH MUSHROOMS

Saucy Chicken-Stuffed Manicotti with Provolone

Pasta casseroles are always a hit at parties, and you can double this recipe to serve 8. If you'd like to make the dish ahead of time and freeze it, line the baking dish with heavy-duty foil before filling it with the manicotti and sauce. Bake as directed; then, after cooling, wrap the manicotti tightly with foil and freeze. Reheat (covered, and without thawing) in a 300°F. oven for 20 to 30 minutes, or until piping hot throughout.

Prep Time: 25 minutes
Cooking Time: 40 minutes
Makes 4 servings

NUTRITION INFORMATION
Per Serving
Calories 780
Total Fat 41g
Saturated Fat 19g
Cholesterol 185mg
Sodium 1733mg
Protein 48g
Carbohydrates 56g

- 8 manicotti (about 6 ounces)
- 2 tablespoons olive oil
- 2 large onions, finely chopped
- ¾ pound ground chicken
- ¾ pound Provolone cheese, shredded (3 cups)
- ⅔ cup chopped fresh basil leaves
- 3 tablespoons grated Parmesan cheese
- ½ teaspoon freshly ground black pepper
- ¾ teaspoon salt
- 1 large egg yolk
- 1 can (35 ounces) tomatoes, chopped with their juice
- 1 teaspoon sugar
- ¼ teaspoon crushed red pepper flakes

1. In large pot of boiling water, cook manicotti according to package directions. Drain and rinse under cold running water.

2. Meanwhile, in large skillet, heat oil over medium heat. Add onions and cook, stirring frequently, 10 minutes or until golden brown and tender. Transfer half of onions to large bowl. Set skillet with remaining onions aside.

3. Let onions in bowl cool to room temperature, then stir in ground chicken, 1½ cups of Provolone, ⅓ cup of basil, the Parmesan, pepper, ¼ teaspoon of salt, and the egg yolk. Fill a pastry bag or large sturdy zip-seal bag with chicken filling (see technique photo, at right). Pipe into cooked manicotti.

4. Preheat oven to 375°F. Add tomatoes, remaining ⅓ cup basil, ½ teaspoon of salt, the sugar, and red pepper flakes to onions in skillet. Bring to a boil, reduce to a simmer, and cook 5 minutes or until slightly thickened.

5. Spoon ½ cup of tomato sauce into bottom of 7 x 11-inch glass baking dish. Arrange stuffed manicotti on top of sauce. Spoon remaining sauce over manicotti and bake for 20 minutes. Sprinkle remaining 1½ cups Provolone on top and bake for 5 minutes until bubbly.

IN A HURRY?

Use 3 cups bottled pasta sauce (preferably basil-flavored) and add to sautéed onions in step 4. Omit remainder of sauce-making step.

FROM THE FRIDGE

Use 2 cups minced cooked chicken thigh instead of ground chicken and add as directed in step 3.

HINTS & TIPS

➤ You don't usually rinse pasta after cooking. In this case, though, the manicotti will be easier to handle if you do. Rinsing removes the surface starch and keeps the manicotti from sticking together after they're cooked.

➤ Before shredding the Provolone, spray the face of the grater with nonstick cooking spray. The cheese won't stick, and clean-up will be much easier.

➤ Chop basil and other herbs with a stainless-steel knife. If you use one with a carbon-steel blade, the chopped herbs will turn black.

TECHNIQUE

HOW TO STUFF MANICOTTI

Fill a sturdy zip-seal plastic bag with the chicken filling. Snip a scant ½-inch piece off one corner of the bag and pipe the mixture into one end of the cooked manicotti until it half fills it. Turn the manicotti around and pipe filling into the other end.

SAUCY CHICKEN-STUFFED MANICOTTI WITH PROVOLONE

Pesto Chicken Meatballs with Tomato-Oregano Sauce

Pesto is the fragrant Genoese pasta sauce made from fresh basil, nuts, and Parmesan. As tasty as it is on fettuccine or penne, pesto is also a delicious seasoning for meatballs in an herbed tomato sauce.

Prep Time: 20 minutes
Cooking Time: 15 minutes
Makes 4 servings

- 2 cloves garlic, peeled
- 1 cup packed fresh basil leaves
- ⅓ cup grated Parmesan cheese
- ¼ cup heavy or whipping cream
- 3 tablespoons pine nuts
- ¾ teaspoon salt
- 1 pound ground chicken
- 1 large egg
- 3 tablespoons plain dried bread crumbs
- ¼ cup flour
- 3 tablespoons olive oil
- 1 can (35 ounces) tomatoes, chopped with their juice
- 3 tablespoons chopped fresh oregano or 1 teaspoon dried
- 10 ounces ziti

1. In small pan of boiling water, blanch garlic 2 minutes. Transfer garlic to food processor. Add basil, Parmesan, cream, pine nuts, and ½ teaspoon of salt. Transfer to large bowl; add chicken, egg, and bread crumbs, and mix well to combine. With moistened hands, shape into 24 meatballs. Dredge meatballs in flour, shaking off excess.

2. In large skillet, heat oil over medium heat. Add meatballs and cook 4 minutes or until golden brown. Stir in tomatoes, oregano, and remaining ¼ teaspoon salt, and bring to a boil. Reduce to a simmer, cover, and cook 5 to 7 minutes or until meatballs are cooked through and sauce is flavorful.

3. Meanwhile, in large pot of boiling water, cook ziti according to package directions. Drain. Top ziti with sauce and meatballs.

NUTRITION INFORMATION
Per Serving
Calories 776
Total Fat 35g
Saturated Fat 10g
Cholesterol 173mg
Sodium 1128mg
Protein 40g
Carbohydrates 78g

Cumin-Spiced Chicken Thighs

This main dish has a mildly exotic flavor, thanks to a spice mixture rubbed on the chicken. Some of the potatoes cooked with the chicken are mashed to thicken the sauce without adding fat.

LOW FAT

Prep Time: 15 minutes
Cooking Time: 55 minutes
Makes 4 servings

- 1 tablespoon ground cumin
- 1½ teaspoons paprika
- ½ teaspoon sugar
- ¾ teaspoon salt
- ½ teaspoon freshly ground black pepper
- 8 bone-in chicken thighs (about 2 pounds), skin removed
- 1 tablespoon olive oil
- 4 scallions, thinly sliced
- 2 cloves garlic, minced
- 1 pound all-purpose potatoes, peeled and cut into ½-inch chunks
- 6 carrots, quartered lengthwise and cut into ½-inch lengths
- 1 cup chicken broth, canned or homemade (page 45)

1. Preheat oven to 350°F. In large bowl, stir together cumin, paprika, sugar, ½ teaspoon of salt, and the pepper. Add chicken and rub spice mixture all over. Let stand for 10 minutes.

2. In Dutch oven, heat oil over medium heat. Add chicken and sauté 3 minutes per side or until golden brown. Push chicken to side of pan. Add scallions and garlic, and cook 1 minute.

3. Add potatoes, carrots, broth, and remaining ¼ teaspoon salt and bring to a boil. Cover, place in oven, and bake for 45 minutes or until chicken and vegetables are cooked through. Transfer chicken to serving platter. With potato masher, slightly mash about one-fourth of vegetables in pot to thicken sauce. Spoon sauce and vegetables over chicken.

NUTRITION INFORMATION
Per Serving
Calories 322
Total Fat 9.5g
Saturated Fat 2g
Cholesterol 107mg
Sodium 858mg
Protein 29g
Carbohydrates 30g

PESTO CHICKEN MEATBALLS WITH TOMATO-OREGANO SAUCE

CHICKEN-JACK ENCHILADAS WITH SALSA VERDE

Prep Time: 15 minutes
Cooking Time: 35 minutes
Makes 4 servings

NUTRITION INFORMATION
Per Serving
Calories 594
Total Fat 33g
Saturated Fat 14g
Cholesterol 138mg
Sodium 974mg
Protein 41g
Carbohydrates 33g

HINTS & TIPS

➤ The words *salsa verde* can be applied to any green sauce, but in Mexican cooking it's usually a cooking sauce and condiment made from *tomatillos* (a type of small, tomato-like fruit that's used when it is still green and hard). The other ingredients in a basic *salsa verde* are green chilies and cilantro. You'll find bottled salsa verde in the Mexican foods section of most supermarkets.

➤ A dollop of sour cream and a cilantro sprig make an appealing garnish for these enchiladas.

Chicken-Jack Enchiladas with Salsa Verde

Mexican food is easy to make at home, and the freshness of the food makes the effort worthwhile. For this casual main dish, corn tortillas are filled with chicken and mellow Monterey Jack cheese and baked in a salsa verde, or green chili sauce. If you end up with more filling than you need— or if some of the filling falls out during baking—just spoon it over the enchiladas as you serve them.

- 3 tablespoons olive oil
- 1 small onion, finely chopped
- 2 cloves garlic, minced
- 2 cups shredded cooked chicken breasts or thighs—leftover or poached (page 17)
- 1 can (4½ ounces) chopped mild green chilies
- ⅓ cup chopped cilantro
- 1 pickled jalapeño pepper, minced with seeds
- ¼ teaspoon salt
- 1 cup bottled salsa verde (tomatillo-based)
- ⅓ cup heavy or whipping cream
- 8 corn tortillas (6-inch diameter)
- 6 ounces Monterey Jack cheese, shredded (1½ cups)

1. In small skillet, heat 1 tablespoon of oil over low heat. Add onion and garlic, and cook 7 minutes or until onion is tender. Stir in chicken, mild green chilies, cilantro, pickled jalapeño, and salt. Stir until combined. In small bowl, combine salsa verde and cream.

2. Preheat oven to 350°F. In large skillet, heat remaining 2 tablespoons oil. Gently heat each tortilla in oil 5 seconds. Drain on paper towels. Dip each tortilla in salsa-verde mixture. Dividing evenly, spoon chicken filling down centers of tortillas. Top each with 1 tablespoon of Monterey Jack and roll enchiladas up.

3. Spread ⅓ cup of salsa-verde mixture onto bottom of 7 x 11-inch glass baking dish. Place enchiladas, seam-side down, in dish. Pour remaining salsa verde on top. Cover with foil and bake for 20 minutes or until piping hot. Uncover, sprinkle remaining 1 cup Monterey Jack on top, and bake for 5 minutes or until cheese has melted.

TO REDUCE THE FAT
Omit 2 tablespoons oil and sautéing of tortillas in step 2. Instead, to soften tortillas for rolling, wrap in foil and heat in 250°F. oven for 10 minutes. Dip into salsa-verde mixture, then stuff and roll as directed at end of step 2. Reduce cheese to 1 cup (4 ounces).

Calories 481, Total Fat 22g, Saturated Fat 10g, Cholesterol 92mg, Sodium 898mg, Protein 37g, Carbohydrates 33g

CHICKEN-CHEDDAR ENCHILADAS Substitute Cheddar
cheese for Monterey Jack. Substitute mild to hot tomato-based salsa for salsa verde. Be sure to use a thick salsa, one that is not too chunky or watery.

Calories 607, Total Fat 34g, Saturated Fat 15g, Cholesterol 137mg, Sodium 1459mg, Protein 41g, Carbohydrates 33g

Greek-Style Stuffed Peppers

Orzo, a rice-shaped pasta, is flavored with pungent Greek feta cheese, lemon, dill, and mint.

- 2 red bell peppers
- 2 green bell peppers
- 1 tablespoon olive oil
- 1 large onion, finely chopped
- 1 cup orzo
- ¼ cup snipped fresh dill
- 2 tablespoons minced fresh mint
- 1 teaspoon grated lemon zest
- ¾ teaspoon salt
- 2 cups cooked shredded chicken thighs or breasts—leftover or poached (page 17)
- 6 ounces crumbled feta cheese
- 1 cup canned crushed tomatoes
- ¼ cup chicken broth
- ½ teaspoon dried oregano

1. Cut a thin slice from bottom of each pepper so that it stands flat. Cut off and reserve pepper tops. Remove and discard seeds. In large pot of boiling water, blanch peppers and tops 4 minutes. Drain peppers, cut-side down, on paper towels.

2. In medium skillet, heat oil over medium heat. Add onion and cook, stirring frequently, 10 minutes or until golden.

3. Meanwhile, in large saucepan of boiling water, cook orzo according to package directions; drain.

4. Preheat oven to 375°F. In large bowl, combine sautéed onion, drained orzo, dill, mint, lemon zest, and salt. Stir in chicken and feta.

5. In 9-inch square glass baking dish, stir together tomatoes, broth, and oregano. Stand peppers in tomato mixture and spoon chicken mixture into them. Place tops on peppers. Tent with foil and bake for 40 minutes or until peppers are very tender and filling is piping hot. To serve, spoon tomato sauce over peppers.

ITALIAN CHICKEN-STUFFED PEPPERS Prepare peppers as directed in step 1. In step 2, use medium saucepan instead of skillet; increase oil to 2 tablespoons and sauté onion as directed. Stir in ½ cup rice until coated; add 1 cup chicken broth and ¼ teaspoon salt, and bring to a boil. Reduce to a simmer, cover, and cook 17 minutes or until rice is tender. Omit orzo and step 3. When rice is cooked, remove from heat and stir in chicken, ½ cup grated Parmesan, and ¼ cup chopped parsley. Omit dill, mint, lemon zest, feta, and ¾ teaspoon salt. In step 5, substitute ½ teaspoon ground ginger for oregano in sauce. Fill and bake as directed.
Calories 401, Total Fat 18g, Saturated Fat 5g, Cholesterol 75mg, Sodium 823mg, Protein 26g, Carbohydrates 32g

LEFTOVERS

Prep Time: 20 minutes
Cooking Time: 55 minutes
Makes 4 servings

NUTRITION INFORMATION
Per Serving
Calories 505
Total Fat 21g
Saturated Fat 9g
Cholesterol 105mg
Sodium 1144mg
Protein 32g
Carbohydrates 46g

Moroccan Chicken

This two-step (note the brevity of the directions) Moroccan stew is richly spiced and highly satisfying.

- 2 tablespoons butter
- 1 teaspoon ground cinnamon
- ½ teaspoon ground ginger
- ½ teaspoon turmeric
- ½ teaspoon paprika
- ½ teaspoon freshly ground black pepper
- 4 whole chicken legs (about 2½ pounds), split into drumsticks and thighs (page 14), skin removed
- 1 onion, finely chopped
- ⅓ cup chopped cilantro
- 1 can (8 ounces) tomato sauce
- 1 can (19 ounces) garbanzos (chick-peas), rinsed and drained
- 1 package (10 ounces) frozen lima beans
- ½ teaspoon salt

1. Preheat oven to 350°F. In Dutch oven, melt butter over low heat. Add cinnamon, ginger, turmeric, paprika, and pepper, and cook 30 seconds. Add chicken, onion, and cilantro; cover and cook 7 minutes or until onion is tender.

2. Stir in tomato sauce, garbanzos, limas, salt, and ⅓ cup of water; bring to a boil. Cover, place in oven, and bake 35 minutes or until chicken is cooked through and limas are tender.

LOW FAT

Prep Time: 15 minutes
Cooking Time: 45 minutes
Makes 4 servings

NUTRITION INFORMATION
Per Serving
Calories 450
Total Fat 14g
Saturated Fat 5g
Cholesterol 145mg
Sodium 1023mg
Protein 43g
Carbohydrates 36g

GREEK-STYLE STUFFED PEPPERS

CHICKEN BRAISED WITH GARLIC & MUSHROOMS

Prep Time: 15 minutes
Cooking Time: 45 minutes
Makes 4 servings

NUTRITION INFORMATION
Per Serving
Calories 690
Total Fat 23g
Saturated Fat 3.5g
Cholesterol 74mg
Sodium 920mg
Protein 38g
Carbohydrates 85g

Cardamom Chicken Casserole

Jasmine rice, grown in Thailand, tastes very much like Indian Basmati rice, but costs less.

3 tablespoons olive oil
1 large onion, finely chopped
2 cloves garlic, minced
4 large carrots, shredded
1½ cups jasmine rice
¾ teaspoon ground cardamom
½ teaspoon ground ginger
½ teaspoon salt
2 cups chicken broth, canned or homemade (page 45)
2½ cups chunks (1-inch) chicken breasts or thighs—leftover or poached (page 17)
½ cup coarsely chopped natural (unblanched) almonds
½ cup golden raisins

1. Preheat oven to 350°F. In Dutch oven, heat oil over low heat. Add onion and garlic, and cook 7 minutes or until onion is tender. Stir in carrots and cook 2 minutes.

2. Stir in rice, cardamom, ginger, and salt until coated. Add broth and 1½ cups of water, and bring to a boil. Stir in chicken, almonds, and raisins. Cover, place in oven, and bake for 35 minutes or until rice is tender.

IN A HURRY?
Instead of cooking rice especially for this casserole, consider making the casserole when you have leftover rice (you'll need 4½ cups cooked). You can also save some time by using preshredded carrots.

Prep Time: 35 minutes
Cooking Time: 55 minutes
4 servings

NUTRITION INFORMATION
Per Serving
Calories 556
Total Fat 13g
Saturated Fat 2.5g
Cholesterol 107mg
Sodium 1225mg
Protein 37g
Carbohydrates 73g

Chicken Braised with Garlic & Mushrooms

Both Japanese shiitake (deeply flavorful, umbrella-shaped mushrooms) and Italian cremini (handsome tan cousins of the white button mushroom) are now grown domestically.

2 tablespoons olive oil
8 bone-in chicken thighs (about 2 pounds), skin removed
2 tablespoons flour
1 green bell pepper, cut into ½-inch squares
10 cloves garlic, slivered
1 pound all-purpose potatoes, peeled and cut into ½-inch cubes
10 ounces button mushrooms, thickly sliced
½ pound shiitake mushrooms, stems trimmed and caps thickly sliced
½ pound cremini mushrooms, thickly sliced
1 package (9 ounces) frozen artichokes, thawed
¾ cup chicken broth
1½ teaspoons salt
½ teaspoon dried tarragon
1 cup rice
1 tablespoon fresh lemon juice

1. Preheat oven to 350°F. In Dutch oven, heat oil over medium heat. Dredge chicken in flour, shaking off excess. Add chicken to pan and sauté 4 minutes per side or until golden brown. With slotted spoon, transfer chicken to plate.

2. Reduce heat to medium-low. Add bell pepper and garlic to pan, and cook 5 minutes or until pepper is crisp-tender. Add potatoes and cook 2 minutes.

3. Add all mushrooms. Cover and cook, stirring occasionally, 5 minutes or until mushrooms begin to release their juices. Stir in artichokes, broth, 1 teaspoon of salt, and the tarragon, and bring to a boil. Return chicken to pan and bring to a boil. Cover, place in oven, and bake for 35 minutes or until chicken and potatoes are tender.

4. Meanwhile, in medium covered saucepan, bring 2¼ cups of water to a boil. Add rice and remaining ½ teaspoon salt. Reduce heat to a simmer, cover, and cook 17 minutes or until rice is tender. Stir lemon juice into Dutch oven. Serve sauce and chicken with rice.

CHICKEN "OSSO BUCO"

Chicken Pot-au-Feu

Prep Time: 30 minutes
Cooking Time: 3 hours 35 minutes
Makes 8 servings

NUTRITION INFORMATION
Per Serving
Calories 790
Total Fat 46g
Saturated Fat 19g
Cholesterol 193mg
Sodium 1638mg
Protein 52g
Carbohydrates 36g

Pot-au-feu, or "pot on the fire," is a phrase that gladdens hearts of the French. It speaks of a warm kitchen, a happy family, and a simmering pot of meat and vegetables—the essence of "home cooking."

6 cups chicken broth, canned or homemade (page 45)

6 carrots, cut into 1½-inch lengths

1 large onion, halved and thinly sliced

1 stalk celery, thinly sliced

3 cloves garlic, peeled

1½ teaspoons salt

1 piece (2½ pounds) beef brisket, well trimmed

1 whole chicken (about 3½ pounds), cut into 8 serving pieces (page 14), skin removed

4 parsnips (12 ounces), peeled and cut into 1½-inch lengths

3 white turnips (¾ pound total), peeled and cut into 8 wedges each

2 pounds small red-skinned potatoes, halved

¼ cup Dijon mustard

⅓ cup heavy or whipping cream

1 tablespoon cornstarch blended with ¼ cup water

1. In stockpot or large soup pot, combine broth and 6 cups of water. Bring to a boil over high heat. Add 2 carrots, the onion, celery, garlic, and salt, and return to a boil. Add beef, reduce to a simmer, partially cover, and cook 2½ hours. Remove and discard vegetables.

2. Add chicken, parsnips, turnips, and remaining 4 carrots to pot; partially cover and cook 1 hour or until chicken is cooked through and vegetables are tender. Meanwhile, in large saucepan of simmering water, cook potatoes until tender. Drain.

3. Remove beef from broth and slice on diagonal. Place meat and chicken on serving platter and surround with vegetables and potatoes.

4. Skim any fat from surface of broth. Measure out 2 cups of broth and transfer to medium saucepan. (Spoon some of broth remaining in cooking pot over chicken, beef, and vegetables to keep them moist.) To broth in saucepan, add mustard and cream, and bring to a boil over medium heat. Boil 2 minutes. Stir in cornstarch mixture and boil 1 minute until slightly thickened. Serve sauce with chicken, beef, and vegetables.

Chicken "Osso Buco"

LOW FAT

Prep Time: 15 minutes
Cooking Time: 40 minutes
Makes 4 servings

NUTRITION INFORMATION
Per Serving
Calories 430
Total Fat 12g
Saturated Fat 2.5g
Cholesterol 107mg
Sodium 799mg
Protein 30g
Carbohydrates 47g

Osso buco is really made with lamb shanks; here, chicken thighs are prepared in the same way: braised in wine, then sprinkled with a lively parsley-lemon-garlic mixture called "gremolata."

2 tablespoons olive oil

8 bone-in chicken thighs (about 2 pounds), skin removed

1 teaspoon salt

¼ teaspoon freshly ground black pepper

¼ cup flour

½ cup dry white wine

1 cup canned tomatoes, chopped with their juice

1 cup rice

2 cloves garlic, minced

½ cup chopped parsley

Grated zest of 1 lemon

1. In Dutch oven, heat oil over medium heat. Sprinkle chicken with ½ teaspoon of salt and the pepper. Dredge chicken in flour, shaking off excess. Add chicken to pan and sauté 3 minutes per side or until chicken is golden brown.

2. Add wine to pan, increase heat to high, and cook 1 minute. Add tomatoes and bring to a boil. Reduce to a simmer, cover, and cook 30 minutes or until chicken is very tender.

3. Meanwhile, in medium covered saucepan, bring 2¼ cups of water to a boil. Add rice and remaining ½ teaspoon salt. Reduce to a simmer, cover, and cook 17 minutes or until rice is tender.

4. In small bowl, stir together garlic, parsley, and lemon zest. Uncover chicken and sprinkle garlic-lemon zest mixture over chicken. Cover and cook 3 minutes. Serve sauce and chicken over rice.

Chicken Chili with Corn Bread Topping

Chili plus corn bread is a natural match, and what easier way to enjoy the combination than to cook them both in the same pot? All you need for a perfectly balanced dinner is a cool cucumber salad on the side. For a taste of Mexico at the close of the meal, serve scoops of cinnamon-dusted chocolate ice cream sprinkled with slivered almonds.

Prep Time: 30 minutes
Cooking Time: 45 minutes
Makes 4 servings

NUTRITION INFORMATION
Per Serving
Calories 741
Total Fat 27g
Saturated Fat 5g
Cholesterol 197mg
Sodium 1656mg
Protein 47g
Carbohydrates 77g

CHILI:

- 1 tablespoon olive oil
- 1 large onion, cut into 1-inch chunks
- 2 large carrots, thinly sliced
- 1 red bell pepper, cut into 1-inch chunks
- 1 tablespoon chili powder
- 1 teaspoon ground cumin
- 1 can (28 ounces) crushed tomatoes
- ½ teaspoon salt
- 1½ pounds skinless, boneless chicken thighs, cut into 1-inch chunks

CORN BREAD TOPPING:

- 1¼ cups flour
- ¾ cup yellow cornmeal
- 1 tablespoon sugar
- 1½ teaspoons baking powder
- ½ teaspoon baking soda
- ¾ teaspoon salt
- 1 cup buttermilk
- ¼ cup vegetable oil
- 1 large egg

1. Preheat oven to 375°F. Prepare Chili: In Dutch oven, heat oil over medium heat. Add onion and cook, stirring frequently, 5 minutes or until golden brown. Add carrots and bell pepper, and cook, stirring frequently, 4 minutes or until carrots are crisp-tender. Add chili powder and cumin, stirring to coat. Add tomatoes and salt, and bring to a boil. Stir in chicken and remove from heat.

2. Make Corn Bread Topping: In large bowl, stir together flour, cornmeal, sugar, baking powder, baking soda, and salt. In measuring cup, stir together buttermilk, oil, and egg. Stir buttermilk mixture into flour mixture until combined.

3. Spoon topping over chicken mixture. Bake, uncovered, 35 minutes or until corn bread is golden brown and chicken is cooked through.

CHICKEN CHILI BUNS Omit corn bread topping and do not preheat oven. Prepare chili in step 1, but do not remove pan from heat after adding chicken. Instead, reduce heat to a simmer and cook, uncovered, 10 minutes or until chicken is cooked through. Spoon chili over toasted sourdough or Kaiser rolls.
Calories 495, Total Fat 14g, Saturated Fat 2.5g, Cholesterol 141mg, Sodium 1109mg, Protein 43g, Carbohydrates 51g

HINTS & TIPS

➤ You can measure and combine the dry ingredients for the topping in advance; store the mixture in a zip-seal bag. When you're ready to proceed, empty the bag into a mixing bowl and stir the flour mixture briefly before adding the buttermilk, oil, and egg.

➤ Yellow and white cornmeal are very similar in flavor and nutritional value. This dish will just be prettier if you use yellow.

CHICKEN CHILI WITH CORN BREAD TOPPING

Chicken Stew with Corn & Limas

You can make the stew a day ahead; reheat it on the stovetop before adding the corn and parsley.

LOW FAT

Prep Time: 25 minutes
Cooking Time: 1 hour
Makes 4 servings

- 6 slices bacon (about 4 ounces), cut crosswise into 1-inch lengths
- 4 whole chicken legs (about 2½ pounds), split into drumsticks and thighs (page 14), skin removed
- ¼ cup flour
- 1 large onion, cut into ½-inch chunks
- 1 pound small red-skinned potatoes, cut into ¼-inch-thick slices
- ¾ cup chicken broth
- 1 can (14½ ounces) stewed tomatoes, chopped with their juice
- 1 cup thawed frozen lima beans
- ½ teaspoon salt
- 1 cup thawed frozen corn kernels
- ¼ cup chopped parsley

1. Preheat oven to 350°F. In Dutch oven, cook bacon over low heat 7 minutes or until crisp; drain on paper towels. Remove all but 2 tablespoons of bacon drippings from pan.

2. Dredge chicken in flour, shaking off excess. Add chicken to pan, increase heat to medium-high, and sauté 4 minutes per side or until golden brown. With slotted spoon, transfer chicken to plate.

3. Add onion to pan and cook, stirring frequently, 7 minutes or until soft. Add potatoes and stir to coat. Add broth, stewed tomatoes, lima beans, salt, and bacon, and bring to a boil. Cover, place in oven, and bake for 35 minutes or until chicken is tender.

4. On stovetop, stir in corn and parsley, and cook over medium heat 3 minutes or just until corn is heated through.

NUTRITION INFORMATION
Per Serving
Calories 541
Total Fat 16g
Saturated Fat 5g
Cholesterol 141mg
Sodium 1048mg
Protein 44g
Carbohydrates 55g

CHICKEN STEW WITH CORN & LIMAS

Prep Time: 25 minutes
Cooking Time: 40 minutes
Makes 4 servings

Chicken & Sausage Casserole

Chicken sausage comes in many different "styles." An Italian-style sausage, with garlic, fennel, and red pepper, is the best choice for this casserole.

- 8 skinless, boneless chicken thighs (about 1½ pounds), cut into 1-inch chunks
- ½ pound fully-cooked chicken sausage, halved lengthwise and sliced ½ inch thick
- 2 stalks broccoli, cut into florets, stalks trimmed and thinly sliced
- ⅓ cup oil-packed sun-dried tomatoes, coarsely chopped
- ⅓ cup golden raisins
- ½ cup chicken broth
- 2 tablespoons olive oil
- ½ teaspoon salt
- ¼ pound Monterey Jack cheese, shredded
- 10 ounces penne or ziti

1. Preheat oven to 375°F. In large bowl, toss together chicken, sausage, broccoli, sun-dried tomatoes, and raisins. In small bowl, stir together broth, oil, and salt. Pour broth mixture over chicken mixture. Add Monterey Jack and toss well.

2. Transfer mixture to 7 x 11-inch glass baking dish. Tent with foil and bake for 30 minutes. Uncover and bake for 10 minutes or until chicken is cooked through and broccoli is tender.

3. Meanwhile, in large pot of boiling water, cook penne according to package directions. Drain. Serve pasta topped with chicken and sausage mixture.

Prep Time: 20 minutes
Cooking Time: 40 minutes
Makes 4 servings

Chicken & Sweet Potato Stew

A last-minute squeeze of lemon juice lightens and brightens the flavors here. Although sweet potatoes are most abundant in the late fall and winter, they can be had at other times, so you don't have to wait for the holiday season to try this recipe.

- 2 teaspoons ground ginger
- 1 teaspoon sugar
- ¾ teaspoon salt
- ½ teaspoon freshly ground black pepper
- ⅛ teaspoon ground allspice
- 1½ pounds skinless, boneless chicken thighs, cut into 1-inch chunks
- 2 tablespoons olive oil
- 2 red bell peppers, cut into 1-inch chunks
- 1½ pounds sweet potatoes, peeled and cut into ½-inch chunks
- ⅔ cup chicken broth
- 2 tablespoons orange marmalade
- 1 tablespoon fresh lemon juice

1. Preheat oven to 350°F. In large bowl, stir together ginger, sugar, ½ teaspoon of salt, the black pepper, and allspice. Add chicken and toss well to coat. Let stand 10 minutes.

2. In Dutch oven, heat oil over medium heat. Add chicken and cook 7 minutes or until golden brown. With slotted spoon, transfer chicken to plate.

3. Add bell peppers to pan and cook, stirring frequently, 5 minutes or until crisp-tender. Stir in sweet potatoes and cook 2 minutes. Add broth, marmalade, and remaining ¼ teaspoon salt, and bring to a boil. Return chicken to pan and bring to a boil. Cover, place in oven, and bake for 20 to 25 minutes or until chicken is cooked through and sweet potatoes are tender. Uncover and stir in lemon juice.

TO REDUCE THE FAT

Use 1½ pounds skinless, boneless chicken breasts instead of thighs. In step 3, cook as directed, but cook it all the way through. Do not return cooked chicken to casserole until the very end when you add lemon juice.

Calories 423, Total Fat 10g, Saturated Fat 1.5g, Cholesterol 99mg, Sodium 745mg, Protein 42g, Carbohydrates 41g

Tandoori-Seasoned Chicken

Dishes baked in a tandoor (an Indian clay oven) are typically seasoned with the spices used here.

1 small onion, peeled and quartered

2 tablespoons chopped fresh ginger

2 cloves garlic, peeled

2 teaspoons paprika

1½ teaspoons ground cumin

1¼ teaspoons salt

½ teaspoon ground cardamom

½ teaspoon cinnamon

8 bone-in chicken thighs (about 2 pounds), skin removed

2 tablespoons butter, melted

1 cup chicken broth, canned or homemade (page 45)

1 can (19 ounces) garbanzos (chick-peas), rinsed and drained

3 carrots, shredded

1½ cups couscous (about 10 ounces)

2 cups boiling water

1. In food processor or blender, combine onion, ginger, garlic, paprika, cumin, ¾ teaspoon of salt, cardamom, cinnamon, and ½ cup of water. Process to smooth paste. Place chicken in large zip-seal plastic bag and pour in onion mixture. Squeeze air out and close bag. Marinate in refrigerator at least 4 hours or up to overnight.

2. Preheat oven to 450°F. Transfer chicken to Dutch oven. Pour melted butter on top. Bake uncovered for 20 minutes. Stir in broth, garbanzos, and carrots. Cover, return to oven, and bake 15 minutes or until chicken is cooked through.

3. Meanwhile, in large bowl, combine couscous, boiling water, and remaining ½ teaspoon salt. Cover and let stand 5 minutes or until liquid has been absorbed. Fluff couscous with a fork. Serve chicken on top of couscous.

LOW FAT

Prep Time: 20 minutes plus marinating time
Cooking Time: 35 minutes
Makes 4 servings

NUTRITION INFORMATION
Per Serving
Calories 615
Total Fat 14g
Saturated Fat 5g
Cholesterol 123mg
Sodium 1336mg
Protein 41g
Carbohydrates 79g

Portuguese Chicken with Greens

This is an interpretation of Portuguese caldo verde, a stew made with kale, potatoes, and sausage.

1 tablespoon olive oil

½ pound spicy pork sausage (preferably Portuguese linguiça), casings removed

1 leek, halved lengthwise and thinly sliced

2 carrots, thinly sliced

1½ pounds all-purpose potatoes, peeled and cut into ½-inch chunks

8 cups torn kale, stems removed

1 cup chicken broth, canned or homemade (page 45)

½ teaspoon salt

½ teaspoon dried thyme

8 skinless, boneless chicken thighs (about 1½ pounds), cut into 1-inch chunks

1. In Dutch oven or 5-quart saucepan, heat oil over medium heat. Add sausage and cook 5 minutes or until lightly browned. With slotted spoon, transfer sausage to plate.

2. Add leek and carrots to pan, and cook, stirring frequently, 7 minutes or until leek is tender. Add potatoes and kale, stirring to coat. Add broth, salt, and thyme, and bring to a boil.

3. Stir chicken and sausage into pan. Reduce to a simmer, cover, and cook 25 minutes or until chicken and sausage are cooked through and potatoes are tender.

TO REDUCE THE FAT

Substitute ½ pound spicy fresh chicken sausage for pork sausage and 4 skinless, boneless chicken breasts for thighs. Cook sausage as directed. Add chicken breasts with broth in step 2 and cook 10 minutes. Remove chicken from pan. In step 3, cook potatoes 10 minutes before returning cooked breasts to pan for last 15 minutes of cooking time.
Calories 501, Total Fat 11g, Saturated Fat 2g, Cholesterol 132mg, Sodium 1037mg, Protein 58g, Carbohydrates 44g

Prep Time: 25 minutes
Cooking Time: 40 minutes
Makes 4 servings

NUTRITION INFORMATION
Per Serving
Calories 636
Total Fat 29g
Saturated Fat 9g
Cholesterol 184mg
Sodium 1197mg
Protein 50g
Carbohydrates 45g

PORTUGUESE CHICKEN WITH GREENS

CHICKEN SHEPHERD'S PIE

Prep Time: 30 minutes
Cooking Time: 1 hour 20 minutes
Makes 4 servings

NUTRITION INFORMATION

Per Serving

Calories 479

Total Fat 17g

Saturated Fat 8g

Cholesterol 172mg

Sodium 1267mg

Protein 40g

Carbohydrates 40g

HINTS & TIPS

➤ Add an extra flavor dimension by sprinkling the potato crust with grated Cheddar cheese before baking.

➤ An electric mixer, especially a stand mixer, is a real labor saver when you're mashing potatoes—but it's best not to use a food processor, which will turn the mashed potatoes gray and gummy. Another option for this task is a hand-cranked food mill.

Chicken Shepherd's Pie

The main ingredient for a traditional shepherd's pie is, naturally, lamb, but tender chicken thighs, sautéed and simmered with onions, carrots, and peas, make a worthy substitute. The mashed-potato topping can be simply spooned over the filling, or piped through a pastry bag for a decorative effect.

1½	pounds all-purpose potatoes, peeled and cut into 1-inch chunks
3	cloves garlic, crushed and peeled
3	tablespoons heavy or whipping cream
1¼	teaspoons salt
2	tablespoons butter
1	small onion, finely chopped
3	carrots, halved lengthwise and thinly sliced
1½	pounds skinless, boneless chicken thighs, cut into ½-inch chunks
2	tablespoons flour
1	cup chicken broth, canned or homemade (page 45)
1	cup frozen peas
¼	cup chopped parsley

1. In medium saucepan of boiling water, cook potatoes and garlic 25 minutes or until tender. Drain. With potato masher or electric mixer, mash potatoes, garlic, cream, and ¾ teaspoon of salt until smooth; set aside.

2. Preheat oven to 350°F. In large skillet, melt butter over low heat. Add onion and cook, stirring frequently, 7 minutes or until tender. Add carrots and cook, stirring frequently, 5 minutes or until tender. Add chicken and cook 4 minutes or until no longer pink.

3. Sprinkle flour over chicken mixture and cook, stirring frequently, 1 minute or until no streaks of flour remain. Gradually add broth and remaining ½ teaspoon salt, and bring to a boil. Reduce to a simmer and cook, stirring frequently, 5 minutes or until slightly thickened. Stir in peas and parsley.

4. Spoon mixture into a 9-inch deep-dish pie plate. Spoon mashed potatoes on top (or, if you prefer, spoon potatoes into pastry bag and pipe potatoes over chicken mixture). Place pie plate on jelly-roll pan to catch any drips and bake for 30 minutes or until potato mixture is golden brown and crusty.

FROM THE FRIDGE

Use 3½ cups shredded cooked chicken thighs or breasts instead of uncooked thighs. In step 3, increase broth to 1¼ cups. Do not add cooked chicken until end of step 3 when stirring in peas.

GOLDEN-TOPPED SHEPHERD'S PIE In step 1, substitute following for potatoes: 3 parsnips (peeled and cut into chunks), ½ pound all-purpose potatoes (peeled and cut into chunks), 1 white turnip (peeled and cut into chunks), 2 cups peeled chunks of butternut squash, and 4 cloves garlic. Cook and mash as directed. In step 2, substitute 2 tablespoons olive oil for butter. Assemble and bake as directed.

Calories 531, Total Fat 19g, Saturated Fat 5.5g, Cholesterol 157mg, Sodium 1230mg, Protein 40g, Carbohydrates 51g

Country Roast Chicken & Vegetables

This one-dish meal roasts for a little over an hour, but there's very little to prepare, so you can get it into the oven in practically no time.

LOW FAT

Prep Time: 15 minutes
Cooking Time: 1 hour 15 minutes
Makes 4 servings

- 1 whole chicken (about 3½ pounds), cut into 8 serving pieces (page 14)
- 16 small red-skinned potatoes (about 1½ pounds), cut into 1½-inch pieces
- 1 small zucchini, cut into 1-inch chunks
- 1 small yellow squash, cut into 1-inch chunks
- ½ pound peeled baby carrots (1¾ cups)
- 1 whole head garlic, loose outer skin removed and top quarter sliced off
- 2 tablespoons vegetable oil or melted butter
- 2 bay leaves
- ½ teaspoon dried sage
- ½ teaspoon dried thyme
- ¾ teaspoon salt
- ¼ teaspoon freshly ground black pepper

1. Preheat oven to 400° F. In large roasting pan, toss chicken, potatoes, zucchini, squash, carrots, garlic, oil, bay leaves, sage, thyme, salt, and pepper together.

2. Roast, turning chicken and tossing vegetables every 15 minutes, for 1 hour 15 minutes or until chicken is cooked through.

3. Transfer chicken to platter and vegetables to bowl. Discard bay leaves. Squeeze out garlic pulp and toss with vegetables. Arrange vegetables around chicken.

SOUTHWESTERN ROAST CHICKEN & VEGETABLES
Omit bay leaves. Substitute ½ teaspoon ground cumin for sage and ½ teaspoon oregano for thyme. If you like, sprinkle with chopped cilantro after baking.
Calories 477, Total Fat 13g, Saturated Fat 2.5g, Cholesterol 133mg, Sodium 620mg, Protein 46g, Carbohydrates 42g

NUTRITION INFORMATION
Per Serving
Calories 477
Total Fat 13g
Saturated Fat 2.5g
Cholesterol 133mg
Sodium 619mg
Protein 46g
Carbohydrates 43g

Chicken Pastitsio

This Greek casserole calls for tubular pasta, such as ditalini ("little thimbles"). The ground chicken is cooked in a spicy tomato sauce, then layered with the pasta and napped with white sauce.

Prep Time: 20 minutes
Cooking Time: 1 hour 5 minutes
Makes 4 servings

- 2 tablespoons olive oil
- 1 large onion, finely chopped
- 2 cloves garlic, minced
- 1 pound ground chicken
- 2 cups chopped canned tomatoes
- 1 teaspoon cinnamon
- 1 teaspoon salt
- ½ teaspoon freshly ground black pepper
- ¼ teaspoon ground allspice
- ⅛ teaspoon ground cloves
- 10 ounces ditalini, penne, or ziti
- 2 tablespoons butter
- 3 tablespoons flour
- 2 cups milk
- ½ cup grated Parmesan cheese

1. In large skillet, heat oil over medium heat. Add onion and garlic, and cook, stirring frequently, 7 minutes or until onion is soft. Stir in chicken. Stir in tomatoes, cinnamon, ¾ teaspoon of salt, the pepper, allspice, and cloves. Reduce heat and simmer 20 minutes or until thick and almost dry.

2. Meanwhile, in large pot of boiling water, cook pasta according to package directions. Drain.

3. Preheat oven to 350°F. In medium saucepan, melt butter over low heat. Whisk in flour until well combined. Gradually whisk in milk, stirring until well combined and smooth. Cook, stirring constantly, 7 minutes or until white sauce is slightly thickened.

4. Spoon ¼ cup of white sauce into 9-inch square glass baking dish. Spoon half of pasta on top, spreading it out to form an even layer. Spoon half chicken sauce on top. Sprinkle with ¼ cup of Parmesan. Top with remaining pasta, chicken sauce, and white sauce. Sprinkle with remaining ¼ cup Parmesan. Place on jelly-roll pan to catch any drips and bake, uncovered, for 35 minutes or until crusty and golden brown.

NUTRITION INFORMATION
Per Serving
Calories 740
Total Fat 31g
Saturated Fat12g
Cholesterol 135mg
Sodium 1424mg
Protein 40g
Carbohydrates 75g

COUNTRY ROAST CHICKEN & VEGETABLES

Pasta with Sausage & Wild Mushroom Sauce

The "wild" mushrooms called for here are now farm-raised, and you'll probably find them in the produce section of your supermarket. But if your local stores don't carry shiitake or cremini, you can use white button mushrooms. The deep flavor of the dried shiitake, however, is important here.

1 package (¼ ounce) dried shiitake mushrooms
½ cup boiling water
2 tablespoons olive oil
¾ pound fully-cooked chicken sausage, halved lengthwise and thinly sliced crosswise
1 leek, cut into ¼-inch dice
1 clove garlic, minced
1¼ pounds fresh wild mushrooms (all shiitake, all cremini, or a mixture), trimmed and thinly sliced
1 cup chicken broth, canned or homemade (page 45)
¾ teaspoon salt
¼ teaspoon freshly ground black pepper
½ cup heavy or whipping cream
10 ounces fusilli pasta

1. In small bowl, combine dried shiitake mushrooms and boiling water. Let stand 20 minutes or until softened. With your fingers, lift mushrooms from their soaking liquid. Strain soaking liquid through paper towel-lined strainer. Reserve soaking liquid. Rinse mushrooms.

2. In large skillet, heat oil over low heat. Add sausage, leek, and garlic, and cook, stirring frequently, 5 minutes or until leek is soft. Add fresh wild mushrooms, dried shiitakes, and reserved mushroom soaking liquid, and cook, stirring frequently, 10 minutes or until fresh mushrooms are tender and all liquid has evaporated.

3. Add broth, salt, and pepper. Bring to a boil, reduce to a simmer, and cook 5 minutes or until slightly reduced. Stir in cream and boil 2 minutes.

4. Meanwhile, in large pot of boiling water, cook fusilli according to package directions. Drain. Return to cooking pot, add sausage mixture, and toss to combine.

Prep Time: 30 minutes
Cooking Time: 25 minutes
Makes 4 servings

NUTRITION INFORMATION
Per Serving
Calories 641
Total Fat 26g
Saturated Fat 10g
Cholesterol 108mg
Sodium 1302mg
Protein 35g
Carbohydrates 66g

Mustard-Tarragon Chicken Sauté

Serve the sautéed chicken breasts with steamed new potatoes or rice, and some crisp-tender asparagus or green beans. Because the scallions are an integral part of the dish, and not just a flavoring, you'll want to choose a nice plump bunch.

2 teaspoons olive oil
4 skinless, boneless chicken breast halves (about 1½ pounds), pounded to ½-inch thickness (page 15)
2 tablespoons flour
5 scallions, cut into 1-inch lengths
¾ cup chicken broth
1 tablespoon red wine vinegar
4 teaspoons Dijon mustard
1 tablespoon chopped fresh tarragon or 1 teaspoon dried
1 small tomato, seeded and diced
¼ cup diced gherkin pickle

1. In large nonstick skillet, heat oil over medium heat. Dredge chicken in flour, shaking off excess. Add chicken to pan and sauté 4 minutes per side or until golden brown. With slotted spoon, transfer chicken to plate.

2. Add scallions to pan and cook 1 minute. Add broth and vinegar, and bring to a boil. Stir in mustard and tarragon, and return to a boil. Stir in tomato and pickle. Return chicken to pan, reduce to a simmer, cover, and cook 5 minutes or until chicken is cooked through and sauce is richly flavored. Serve chicken with sauce spooned on top.

LOW FAT
QUICK TO FIX

Prep Time: 10 minutes
Cooking Time: 15 minutes
Makes 4 servings

NUTRITION INFORMATION
Per Serving
Calories 265
Total Fat 5g
Saturated Fat 1g
Cholesterol 99mg
Sodium 542mg
Protein 41g
Carbohydrates 11g

MUSTARD-TARRAGON CHICKEN SAUTÉ

PARMESAN-CRUSTED CHICKEN CUTLETS

Prep Time: 15 minutes
Cooking Time: 45 minutes
Makes 4 servings

Mushroom-Smothered Chicken with Caramelized Onions

When onions are cooked slowly with a little sugar, they turn soft, golden, and miraculously sweet. Add some wine or spirits, and the flavor becomes totally sublime. Here, a splash of brandy is cooked with the onions and mushrooms. Most of the alcohol evaporates, but the tantalizing flavor lingers.

3 tablespoons olive oil

4 bone-in chicken breast halves (about 2 pounds), skin removed

4 tablespoons flour

1 Spanish onion, cut into ½-inch chunks

2 teaspoons sugar

1 pound mushrooms, thinly sliced

¼ cup brandy

1¼ cups chicken broth, canned or homemade (page 45)

½ teaspoon freshly ground black pepper

¼ teaspoon salt

¼ teaspoon dried sage

1. In large skillet, heat oil over medium heat. Dredge chicken in 2 tablespoons of flour, shaking off excess. Add chicken to pan and sauté 5 minutes per side or until golden brown. With slotted spoon, transfer chicken to plate.

2. Add onion to pan, sprinkle with sugar, and cook, stirring frequently, 12 minutes or until golden brown and tender. Add mushrooms and cook, stirring frequently, 10 minutes or until tender and liquid has evaporated. Add brandy to pan, increase heat to high, and cook 1 minute to evaporate alcohol.

3. Add remaining 2 tablespoons flour, stirring to evenly coat vegetables. Whisk in broth, pepper, salt, and sage, and bring to a boil. Reduce to a simmer, return chicken to pan, and simmer 7 minutes or until cooked through.

LOW FAT

Prep Time: 15 minutes plus
  chilling time
Cooking Time: 10 minutes
Makes 4 servings

Parmesan-Crusted Chicken Cutlets

Who'd have guessed that a mere six ingredients could add up to so much flavor! These Parmesan-breaded chicken breasts are delicious hot from the pan, served with a green salad, potato salad, or cole slaw. Warm or cold, the crisp-crusted chicken also makes spectacular sandwiches. For best results, let the uncooked, breaded chicken stand for a few hours before sautéing, as the coating will adhere better.

4 slices firm-textured white bread (4 ounces)

½ cup grated Parmesan cheese

2 eggs lightly beaten with 1 tablespoon water

4 skinless, boneless chicken breast halves (about 1½ pounds), pounded to ½-inch thickness (page 15)

3 tablespoons olive oil

4 lemon wedges

1. In food processor, process bread to fine crumbs. Transfer to shallow bowl. Place Parmesan in second bowl and egg mixture in third. Dip chicken first in Parmesan, pressing cheese into chicken. Then dip chicken in egg and finally in breadcrumbs, pressing crumbs into chicken. Place on plate and refrigerate uncovered 30 minutes or up to 4 hours.

2. In large skillet, heat oil over medium heat. Add chicken and sauté 5 minutes per side or until golden brown and cooked through. Serve with lemon wedges.

IN A HURRY?

Omit the chilling time in step 1 and go straight to step 2, but use a nonstick skillet and be careful when turning cutlets so breading does not fall off.

Chicken Roll-Ups
with Ham & Provolone

If you've ever eaten saltimbocca at an Italian restaurant, you'll recognize the source of this recipe. Instead of veal scaloppine rolled with sage leaves and prosciutto, this appealing entrée is made with pounded chicken breasts, Virginia ham, Provolone, and fresh basil.

4 skinless, boneless chicken breast halves (about 1½ pounds), pounded to ¼-inch thickness (page 15)

½ teaspoon salt

¼ pound thinly sliced Virginia ham

2 ounces thinly sliced Provolone cheese

12 large fresh basil leaves

1 tablespoon olive oil

½ cup chicken broth

2 tablespoons fresh lemon juice

1 tablespoon unsalted butter, cut up

1. Sprinkle chicken with salt. Place chicken breasts smooth-side down. Place ham on top of chicken. Top with Provolone and basil leaves. Starting at short end, roll each chicken breast up and secure with toothpicks.

2. In large skillet, heat oil over medium-low heat. Add chicken roll-ups and sauté, turning chicken over as it cooks, 10 minutes or until golden.

3. Add broth to pan, cover, and cook, turning chicken over, 5 to 7 minutes or until cooked through. Transfer chicken to cutting board and slice crosswise into ½-inch slices. Transfer to dinner plates.

4. Add lemon juice and butter to pan and swirl over very low heat until creamy. Spoon over chicken.

Prep Time: 15 minutes
Cooking Time: 20 minutes
Makes 4 servings

NUTRITION INFORMATION
Per Serving
Calories 353
Total Fat 15g
Saturated Fat 6g
Cholesterol 136mg
Sodium 1421mg
Protein 51g
Carbohydrates 1g

Chicken with
Red Grapes & Rosemary

The "Véronique" presentation in French cuisine uses green grapes as a garnish for fish or chicken (see our dinner-party version of a Véronique on page 318). Here, the grapes are red—a highly interesting addition to the heady red-wine sauce.

2 tablespoons olive oil

4 bone-in chicken breast halves (about 2 pounds), skin removed

2 tablespoons flour

2 shallots, minced

2 cloves garlic, minced

3 tablespoons brandy

1 cup dry red wine

1 tablespoon tomato paste

1½ teaspoons chopped fresh rosemary or ½ teaspoon dried, crumbled

½ teaspoon salt

2 cups seedless red grapes, halved

¼ cup chopped parsley

1. In large skillet, heat oil over medium heat. Dredge chicken in flour, shaking off excess. Add chicken to pan and sauté 4 minutes per side or until golden brown. With slotted spoon, transfer chicken to plate.

2. Reduce heat to medium-low. Add shallots and garlic, and stir-fry 3 minutes or until shallots are tender. Add brandy and cook 30 seconds to evaporate alcohol. Add wine, bring to a boil, and cook 2 minutes or until slightly reduced.

3. Stir in tomato paste, rosemary, and salt. Add chicken and grapes, and reduce to a simmer. Cover and cook, turning chicken as it cooks, 12 minutes or until cooked through.

4. Transfer chicken to dinner plates. Stir parsley into sauce and spoon over chicken.

LOW FAT

Prep Time: 20 minutes
Cooking Time: 30 minutes
Makes 4 servings

NUTRITION INFORMATION
Per Serving
Calories 346
Total Fat 9g
Saturated Fat 1.5g
Cholesterol 86mg
Sodium 425mg
Protein 36g
Carbohydrates 20g

CHICKEN ROLL-UPS WITH HAM & PROVOLONE

RASPBERRY CHICKEN BREASTS

Prep Time: 10 minutes
Cooking Time: 20 minutes
Makes 4 servings

NUTRITION INFORMATION
Per Serving
Calories 309
Total Fat 9.5g
Saturated Fat 1.5g
Cholesterol 99mg
Sodium 600mg
Protein 40g
Carbohydrates 14g

Raspberry Chicken Breasts

A sophisticated step up from applesauce, raspberry sauce is wonderful with chicken. Here, raspberry vinegar is the basis of the lightly thickened sauce, and fresh berries are a final flourish.

2	tablespoons olive oil
4	skinless, boneless chicken breast halves (about 1½ pounds)
2	tablespoons flour
4	scallions, thinly sliced
4	teaspoons sugar
⅓	cup raspberry vinegar or red wine vinegar
¾	cup chicken broth
½	teaspoon dried tarragon
½	teaspoon salt
1½	teaspoons cornstarch blended with 1 tablespoon water
½	pint raspberries

1. In large skillet, heat oil over medium heat. Dredge chicken in flour, shaking off excess. Add chicken to pan and sauté 4 minutes per side or until golden brown. With slotted spoon, transfer chicken to plate.

2. Add scallions to pan and cook 1 minute or until soft. Add sugar and cook 4 minutes or until sugar has melted and is amber in color. Add vinegar and bring to a boil.

3. Add broth, tarragon, and salt, and bring to a boil. Return chicken to pan, reduce to a simmer, cover, and cook 5 minutes or until chicken is cooked through.

4. Transfer chicken to dinner plates. Return sauce to a boil, whisk in cornstarch mixture, and cook, stirring constantly, 1 minute or until sauce is slightly thickened. Stir in raspberries. Spoon sauce over chicken.

Prep Time: 10 minutes
Cooking Time: 15 minutes
Makes 4 servings

NUTRITION INFORMATION
Per Serving
Calories 330
Total Fat 13g
Saturated Fat 5.5g
Cholesterol 126mg
Sodium 540mg
Protein 40g
Carbohydrates 2g

Black Pepper Chicken Breasts with Cognac Cream Sauce

Chicken breasts "au poivre" are served with a cream-enriched sauce that balances the pungency of the pepper. You can buy coarsely ground black pepper in a jar in your supermarket, or set your peppermill to yield a coarse grind and mill fresh black peppercorns yourself. Although already relatively low in fat, you can cut the fat in this dish in half by using the reduced-fat version below.

1	tablespoon coarsely ground black pepper
½	teaspoon dried thyme
½	teaspoon salt
⅛	teaspoon cayenne pepper
4	skinless, boneless chicken breast halves (about 1½ pounds), pounded to a ½-inch thickness (page 15)
1	tablespoon olive oil
¼	cup Cognac or other brandy
½	cup chicken broth
⅓	cup heavy or whipping cream
2	tablespoons snipped chives

1. On plate, combine black pepper, thyme, ¼ teaspoon of salt, and the cayenne. Dip chicken breasts in pepper mixture, pressing it into chicken.

2. In large skillet, heat oil over medium heat. Add chicken and cook 3 minutes per side or until cooked through. Transfer to dinner plates.

3. Add Cognac to pan and cook 30 seconds to evaporate alcohol. Pour broth into skillet and boil 1 minute. Add cream and remaining ¼ teaspoon salt, and boil 3 minutes or until slightly reduced. Stir in chives.

TO REDUCE THE FAT
Use nonstick skillet and reduce oil to 2 teaspoons. Omit heavy cream. In step 3, boil broth 3 minutes. Remove from heat and whisk in ¼ cup reduced-fat sour cream.
Calories 277, Total Fat 6.5g, Saturated Fat 2g, Cholesterol 104mg, Sodium 540mg, Protein 41g, Carbohydrates 2g

Chicken Breasts Stuffed with Pistachios

When you don't have the time to roast a whole stuffed chicken—or when it's too hot to turn on the oven—serve these plump chicken breasts filled with a creamy, lemon-scented pistachio stuffing. To serve, cut the stuffed breasts crosswise, arrange the slices on plates, and top with the pan sauce.

- 4 skinless, boneless chicken breast halves (about 1½ pounds)
- 1 package (3 ounces) cream cheese
- ⅓ cup shredded fresh basil leaves
- 1 teaspoon grated lemon zest
- ¾ teaspoon salt
- ⅓ cup shelled pistachios
- 2 tablespoons plain dried breadcrumbs
- 4 teaspoons olive oil
- 3 tablespoons flour
- 1 cup chicken broth, canned or homemade (page 45)
- 3 tablespoons fresh lemon juice

1. With sharp chef's knife, make a pocket in each chicken breast half (see technique photo, at right).

2. In food processor, combine cream cheese, basil, lemon zest, and ¼ teaspoon of salt, and process until smooth. Add pistachios and breadcrumbs and process until coarsely chopped. Sprinkle remaining ½ teaspoon salt inside pockets and on outsides of chicken breasts. Spoon pistachio mixture into pockets and secure with toothpicks.

3. In large nonstick skillet, heat oil over medium heat. Dredge chicken in flour, shaking off excess. Add chicken to skillet and sauté, turning chicken over as it colors, 15 minutes or until richly browned and almost cooked through.

4. Add broth and lemon juice to pan and bring to a simmer. Cover and cook 7 minutes or until chicken is cooked through. Remove toothpicks from chicken. Serve chicken with sauce spooned on top.

TO REDUCE THE FAT

Use reduced-fat cream cheese (Neufchâtel) instead of regular cream cheese. Reduce pistachios to ¼ cup. Increase breadcrumbs to 3 tablespoons.

Calories 378, Total Fat 16g, Saturated Fat 5g, Cholesterol 114mg, Sodium 944mg, Protein 45g, Carbohydrates 12g

Prep Time: 20 minutes
Cooking Time: 25 minutes
Makes 4 servings

NUTRITION INFORMATION
Per Serving

Calories 408

Total Fat 20g

Saturated Fat 6.5g

Cholesterol 122mg

Sodium 902mg

Protein 45g

Carbohydrates 12g

TECHNIQUE

CUTTING A POCKET

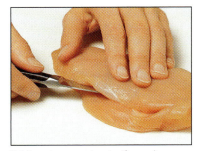

With a sharp paring knife, make a horizontal slit in the fatter side of a chicken breast, stopping ½ inch short of either end. Insert the blade into the slit, and with a back and forth swiveling motion, cut a pocket in the breast without cutting through the opposite side.

CHICKEN BREASTS STUFFED WITH PISTACHIOS

FETTUCCINE WITH CHICKEN & ASPARAGUS

Prep Time: 15 minutes
Cooking Time: 15 minutes
Makes 4 servings

NUTRITION INFORMATION
Per Serving
Calories 548
Total Fat 18g
Saturated Fat 10g
Cholesterol 103mg
Sodium 647mg
Protein 36g
Carbohydrates 59g

Fettuccine with Chicken & Asparagus

Pasta and chicken have light flavors that will not overwhelm delicate asparagus. When fresh asparagus is out of season, you can use frozen; just be careful not to overcook it.

1	pound asparagus, cut on the diagonal into 1-inch lengths
10	ounces fettuccine
1	tablespoon butter
¼	cup minced onion
¾	pound skinless, boneless chicken breasts, cut for stir-fry (page 15)
½	cup chicken broth
½	cup heavy cream
½	teaspoon salt
½	teaspoon dried tarragon
½	teaspoon freshly ground black pepper
⅓	cup grated Parmesan

1. In large pot of boiling water, cook asparagus 3 minutes. With slotted spoon, remove asparagus and rinse under cold water to stop cooking. In same pot of boiling water, cook fettuccine according to package directions; drain, reserving ¼ cup of pasta cooking water.

2. Meanwhile, in large skillet, melt butter over low heat. Add onion and cook, stirring frequently, 5 minutes or until onion is tender and golden brown. Add chicken and cook 1 minute.

3. Increase heat to medium. Add broth, cream, salt, tarragon, and pepper, and bring to a boil. Cook 3 minutes or until sauce is slightly thickened and chicken is cooked through. Add asparagus and cook 30 seconds, just until heated through.

4. Transfer mixture to large bowl. Add hot pasta, Parmesan, and reserved pasta cooking water, and toss well to combine.

Prep Time: 20 minutes
Cooking Time: 15 minutes
Makes 4 servings

NUTRITION INFORMATION
Per Serving
Calories 499
Total Fat 13g
Saturated Fat 2g
Cholesterol 94mg
Sodium 909mg
Protein 33g
Carbohydrates 62g

Spicy Chicken & Eggplant with Couscous

Will couscous someday replace rice or potatoes in America's dinner fare? Maybe not. But this quick-cooking North African pasta certainly deserves more frequent appearances on our plates.

2	tablespoons olive oil
1	tablespoon chili powder
1	teaspoon ground cumin
1	teaspoon ground coriander
2	zucchini (6 ounces each), quartered lengthwise and cut into 2 x ½-inch matchsticks
1	small eggplant, peeled and cut into 2 x ½-inch matchsticks
1	red bell pepper, cut into thin 2-inch-long strips
1	teaspoon salt
½	teaspoon cayenne pepper
4	skinless, boneless chicken thighs (about 1 pound)
¾	cup chicken broth
1½	cups couscous
2	cups boiling water

1. In large skillet, heat oil over low heat. Add chili powder, cumin, and coriander, and cook 1 minute. Add zucchini, eggplant, and bell pepper. Sprinkle with ½ teaspoon of salt and the cayenne and stir-fry 7 minutes or until vegetables are crisp-tender.

2. Add chicken to pan and stir to coat. Add broth, bring to a boil, reduce to a simmer, and cook 5 to 7 minutes or until chicken is cooked through.

3. Meanwhile, in large bowl, combine couscous, boiling water, and remaining ½ teaspoon salt. Cover and let stand 5 minutes or until liquid has been absorbed. Fluff with fork. Transfer to large platter. Spoon some of the sauce over couscous and top with vegetables and chicken.

HERB-CRUSTED CHICKEN BREASTS WITH FRESH SHIITAKES

Prep Time: 35 minutes plus
    chilling time
Cooking Time: 15 minutes
Makes 4 servings

NUTRITION INFORMATION

Per Serving

Calories 471

Total Fat 25g

Saturated Fat 4g

Cholesterol 136mg

Sodium 681mg

Protein 40g

Carbohydrates 23g

HINTS & TIPS

➤ Shiitake mushrooms, also called Chinese black mushrooms, were originally gathered from the wild in Asia, their home territory. Today, these broad-capped, dark brown mushrooms are cultivated in the United States, making them more widely available and cheaper, too.

➤ Wash shiitakes thoroughly but quickly so they don't become waterlogged. Trim off the stems, which are too tough to eat. Discard them, or save them for flavoring stocks and soups.

Herb-Crusted Chicken Breasts with Fresh Shiitakes

There's quite a flavor-fest going on here, with the herb-breaded sautéed chicken served on a bed of tart-bitter arugula and rich garlic-sautéed mushrooms. There's a pleasant contrast of temperatures and textures, too, because the arugula-shiitake salad is just warm, while the chicken breasts are hot from the pan. Add thickly sliced French or Italian bread and you have an unbeatable dinner.

- 3 slices firm-textured white bread (3 ounces)
- ½ cup fresh basil leaves
- 2 tablespoons fresh oregano or ½ teaspoon dried
- ¾ teaspoon grated lemon zest
- ¾ teaspoon salt
- 1 large egg, lightly beaten with 1 tablespoon water
- 4 small skinless, boneless chicken breast halves (about 1¼ pounds), pounded to ¼-inch thickness (page 15)
- 6 tablespoons olive oil
- ¾ pound fresh shiitake mushrooms, stems discarded and caps thinly sliced
- 3 cloves garlic, minced
- 1 pound plum tomatoes, cut into ½-inch chunks
- 1 bunch arugula, tough stems trimmed
- 2 tablespoons fresh lemon juice

1. In food processor, combine bread, basil, oregano, lemon zest, and ½ teaspoon of salt, and process until bread has become fine crumbs. Transfer to shallow plate or sheet of waxed paper.

2. Place egg mixture in shallow bowl. Dip chicken first in egg mixture, then in bread-crumb mixture, pressing crumbs into chicken. Transfer chicken to baking sheet and refrigerate at least 1 hour or up to 4 hours.

3. In large nonstick skillet, heat 1 tablespoon of oil over medium heat. Add shiitakes and garlic, and cook 7 minutes or until mushrooms are tender. Transfer mushrooms and garlic to large bowl. Add tomatoes, arugula, lemon juice, 1 tablespoon of oil, and remaining ¼ teaspoon salt, and toss to combine.

4. In large nonstick skillet, heat 2 tablespoons of oil over medium heat. Add 2 chicken breast halves and cook 1½ minutes per side or until golden brown and cooked through. Repeat with remaining 2 tablespoons oil and chicken. Divide mushroom mixture evenly among 4 dinner plates and top with chicken.

IN A HURRY?

Omit the chilling time in step 2 and go straight to step 3, but use a nonstick skillet and be careful when turning cutlets so breading does not fall off.

Pasta Pesto with Chicken & Tomatoes

When summer arrives, grab a big bunch of fresh basil and a basket of cherry tomatoes, and treat yourself to this superb chicken-and-pasta dish. The pesto can sauce any kind of pasta, and you can add other vegetables and slivers of smoked chicken for a variation on this meal.

- 10 ounces penne pasta
- 1 cup packed fresh basil leaves
- 4 tablespoons olive oil
- 2 tablespoons pine nuts
- 1 large clove garlic
- ¾ teaspoon salt
- ½ cup grated Parmesan cheese
- ¾ pound skinless, boneless chicken breasts, cut for stir-fry (page 15)
- 2 cups cherry tomatoes, halved

1. In large pot of boiling water, cook penne according to package directions. Drain, reserving ¼ cup of pasta cooking water.

2. Meanwhile, in food processor or blender, combine basil, 3 tablespoons of olive oil, the pine nuts, garlic, and salt. Process until smooth. Add ¼ cup of Parmesan and process until combined.

3. In large skillet, heat remaining 1 tablespoon oil over medium heat. Add chicken and stir-fry 2 minutes or until no longer pink. Add cherry tomatoes and cook 3 minutes or until chicken is cooked through and cherry tomatoes have started to collapse. Add pesto and reserved pasta cooking water, and toss to coat well.

4. Transfer chicken mixture to large bowl. Add hot pasta and remaining ¼ cup Parmesan, and toss well.

CILANTRO PESTO WITH CHICKEN & PEPPERS

Cook the pasta as directed. In step 2, substitute 1 cup cilantro leaves (and tender stems) for basil and ¼ cup natural (unblanched) almonds for pine nuts; increase salt to 1 teaspoon and garlic to 2 cloves; add 1 pickled jalapeño pepper. Process as directed, but omit the ¼ cup Parmesan. In step 3, sauté chicken as directed, but omit cherry tomatoes. Add cilantro pesto and reserved pasta cooking water and cook 1 minute. In step 4, substitute ¾ cup grated Manchego cheese for the Parmesan and add 1 cup thinly sliced bottled roasted red peppers; toss well.

Calories 630, Total Fat 27g, Saturated Fat 8g, Cholesterol 72mg, Sodium 893mg, Protein 36g, Carbohydrates 59g

QUICK TO FIX

Prep Time: 15 minutes
Cooking Time: 15 minutes
Makes 4 servings

NUTRITION INFORMATION
Per Serving
Calories 568
Total Fat 21g
Saturated Fat 4.5g
Cholesterol 57mg
Sodium 689mg
Protein 35g
Carbohydrates 58g

Skillet Chicken Breasts with Lemon & Dill

Lemon and dill are frequently partners for fish, but this spring-fresh combination is equally delicious with chicken. Do use fresh lemon juice—not the juice that comes in a bottle.

- 2 tablespoons butter
- 1 tablespoon olive oil
- 4 skinless, boneless chicken breast halves (about 1½ pounds)
- 2 tablespoons flour
- 2 scallions, thinly sliced
- ⅔ cup chicken broth
- 3 tablespoons fresh lemon juice
- ⅓ cup snipped dill
- ½ teaspoon salt

1. In large skillet, heat 1 tablespoon of butter and the oil over medium heat. Dredge chicken in flour, shaking off excess. Add chicken to pan and sauté, turning it over as it colors, 12 minutes or until golden brown and cooked through. With slotted spoon, transfer chicken to plate.

2. Add scallions to pan and cook 1 minute. Add broth, lemon juice, dill, and salt, and bring to a boil. Remove from heat and swirl in remaining 1 tablespoon butter. Return chicken to skillet and spoon sauce over chicken, turning to coat. Transfer chicken to dinner plates and drizzle any sauce remaining in skillet over them.

QUICK TO FIX

Prep Time: 10 minutes
Cooking Time: 15 minutes
Makes 4 servings

NUTRITION INFORMATION
Per Serving
Calories 297
Total Fat 12g
Saturated Fat 4.5g
Cholesterol 114mg
Sodium 637mg
Protein 40g
Carbohydrates 8g

SKILLET CHICKEN BREASTS WITH LEMON & DILL

THAI CHICKEN STIR-FRY

Thai Chicken Stir-Fry

Prep Time: 15 minutes
Cooking Time: 10 minutes
Makes 4 servings

NUTRITION INFORMATION

Per Serving

Calories 262

Total Fat 12g

Saturated Fat 2g

Cholesterol 67mg

Sodium 815mg

Protein 29g

Carbohydrates 8g

The long ingredient list for this simple stir-fry is deceiving: More than half of the components go right into the blender to make a super-quick herb paste. There's time to cook a pot of rice while you put together the stir-fry. Mango sorbet is the perfect dessert.

- 2 teaspoons anchovy paste
- 4 cloves garlic, coarsely chopped
- 4 scallions, cut into 1-inch lengths
- ⅓ cup packed cilantro leaves
- ½ teaspoon salt
- ½ teaspoon crushed red pepper flakes
- 3 tablespoons vegetable oil
- 1 pound skinless, boneless chicken breast halves, cut for stir-fry (page 15)
- 1 cup canned baby corn, rinsed and drained
- 2 plum tomatoes, cut into ½-inch chunks
- 2 tablespoons lower-sodium soy sauce
- 1½ teaspoons sugar
- ½ cup packed fresh basil leaves, shredded

1. In food processor or blender, combine anchovy paste, garlic, scallions, cilantro, salt, red pepper flakes, 1 tablespoon of oil, and 2 teaspoons of water. Process to smooth paste.

2. In large skillet, heat remaining 2 tablespoons oil over medium-high heat. Add herb paste and cook 1 minute. Add chicken and stir-fry 4 minutes or until chicken is no longer pink.

3. Add corn, tomatoes, soy sauce, sugar, and basil, and cook, stirring constantly, 2 minutes or until chicken is just cooked through.

Sicilian Linguine with Chicken & Broccoli Rabe

Prep Time: 25 minutes
Cooking Time: 20 minutes
Makes 4 servings

NUTRITION INFORMATION

Per Serving

Calories 764

Total Fat 27g

Saturated Fat 6g

Cholesterol 94mg

Sodium 1273mg

Protein 51g

Carbohydrates 81g

The favorite Italian combination of pasta, broccoli rabe, and spicy sausage makes a satisfying meal. Here, chicken sausage flavors the pasta and strips of sautéed chicken breast. If you don't care for broccoli rabe's assertive bite, use regular broccoli, cut into florets; chop the stems into small pieces.

- 10 ounces linguine
- 3 tablespoons olive oil
- 3 cloves garlic, slivered
- 1 bunch broccoli rabe (1 pound), trimmed and chopped (8 cups)
- 6 ounces fully-cooked spicy chicken sausage, coarsely chopped
- ¾ pound skinless, boneless chicken breast halves, cut for stir-fry (page 15)
- ½ teaspoon salt
- ⅔ cup grated Parmesan cheese
- ½ cup golden raisins
- ½ cup oil-packed sun-dried tomatoes, drained and coarsely chopped
- 3 tablespoons pine nuts

1. In large pot of boiling water, cook linguine according to package directions. Drain, reserving 1 cup of pasta cooking water.

2. Meanwhile, in large skillet, heat oil over low heat. Add garlic and cook 2 minutes. Add broccoli rabe and sausage, and cook, stirring frequently, 12 minutes or until broccoli rabe is very tender.

3. Add chicken and salt, and cook 5 minutes or until cooked through. Stir in reserved pasta cooking water and bring to a boil. Transfer to large bowl. Add Parmesan, raisins, sun-dried tomatoes, pine nuts, and hot cooked pasta, and toss well.

Chicken Breasts in
Cheese Sauce with Spinach

For this quick sauté, tender spinach is bathed in a rich and creamy Parmesan sauce.
Even those who are not the most ardent of spinach lovers will ask for seconds.

- 2 tablespoons butter
- 3 scallions, thinly sliced
- 2 cloves garlic, minced
- 4 skinless, boneless chicken breast halves (about 1½ pounds)
- 3 tablespoons flour
- 1 package (10 ounces) frozen chopped spinach, thawed and squeezed dry
- 1½ cups milk
- 2 teaspoons Dijon mustard
- ½ teaspoon salt
- ⅓ cup grated Parmesan cheese

1. In large skillet, melt butter over low heat. Add scallions and garlic, and cook, stirring frequently, 2 minutes or until scallions are soft.

2. Dredge chicken in 2 tablespoons of flour, shaking off excess. Push scallion mixture to one side of pan. Increase heat to medium, add chicken, and sauté 4 minutes per side or until golden brown. With slotted spoon, transfer chicken to plate.

3. Stir spinach into pan and cook 5 minutes or until tender. Sprinkle scallion mixture and spinach with remaining 1 tablespoon flour. Stir in milk, mustard, and salt, and bring to a boil. Reduce to a simmer, return chicken to pan, cover, and simmer 5 minutes or until chicken is cooked through.

4. Transfer chicken to plate. Stir Parmesan into spinach mixture and stir until cheese has melted. Spoon Parmesan-spinach mixture onto dinner plates and top with chicken.

QUICK TO FIX

Prep Time: 10 minutes
Cooking Time: 20 minutes
Makes 4 servings

NUTRITION INFORMATION
Per Serving
Calories 371
Total Fat 13g
Saturated Fat 7.5g
Cholesterol 132mg
Sodium 741mg
Protein 48g
Carbohydrates 13g

Chicken Breasts in
Garlic Butter with Chives

Don't let a drop of the lemony garlic butter go to waste; serve the chicken with pasta, potatoes, or
bread to soak up the sauce. One option (shown here) is broad egg noodles. Toss the cooked noodles
with a bit of butter, divide them among dinner plates, and serve the chicken and sauce on top.

- 1 head of garlic (2 ounces)
- ⅔ cup chicken broth
- 1 teaspoon grated lemon zest
- 1 tablespoon fresh lemon juice
- ¼ teaspoon salt
- ¼ teaspoon freshly ground black pepper
- 2 teaspoons olive oil
- 4 skinless, boneless chicken breast halves (about 1½ pounds)
- 2 tablespoons flour
- 1 tablespoon butter, cut up
- ¼ cup snipped chives

1. Preheat oven to 400°F. Wrap garlic in foil and bake for 30 minutes or until packet feels soft when squeezed. When cool enough to handle, remove foil, snip off top of head of garlic, and squeeze garlic pulp into small bowl. Whisk broth, lemon zest, lemon juice, salt, and pepper into garlic; set aside.

2. Meanwhile, in large nonstick skillet, heat oil over medium heat. Dredge chicken in flour, shaking off excess. Add chicken to pan and sauté 4 minutes per side or until golden brown. With slotted spoon, transfer chicken to plate.

3. Whisk garlic mixture to combine and pour into skillet. Bring to a boil, return chicken to pan, reduce to a simmer, cover, and cook 5 minutes or until chicken is cooked through. Transfer chicken to dinner plates.

4. Return sauce to a simmer. Remove from heat and swirl in butter until creamy. Stir in chives and spoon sauce over chicken.

LOW FAT

Prep Time: 10 minutes
Cooking Time: 45 minutes
Makes 4 servings

NUTRITION INFORMATION
Per Serving
Calories 272
Total Fat 7.5g
Saturated Fat 2.5g
Cholesterol 107mg
Sodium 461mg
Protein 41g
Carbohydrates 8g

CHICKEN BREASTS IN GARLIC BUTTER WITH CHIVES

Chicken Hash

For a quicker hash, microwave the potatoes instead of boiling them (follow the instructions for your oven). If you have leftover boiled potatoes on hand, use 3 cups diced.

- 1 pound all-purpose potatoes
- 2 tablespoons butter
- 1 tablespoon olive oil
- 1 onion, finely chopped
- 1 small green bell pepper, cut into small chunks
- 1 clove garlic, minced
- 1 pickled jalapeño pepper, minced with seeds
- 2½ cups cubed (½-inch) cooked chicken breasts or thighs—leftover or poached (page 17)
- ¾ teaspoon salt
- ¼ teaspoon freshly ground black pepper
- ¼ teaspoon dried thyme
- ⅓ cup heavy or whipping cream

1. In large pot of boiling salted water, cook potatoes 25 minutes or until tender but not falling apart. Drain. When cool enough to handle, peel and cut potatoes into ½-inch chunks.

2. In large skillet, heat butter and oil over medium-low heat. Add onion, bell pepper, and garlic, and cook, stirring frequently, 10 minutes or until onion is soft and golden brown. Add jalapeño and stir to combine. Add potatoes and cook, stirring occasionally, 10 minutes or until lightly browned.

3. Stir in chicken, salt, black pepper, and thyme, and cook until chicken is hot. Add cream, press hash into skillet, and increase heat to medium. Cook, without stirring, 10 minutes or until light crust has formed on bottom.

RED-FLANNEL HASH In step 1, cook potatoes as directed. In step 2, omit butter and use total of 3 tablespoons olive oil. Use 2 onions and 2 cloves garlic; omit bell pepper and jalapeño. In step 3, cook chicken as directed, with these changes: Add 1 can (15 ounces) whole beets, drained and diced; increase salt to 1 teaspoon and black pepper to ½ teaspoon; omit cream. Continue cooking as directed. *Calories 382, Total Fat 14g, Saturated Fat 2.5g, Cholesterol 74mg, Sodium 827mg, Protein 31g, Carbohydrates 34g*

LEFTOVERS

Prep Time: 15 minutes
Cooking Time: 55 minutes
Makes 4 servings

NUTRITION INFORMATION
Per Serving
Calories 405
Total Fat 20g
Saturated Fat 9.5g
Cholesterol 117mg
Sodium 628mg
Protein 30g
Carbohydrates 26g

Orange Chicken with Red & Green Peppers

Broccoli, snow peas, and fresh ginger (plus the bell peppers) make this a colorful and healthful meal.

- 1½ teaspoons cornstarch
- 1 teaspoon grated orange zest
- ½ cup orange juice
- 3 tablespoons lower-sodium soy sauce
- ¾ teaspoon salt
- 2 tablespoons vegetable oil
- 2 tablespoons minced fresh ginger
- 3 cloves garlic, minced
- 2 cups broccoli florets
- 1 red bell pepper, cut into 1-inch chunks
- 1 green bell pepper, cut into 1-inch chunks
- ¼ pound snow peas, strings removed, halved crosswise
- ¾ pound skinless, boneless chicken breasts, cut for stir-fry (page 15)

1. In small bowl, whisk together cornstarch, orange zest, orange juice, soy sauce, and salt; set aside.

2. In large skillet, heat oil over medium heat. Add ginger and garlic, and cook 30 seconds. Add broccoli, bell peppers, snow peas, and ¼ cup of water, and stir-fry 4 minutes or until broccoli is crisp-tender.

3. Stir in chicken, increase heat to medium-high, and stir-fry 2 minutes or until chicken is just cooked through. Stir cornstarch mixture and pour into skillet. Bring to a boil and cook, stirring, 1 minute or until slightly thickened.

QUICK TO FIX

Prep Time: 20 minutes
Cooking Time: 10 minutes
Makes 4 servings

NUTRITION INFORMATION
Per Serving
Calories 227
Total Fat 8.5g
Saturated Fat 1g
Cholesterol 49mg
Sodium 972mg
Protein 24g
Carbohydrates 14g

ORANGE CHICKEN WITH RED & GREEN PEPPERS

ITALIAN CHICKEN BURGERS WITH PROVOLONE

Prep Time: 25 minutes
Cooking Time: 25 minutes
Makes 4 servings

NUTRITION INFORMATION
Per Serving

Calories 525

Total Fat 24g

Saturated Fat 7g

Cholesterol 138mg

Sodium 1299mg

Protein 30g

Carbohydrates 46g

HINTS & TIPS

➤ Provolone, like mozzarella, is an Italian cheese that was once made from water-buffalo's milk. Today's Provolone is made from cow's milk. Mild and soft when young, Provolone develops a sharper flavor with aging. Smoked Provolone is also available; try it in this recipe for a change of pace.

➤ In place of orzo, you could use another pasta of the type called *pastina*—tiny shapes usually served in broth. They include *acini di pepe* (peppercorns) and *stelline* (little stars).

Italian Chicken Burgers with Provolone

In addition to breadcrumbs, the ground chicken is mixed with pasta. How very Italian! Both starches help keep the burgers moist and light. To carry through with the Italian theme, the chicken mixture is seasoned with basil and tomato paste, and the topping is Provolone rather than Cheddar. In the variation below, homage is paid to Milan, where rice is often the starch of choice in place of pasta.

¼   cup orzo

¾   pound ground chicken

6   tablespoons chopped fresh basil

2   tablespoons plain dried breadcrumbs

4½   teaspoons tomato paste

1   large egg

½   teaspoon salt

1   large tomato, seeded and chopped

¼   cup Gaeta or Calamata olives, pitted and coarsely chopped

1   clove garlic, minced

1   tablespoon olive oil

3   ounces sliced Provolone cheese

4   hard rolls, split

1. In medium pot of boiling water, cook orzo according to package directions; rinse under cold water and drain well.

2. Meanwhile, in large bowl, combine chicken, 2 tablespoons of basil, the breadcrumbs, tomato paste, egg, ¼ teaspoon of salt, and the orzo. Mix well to combine; shape into 4 burgers.

3. In medium bowl, stir together tomato, olives, garlic, remaining ¼ cup basil, and ¼ teaspoon salt. Cover tomato-olive mixture and refrigerate.

4. In large nonstick skillet, heat oil over medium heat. Add burgers to skillet and sauté, turning them over as they cook, 10 minutes or until cooked through.

5. Top each burger with Provolone. Cover skillet and cook 1 to 2 minutes or until cheese has melted. Place burgers on rolls and spoon tomato-olive mixture on top.

TO REDUCE THE FAT

Instead of using store-bought ground chicken, grind ¾ pound of chicken breast yourself. Cook it as you would ground chicken. In step 2, use 2 egg whites in place of whole egg. In step 3, omit olives.

Calories 447, Total Fat 13g, Saturated Fat 5g, Cholesterol 64mg, Sodium 1001mg, Protein 35g, Carbohydrates 45g

MILANESE CHICKEN BURGERS Omit orzo. Instead, in medium pot of boiling salted water, cook ¼ cup rice along with 2 cloves minced garlic until rice is very tender. Drain well if any liquid remains. Transfer to large bowl, stir in ½ cup grated Parmesan cheese and ½ teaspoon freshly ground black pepper; cool to room temperature. In step 2, omit tomato paste (and orzo); add remaining step 2 ingredients to bowl of rice; mix well and shape into 4 burgers. Complete steps 3 and 4 as directed. Omit Provolone and serve burgers with tomato-olive mixture.

Calories 496, Total Fat 21g, Saturated Fat 5.5g, Cholesterol 132mg, Sodium 1250mg, Protein 29g, Carbohydrates 47g

Stir-Fried Velvet Chicken

The Chinese technique called "velveting" firms chicken for stir-frying and gives it a velvety texture. For this preliminary step, the chicken is coated with a mixture of egg white and cornstarch, then cooked briefly. You can "velvet" the chicken well in advance and refrigerate it until needed.

Prep Time: 20 minutes plus
    marinating time
Cooking Time: 5 minutes
Makes 4 servings

1   large egg white
2   tablespoons dry sherry
1   tablespoon cornstarch
½   teaspoon salt
1   pound skinless, boneless chicken breasts, cut into 1-inch chunks
2   teaspoons plus 2 tablespoons vegetable oil
2   bell peppers (mixed colors), cut into 1-inch chunks
1   can (8 ounces) bamboo shoots, drained
3   scallions, thinly sliced
2   tablespoons minced fresh ginger
2   cloves garlic, minced
2   tablespoons lower-sodium soy sauce

1. In food processor or blender, combine egg white, 1 tablespoon of sherry, the cornstarch, and ¼ teaspoon of salt. Process 30 seconds or until smooth and creamy. Transfer egg white mixture to large bowl. Add chicken and toss to coat well. Cover and refrigerate at least 8 hours or up to overnight.

2. In large saucepan, bring 4 cups of water and 2 teaspoons of oil to a boil. Reduce to a simmer. Lift chicken from its marinade, add to saucepan, and simmer gently 45 seconds. With skimmer or slotted spoon, remove chicken and drain well.

3. In large skillet, heat remaining 2 tablespoons oil over medium-high heat. Add bell peppers, bamboo shoots, and remaining ¼ teaspoon salt, and stir-fry 2 minutes. Add scallions, ginger, and garlic, and cook 1 minute. Add chicken, soy sauce, and remaining 1 tablespoon sherry, and cook 30 seconds or until chicken is hot and cooked through.

CHICKEN WITH CASHEWS & LEEKS Complete steps 1 and 2 as directed. In step 3, use only 1 red bell pepper and substitute 1 can (5 ounces) sliced water chestnuts for bamboo shoots. When sautéing bell pepper, add 2 leeks cut into ½-inch lengths. Add ginger and garlic as directed, but omit scallions. Add chicken, soy sauce, and sherry as directed, along with ½ cup coarsely chopped roasted, salted cashews. *Calories 379, Total Fat 19g, Saturated Fat 3g, Cholesterol 66mg, Sodium 794mg, Protein 32g, Carbohydrates 20g*

NUTRITION INFORMATION
Per Serving
Calories 255
Total Fat 11g
Saturated Fat 1.5g
Cholesterol 66mg
Sodium 683mg
Protein 29g
Carbohydrates 8g

Southern Fried Chicken

Every Southern cook claims a "secret" for perfect fried chicken. But all you really need is a simple, foolproof recipe like this one. The chicken pieces are soaked in buttermilk for optimal tenderness and flavor; after flouring, they're left to "rest" so the coating won't flake off when the chicken is fried.

Prep Time: 5 minutes plus
    marinating and chilling time
Cooking Time: 30 minutes
Makes 4 servings

1½ cups buttermilk
½   teaspoon freshly ground black pepper
¾   teaspoon salt
4   whole chicken legs (about 2½ pounds), split into drumsticks and thighs (page 14)
1   cup flour
½   cup vegetable oil

1. In large bowl, stir together buttermilk, pepper, and ¼ teaspoon of salt. Add chicken, cover, and refrigerate at least 30 minutes or up to 8 hours.

2. In large shallow pan, stir together flour and ¼ teaspoon of salt. Lift chicken from its marinade and dip into seasoned flour, patting flour into chicken. Place chicken on plate and refrigerate uncovered 30 minutes or up to 4 hours for coating to set.

3. Divide oil between 2 large, deep skillets and heat over medium-low heat. (Oil is ready for frying when a piece of bread sizzles as it hits the surface.) Add chicken and cook, carefully turning pieces as they color, 30 minutes or until richly browned and cooked through. Transfer chicken to paper towels to drain. Sprinkle remaining ¼ teaspoon salt over chicken before serving.

NUTRITION INFORMATION
Per Serving
Calories 558
Total Fat 37g
Saturated Fat 7.5g
Cholesterol 130mg
Sodium 536mg
Protein 39g
Carbohydrates 14g

SOUTHERN FRIED CHICKEN

Chicken & Broccoli with Black Bean Sauce

The wonderful savor of Chinese fermented black beans is a shortcut to tasty stir-fries. Made by fermenting beans with salt and spices, this versatile ingredient is sold in many supermarkets. Once you open the container, transfer the contents to a covered jar. The beans will keep indefinitely.

- 1 pound skinless, boneless chicken breasts, cut for stir-fry (page 15)
- 3 tablespoons lower-sodium soy sauce
- 1 tablespoon dry sherry
- 1 tablespoon cornstarch
- 2 teaspoons sesame oil
- 3 tablespoons peanut or other vegetable oil
- 2 tablespoons fermented black beans
- 3 cups small broccoli florets
- 1 red bell pepper, cut into thin strips
- 1 pickled jalapeño pepper, chopped with seeds
- 2 tablespoons minced fresh ginger
- 2 cloves garlic, minced

1. In large bowl, stir together chicken, 2 tablespoons of soy sauce, the sherry, and cornstarch until well coated. Add 1 teaspoon of sesame oil and toss again.

2. In large skillet, heat 2 tablespoons of peanut oil over medium-high heat. Add chicken mixture and stir-fry 4 minutes or until chicken is lightly browned and cooked through. With slotted spoon, transfer chicken to plate.

3. Meanwhile, rinse black beans in several changes of cold water. Drain well; mash half the black beans with the flat side of a knife.

4. Add remaining 1 tablespoon peanut oil to skillet along with broccoli, bell pepper, jalapeño, ginger, garlic, and black beans, and stir to combine. Add remaining 1 tablespoon soy sauce, 1 teaspoon sesame oil, and ½ cup of water, and cook, stirring constantly, 3 minutes or until broccoli is crisp-tender. Return chicken to pan and cook, stirring constantly, 1 minute or until heated through.

Prep Time: 20 minutes
Cooking Time: 10 minutes
Makes 4 servings

NUTRITION INFORMATION
Per Serving
Calories 301
Total Fat 15g
Saturated Fat 2.5g
Cholesterol 66mg
Sodium 839mg
Protein 31g
Carbohydrates 11g

Chicken Marengo

It's said that this dish was created by Napoleon's chef following the Battle of Marengo, which took place in Italy in 1800. All you need to know, however, is that the chicken is simmered in a lush tomato-wine sauce with tender mushrooms. Serve the chicken and sauce over rice, noodles, or polenta.

- 3 tablespoons olive oil
- 4 bone-in chicken breast halves (about 2 pounds), halved crosswise
- ¼ cup flour
- 1 red onion, finely chopped
- 2 cloves garlic, minced
- ½ pound mushrooms, quartered
- ½ cup dry white wine
- ¾ cup canned crushed tomatoes
- 2 tablespoons tomato paste
- ½ teaspoon salt

1. In large nonstick skillet, heat 2 tablespoons of oil over medium-high heat. Dredge chicken in flour, shaking off excess. Add chicken to skillet and sauté 5 minutes per side or until golden brown. With slotted spoon, transfer chicken to plate.

2. Add remaining 1 tablespoon oil to pan and heat over medium heat. Add onion and garlic, and cook, stirring frequently, 7 minutes or until onion is soft. Add mushrooms and cook 5 minutes or until firm-tender.

3. Stir in wine and bring to a boil. Add tomatoes, tomato paste, and salt, and return to a boil. Return chicken to pan, reduce to a simmer, cover, and cook, turning chicken as it cooks, 20 minutes or until cooked through.

Prep Time: 15 minutes
Cooking Time: 45 minutes
Makes 4 servings

NUTRITION INFORMATION
Per Serving
Calories 493
Total Fat 27g
Saturated Fat 6g
Cholesterol 116mg
Sodium 551mg
Protein 41g
Carbohydrates 15g

CHICKEN MARENGO

CHICKEN RISOTTO WITH WINTER SQUASH

Prep Time: 25 minutes
Cooking Time: 45 minutes
Makes 4 servings

NUTRITION INFORMATION

Per Serving

Calories 512

Total Fat 17g

Saturated Fat 8.5g

Cholesterol 102mg

Sodium 1208mg

Protein 29g

Carbohydrates 62g

HINTS & TIPS

➤ Risotto is traditionally made with Italy's own Arborio rice. Arborio's plump, pearly grains have a uniquely starchy outer coat that cooks into a creamy "sauce" while the inner part of the kernel stays firm. This gives risotto its luxurious texture—nothing like the fluffy, separate grains that are desirable in some other rice dishes.

➤ You can substitute regular long- or short-grain rice (not converted rice) in this recipe, if necessary, but the risotto will not be quite so velvety.

Chicken Risotto with Winter Squash

This risotto—a slow-cooked Italian rice dish—was inspired by a classic ravioli filling: herbed pumpkin purée combined with crushed Amaretti cookies. These ultra-crisp Italian macaroons add a touch of sweetness along with their almond flavor. You can also make this dish without the Amaretti.

3 tablespoons butter

1 small onion, finely chopped

1 red bell pepper, cut into ½-inch chunks

2 cups cubed (1-inch) peeled butternut squash

2 cups chicken broth, canned or homemade (page 45)

½ teaspoon salt

1⅓ cups Arborio rice

⅔ cup dry white wine

¾ pound skinless, boneless chicken thighs, cut into ½-inch chunks

1 cup frozen peas, thawed

½ cup grated Parmesan cheese

6 large or 12 small Amaretti cookies, finely crumbled (optional)

½ teaspoon ground black pepper

1. In large saucepan, melt 2 tablespoons of butter over low heat. Add onion and cook, stirring frequently, 7 minutes or until soft. Add bell pepper and squash, and cook, stirring frequently, 10 minutes or until squash is firm-tender.

2. Meanwhile, in separate saucepan, combine broth, salt, and 1 cup of water, and bring to a simmer over low heat.

3. Add rice to sautéed vegetables and stir until well coated. Add wine and cook, stirring constantly, 2 minutes or until wine is reduced by half. Stir in chicken. Add ½ cup of simmering broth mixture to pan and cook, stirring until absorbed. Continue adding broth mixture ½ cup at time, only adding more liquid when previous amount has been absorbed. Cook, stirring constantly, until sauce surrounding rice is creamy but rice is not mushy. Total cooking time for rice will be about 25 minutes.

4. Stir in peas and cook just until heated through. Stir in Parmesan, Amaretti cookie crumbs, black pepper, and remaining 1 tablespoon butter.

FROM THE FRIDGE

Use 3 cups diced cooked chicken thighs in place of uncooked chicken. Stir in cooked chicken along with peas in step 4.

CHICKEN RISOTTO WITH MUSHROOMS In step 1, omit squash; add ½ pound thinly sliced mushrooms along with bell pepper and cook only 7 minutes or until bell pepper is tender. Proceed as directed, but omit Amaretti cookies.

Calories 504, Total Fat 17g, Saturated Fat 9g, Cholesterol 103mg, Sodium 1245mg, Protein 30g, Carbohydrates 56g

Sweet & Sour Chicken

If you'd prefer, you can cut the chicken into strips for this fresh take on a Chinese restaurant classic.

- 1 can (20 ounces) juice-packed pineapple wedges, drained, juice reserved
- ½ cup chicken broth
- 2 tablespoons rice vinegar
- 1 tablespoon lower-sodium soy sauce
- ½ teaspoon salt
- ½ teaspoon crushed red pepper flakes
- 3 tablespoons vegetable oil
- 8 skinless, boneless chicken thighs (about 2 pounds)
- 2 tablespoons plus 1½ teaspoons cornstarch
- 2 stalks celery, thinly sliced
- ¼ pound snow peas, strings removed
- 1 yellow bell pepper, cut into 1-inch chunks
- 1 red bell pepper, cut into ¼-inch-wide matchsticks
- 1 large tomato, cut into 8 wedges

1. In medium bowl, stir together ¼ cup of reserved pineapple juice, broth, rice vinegar, soy sauce, salt, and red pepper flakes.

2. In large nonstick skillet, heat 2 tablespoons of oil over medium-high heat. Dredge chicken in 2 tablespoons of cornstarch, shaking off excess. Add chicken to skillet and sauté, turning pieces as they color, 10 minutes or until golden brown and cooked through. Transfer chicken to plate.

3. Add remaining 1 tablespoon oil to pan along with celery, snow peas, and bell peppers, and stir-fry 4 minutes or until peppers are crisp-tender. Add tomato to pan and toss to combine. Stir pineapple juice mixture and add to pan along with pineapple chunks; bring to a boil.

4. In small bowl, stir together remaining 1½ teaspoons cornstarch and 1 tablespoon of water. Stir cornstarch mixture into pan. Bring to a boil and cook, stirring constantly, 1 minute or until slightly thickened. Return chicken to pan and cook 2 minutes or until coated and heated through.

SPICY PLUM CHICKEN In step 1, omit pineapple and its juice; add ¼ cup plum jam. Cook chicken as directed in step 2. In step 3, omit celery, snow peas, and tomato; instead, sauté 1 pound plums (pitted and cut into ½-inch wedges) along with bell peppers. Stir plum-jam mixture into pan in place of pineapple and juice mixture. Continue as directed. *Calories 503, Total Fat 20g, Saturated Fat 3.5g, Cholesterol 188mg, Sodium 775mg, Protein 46g, Carbohydrates 34g*

Prep Time: 15 minutes
Cooking Time: 20 minutes
Makes 4 servings

NUTRITION INFORMATION
Per Serving
Calories 508
Total Fat 20g
Saturated Fat 3.5g
Cholesterol 188mg
Sodium 792mg
Protein 47g
Carbohydrates 35g

Curried Chicken with Butternut Squash

Heating the spices in sizzling oil is a crucial step in authentic Indian cooking.

- 2 tablespoons olive oil
- 2 teaspoons curry powder
- 1 teaspoon ground coriander
- ½ teaspoon ground ginger
- 1 large onion, finely chopped
- 2 pounds skinless, boneless chicken thighs, cut into 1-inch chunks
- 1 butternut squash (1½ pounds), peeled, seeded, and cut into 1-inch chunks
- ½ cup chicken broth
- ½ cup canned tomatoes, chopped with their juice
- 2 tablespoons mango chutney, finely chopped
- ½ teaspoon salt
- ¼ cup chopped cilantro

1. In large skillet, heat oil over medium heat. Add curry powder, coriander, and ginger, and cook 30 seconds. Add onion and cook, stirring frequently, for 7 minutes or until soft. Add chicken and squash, and stir to coat well.

2. Add broth, tomatoes, chutney, and salt, and bring to a boil. Reduce to a simmer, cover, and cook 20 minutes or until chicken and squash are tender. Stir in cilantro.

Prep Time: 20 minutes
Cooking Time: 30 minutes
Makes 4 servings

NUTRITION INFORMATION
Per Serving
Calories 459
Total Fat 16g
Saturated Fat 3.5g
Cholesterol 188mg
Sodium 758mg
Protein 47g
Carbohydrates 31g

SWEET & SOUR CHICKEN

POACHED CHICKEN BREASTS WITH TANGERINE SAUCE

Poached Chicken Breasts with Tangerine Sauce

These citrusy chicken breasts are delicious hot or cold. You can use orange juice instead of tangerine.

2 teaspoons plus 2 tablespoons olive oil
2 shallots, minced, or 2 scallions, thinly sliced
1 cup tangerine juice (about 4 tangerines)
2 tablespoons balsamic vinegar
½ teaspoon salt
½ teaspoon dried rosemary, crumbled
¼ teaspoon freshly ground black pepper
4 skinless, boneless chicken breast halves (about 1½ pounds)
1 plum tomato, finely diced
¼ cup chopped parsley

1. In large skillet, heat 2 teaspoons of oil over low heat. Add shallots and cook, stirring frequently, 4 minutes or until tender. Add tangerine juice, vinegar, salt, rosemary, and pepper. Increase heat to high and bring to a boil. Add chicken, reduce heat to a bare simmer, cover, and cook, turning chicken over midway through cooking, 15 minutes or until done.

2. With slotted spoon, transfer chicken to dinner plates. Increase heat to high, add tomato and remaining 2 tablespoons oil, and boil 5 minutes or until oil and juice are no longer separate (they've emulsified) and sauce is slightly thickened. Stir in parsley. Serve warm, at room temperature, or chilled. (If sauce separates after chilling, whisk to recombine.)

CHICKEN WITH CREAMY PEACH SAUCE In step 1, substitute 1 small diced red onion for shallots; increase olive oil to 1 tablespoon; add 1 clove minced garlic. Omit tangerine juice. When adding vinegar and spices, add 2 cups frozen (no need to thaw) sliced peaches, ⅓ cup peach jam, and ½ cup chicken broth. Bring to a boil as directed. Add chicken and cook as directed. In step 2, remove chicken from pan. Omit tomato and olive oil. Stir in ⅓ cup heavy cream and bring to a boil. Boil until sauce is of a light coating consistency. Stir in 2 tablespoons chopped parsley and spoon sauce over chicken.

Calories 405, Total Fat 13g, Saturated Fat 5.5g, Cholesterol 126mg, Sodium 555mg, Protein 41g, Carbohydrates 31g

---

Chicken & Broccoli Potato Topper

Use leftover broccoli (or green beans, spinach, or asparagus) if you have some on hand.

4 large baking potatoes (8 to 10 ounces each)
2 tablespoons butter
1 small onion, finely chopped
2 cups small broccoli florets
2 tablespoons flour
1 cup milk
½ teaspoon salt
¼ teaspoon cayenne pepper
3 cups shredded cooked chicken breasts or thighs—leftover or poached (page 17)
¼ pound shredded sharp Cheddar cheese (1 cup)

1. Preheat oven to 400°F. With fork, prick potatoes in several places. Place in oven and bake for 1 hour or until fork-tender.

2. Meanwhile, in large skillet, heat butter over low heat. Add onion and cook, stirring frequently, 7 minutes or until onion is soft. Add broccoli and cook 4 to 5 minutes or until broccoli is crisp-tender. Stir in flour until vegetables are well coated. Gradually stir in milk. Add salt and cayenne, and cook, stirring frequently, 5 minutes or until slightly thickened. Stir in chicken and cook 1 minute or until heated through. Stir in Cheddar and remove from heat.

3. With fork, split skin down length of each potato. With your fingers, push on each end toward the middle so that the potato opens up. Place one potato on each of 4 dinner plates. Spoon chicken mixture on top.

IN A HURRY?
Cook the potatoes in the microwave (15 to 20 minutes on high power; follow instructions for your oven) and use frozen broccoli, thawed and drained.

Chicken & Green Bean Frittata

Take a couple of eggs, a splash of good olive oil, some grated cheese, and a few choice leftovers, and you have a frittata—an Italian-style open-faced omelette. This one makes a great light supper.

½ pound green beans, cut into 1-inch lengths
2 tablespoons olive oil
1 small onion, finely chopped
¾ teaspoon salt
6 large eggs, lightly beaten
⅓ cup grated Parmesan cheese
½ teaspoon freshly ground black pepper
1½ cups shredded cooked chicken breasts
   or thighs—leftover or poached (page 17)

1. In large pot of boiling salted water, blanch green beans for 4 minutes; drain well. Meanwhile, in large ovenproof skillet, heat 1 tablespoon of oil over low heat. Add onion and stir-fry 7 minutes or until soft. Add beans and ¼ teaspoon of salt, and cook 3 minutes or until tender. Cool slightly.

2. In large bowl, whisk together eggs, all but 1 tablespoon of Parmesan, the pepper, and remaining ½ teaspoon salt. Stir in chicken and green-bean mixture.

3. Add remaining 1 tablespoon oil to skillet and heat over medium heat. Pour in egg mixture, reduce heat to low, and cook without stirring for 12 minutes or until egg is set around edges and almost set in center.

4. Preheat broiler with rack 8 inches from heat. Sprinkle remaining 1 tablespoon Parmesan over egg mixture and broil for 1 to 2 minutes or until set and slightly browned. With metal spatula, release sides of frittata and slide onto platter. Cut into wedges to serve.

FRITTATA WITH POTATOES & MANCHEGO CHEESE
In step 1, omit green beans and cook ¾ pound all-purpose potatoes (peeled and cut into ¼-inch-thick rounds) in boiling salted water 5 to 7 minutes or until tender. Cook onion as directed; add potatoes and cook 2 minutes. Transfer to large bowl. In step 2, substitute ½ cup (2 ounces) shredded Manchego cheese for Parmesan. Complete steps 3 and 4 as directed, but substitute 2 tablespoons shredded Manchego for the Parmesan.
Calories 395, Total Fat 22g, Saturated Fat 8g, Cholesterol 382mg, Sodium 680mg, Protein 32g, Carbohydrates 15g

LEFTOVERS

Prep Time: 10 minutes
Cooking Time: 30 minutes
Makes 4 servings

NUTRITION INFORMATION
Per Serving
Calories 317
Total Fat 18g
Saturated Fat 5g
Cholesterol 369mg
Sodium 697mg
Protein 30g
Carbohydrates 8g

Chicken with Peanut & Pepper Sauce

There's a suggestion of Szechuan about this quick stir-fry, but the peppers are sweet ones, not chilies.

4 small skinless, boneless chicken breast halves
   (about 1¼ pounds), pounded to ¼-inch
   thickness (page 15)
2 tablespoons flour
2 tablespoons olive oil
1 yellow bell pepper, cut into ½-inch squares
2 scallions, thinly sliced
½ cup canned tomatoes, chopped with their juice
½ cup chicken broth
3 tablespoons peanut butter
1 tablespoon soy sauce
1 tablespoon fresh lime juice
¾ teaspoon ground ginger
½ teaspoon salt
½ teaspoon sugar
¼ cup chopped cilantro

1. Dredge chicken in flour, shaking off excess. In large non-stick skillet, heat oil over medium-high heat. Add chicken to pan and cook 1½ minutes per side or until golden brown and cooked through. With slotted spoon, transfer chicken to plate.

2. Add bell pepper and scallions to pan, and stir-fry 3 minutes or until crisp-tender. Add tomatoes, broth, peanut butter, soy sauce, lime juice, ginger, salt, and sugar, and bring to a boil. Reduce to a simmer and cook 5 minutes or until sauce is well flavored. Return chicken to pan and cook 1 minute or just until chicken is heated through. Transfer chicken to dinner plates. Stir cilantro into sauce and spoon over chicken.

QUICK TO FIX

Prep Time: 15 minutes
Cooking Time: 15 minutes
Makes 4 servings

NUTRITION INFORMATION
Per Serving
Calories 325
Total Fat 15g
Saturated Fat 2.5g
Cholesterol 82mg
Sodium 878mg
Protein 38g
Carbohydrates 10g

CHICKEN & GREEN BEAN FRITTATA

CHICKEN BREASTS WITH TOMATO-BASIL SAUCE

Braised Chicken with Artichokes

Prep Time: 15 minutes
Cooking Time: 40 minutes
Makes 4 servings

Frozen artichoke hearts are your secret weapon here: They're among the priciest of frozen vegetables, but worth it, because preparing fresh ones is so tricky. A compound in artichokes makes anything you eat with them taste sweeter, so just imagine how delicious the slow-simmered garlic will be.

2 tablespoons olive oil

12 cloves garlic, peeled

4 whole chicken legs (about 2½ pounds), split into drumsticks and thighs (page 14), skin removed

2 tablespoons flour

1 package (9 ounces) frozen artichoke hearts, thawed

½ cup chicken broth

2 tablespoons fresh lemon juice

½ teaspoon dried rosemary, crumbled

½ teaspoon salt

1. In large skillet, heat oil over low heat. Add garlic and cook, turning as it colors, 5 minutes or until golden brown.

2. Dredge chicken in flour, shaking off excess. Add to pan and sauté 5 minutes per side or until golden brown.

3. Add artichoke hearts and stir to combine. Add broth, lemon juice, rosemary, and salt, and bring to a boil. Reduce to a simmer, cover, and cook 25 minutes or until chicken is tender and cooked through.

Chicken Breasts with Tomato-Basil Sauce

Prep Time: 15 minutes
Cooking Time: 30 minutes
Makes 4 servings

To make the most of the fresh basil, some is simmered with the chicken, but a handful of the fragrant herb is added at the last minute. Serve the chicken with a summery vegetable accompaniment, such as steamed zucchini, yellow squash, or corn on the cob.

2 tablespoons olive oil

4 skinless, bone-in chicken breast halves (about 2 pounds)

2 tablespoons flour

1 small onion, diced

4 cloves garlic, minced

½ cup dry red wine or chicken broth

1½ cups canned tomatoes, chopped with their juice

½ cup chopped fresh basil

½ teaspoon salt

½ teaspoon crushed red pepper flakes

1. In large skillet, heat oil over medium heat. Dredge chicken in flour, shaking off excess. Add chicken to pan and sauté 5 minutes per side or until golden brown. With slotted spoon, transfer chicken to plate.

2. Add onion and garlic to pan, and cook, stirring frequently, 7 minutes or until onion is tender. Add wine, increase heat to high, and boil 2 minutes. Stir in tomatoes, ¼ cup of basil, the salt, and red pepper flakes. Bring to a boil and return chicken to pan. Reduce to a simmer, cover, and cook, turning chicken as it cooks, 10 minutes or until cooked through.

3. Transfer chicken to dinner plates. Add remaining ¼ cup basil to pan and cook 1 minute. Spoon sauce over chicken.

CHICKEN BREASTS WITH SPINACH & MOZZARELLA Sauté chicken as directed in step 1. In step 2, once onion and garlic are tender, stir in 1 package (10 ounces) frozen chopped spinach (thawed and squeezed dry). Omit wine, tomatoes, and red pepper flakes. Stir in ¼ cup chopped basil, ½ teaspoon salt, and ⅔ cup chicken broth, and bring to a boil. Return chicken to pan, cover, and cook 7 minutes or until almost cooked through. Top each piece of chicken with ¼ cup diced fresh tomatoes, 2 basil leaves, and ⅓ cup shredded mozzarella. Cover and cook 2 minutes or until cheese has melted. Omit step 3.
Calories 420, Total Fat 18g, Saturated Fat 6.5g, Cholesterol 131mg, Sodium 1067mg, Protein 51g, Carbohydrates 13g

Chicken, Corn & Broccoli Skillet

Imported Spanish Manchego, a dry, salty cheese from sheep's milk, adds a wonderfully snappy tang to this family-pleasing dinner. If you can't get Manchego, use freshly-grated Parmesan. Warmed flour tortillas or squares of corn bread go very well with this dish.

Prep Time: 20 minutes
Cooking Time: 15 minutes
Makes 4 servings

4 teaspoons cornstarch

2 tablespoons fresh lime juice

½ teaspoon salt

1 pound skinless, boneless chicken breasts (about 3), cut for stir-fry (page 15)

2 tablespoons olive oil

3 cups small broccoli florets

1 package (10 ounces) frozen corn kernels

4 scallions, thinly sliced

2 cloves garlic, minced

1½ cups mild to medium bottled salsa

⅓ cup chopped cilantro

½ cup grated Manchego cheese (2 ounces) or freshly grated Parmesan cheese

1. In large bowl, whisk together cornstarch, lime juice, and salt. Add chicken and toss to coat.

2. In large nonstick skillet, heat oil over medium heat. Add chicken and cook, stirring constantly, 4 minutes or until just cooked through. With slotted spoon, transfer chicken to plate.

3. Add broccoli, corn, scallions, and garlic to pan, and cook 3 minutes or until corn is heated through. Add salsa, cover, and cook 4 minutes or until broccoli is crisp-tender.

4. Return chicken to pan and cook 1 minute or just until heated through. Stir in cilantro. Spoon onto dinner plates and sprinkle with Manchego.

NUTRITION INFORMATION
Per Serving
Calories 386
Total Fat 14g
Saturated Fat 5g
Cholesterol 81mg
Sodium 1455mg
Protein 36g
Carbohydrates 30g

Spanish Rice with Chicken

Start with rice cooked Spanish style—flavored with garlic, tomatoes, and oregano—then add some leftover chicken, and you have a fast, filling dinner. If you prefer to use converted rice, be aware that it takes slightly longer—about 20 minutes total—to cook.

LOW FAT
LEFTOVERS

Prep Time: 10 minutes
Cooking Time: 25 minutes
Makes 4 servings

2 tablespoons olive oil

1 green bell pepper, cut into ½-inch chunks

3 scallions, thinly sliced

2 cloves garlic, minced

1¼ cups rice

1½ cups chicken broth, canned or homemade (page 45)

1 cup canned crushed tomatoes

½ teaspoon dried oregano

½ teaspoon salt

2 cups chunks (½-inch) cooked chicken breasts or thighs—leftover or poached (page 17)

2 tablespoons capers, chopped

1. In medium saucepan, heat oil over medium-low heat. Add bell pepper, scallions, and garlic, and cook, stirring frequently, 5 minutes or until pepper is tender.

2. Add rice and stir to coat. Add broth, tomatoes, oregano, salt, and 1 cup of water, and bring to a boil. Reduce to a simmer, stir in chicken and capers, cover, and simmer 17 minutes or until rice is tender.

CHICKEN PILAF WITH VIRGINIA HAM In step 1, add ¼ pound diced Virginia ham to vegetables. In step 2, substitute brown rice for white rice, and use 2 cups chicken broth and 1 cup of water. Add tomatoes, oregano, and salt as directed, but add ½ teaspoon dried thyme. Bring to a boil. Add chicken, but omit capers; reduce to a simmer, cover, and cook 45 minutes or until rice is tender. Stir in ½ cup slivered almonds.
Calories 580, Total Fat 23g, Saturated Fat 4g, Cholesterol 79mg, Sodium 1737mg, Protein 39g, Carbohydrates 54g

NUTRITION INFORMATION
Per Serving
Calories 421
Total Fat 10g
Saturated Fat 2g
Cholesterol 60mg
Sodium 1028mg
Protein 27g
Carbohydrates 52g

CHICKEN, CORN & BROCCOLI SKILLET

CHICKEN WITH ONIONS & APPLE CIDER VINEGAR

LOW FAT

Prep Time: 15 minutes plus
   marinating time
Cooking Time: 35 minutes
Makes 4 servings

NUTRITION INFORMATION

Per Serving
Calories 250
Total Fat 8.5g
Saturated Fat 1.5g
Cholesterol 94mg
Sodium 1032mg
Protein 27g
Carbohydrates 17g

Chinese 5-Spice Drumsticks

The Chinese seasoning called 5-spice powder is a blend of ground anise or fennel seed, star anise, cloves, cinnamon, and Szechuan peppercorns. Most supermarkets sell 5-spice powder, and it's also available at Asian markets and gourmet shops.

- 2 tablespoons Chinese 5-spice powder
- 2 tablespoons lower-sodium soy sauce
- 2 tablespoons packed light brown sugar
- ¾ teaspoon salt
- 8 chicken drumsticks (about 2 pounds), skin removed
- 1 tablespoon vegetable oil
- 6 scallions, thinly sliced
- 3 cloves garlic, minced
- ½ cup canned sliced water chestnuts, halved
- ⅔ cup chicken broth
- 1½ teaspoons cornstarch blended with 1 tablespoon water

1. In large bowl, stir together 5-spice powder, soy sauce, brown sugar, and ½ teaspoon of salt. Add chicken and toss to coat. Cover and refrigerate 1 hour or up to overnight.

2. In large skillet, heat oil over medium heat. Lift chicken from its marinade, reserving any marinade. Add chicken to pan and cook, turning, 7 minutes or until firm.

3. Add scallions and garlic to pan, and cook 1 minute. Add water chestnuts, broth, remaining ¼ teaspoon salt, and any marinade remaining in bowl. Bring to a boil, reduce to a simmer, cover, and cook 20 to 25 minutes or until chicken is cooked through.

4. With slotted spoon, transfer chicken to dinner plates. Bring cooking juices in skillet to a boil over high heat. Stir in cornstarch mixture and cook, stirring constantly, 1 minute or until slightly thickened. Spoon sauce over chicken.

QUICK TO FIX

Prep Time: 10 minutes
Cooking Time: 20 minutes
Makes 4 servings

NUTRITION INFORMATION

Per Serving
Calories 345
Total Fat 12g
Saturated Fat 3.5g
Cholesterol 107mg
Sodium 379mg
Protein 40g
Carbohydrates 17g

Chicken with Onions & Apple Cider Vinegar

You could call this a "triple-apple" chicken sauté, because the recipe includes cubes of apple, apple cider vinegar, and apple jelly. Accompany the chicken with rice, pasta, or mashed potatoes.

- 2 tablespoons olive oil
- 4 skinless, boneless chicken breast halves (about 1½ pounds)
- 2 tablespoons flour
- 4 scallions, cut into 1-inch lengths
- 1 large apple, peeled and cut into ½-inch cubes
- ⅓ cup apple cider vinegar
- 2 tablespoons apple jelly
- 1 tablespoon Dijon mustard
- ¼ teaspoon salt
- 1 tablespoon butter

1. In large skillet, heat oil over medium heat. Dredge chicken in flour, shaking off excess. Add chicken to pan and sauté, turning chicken as it cooks, 15 minutes or until golden brown and cooked through. With slotted spoon, transfer chicken to plate.

2. Add scallions and apple to pan, and cook, stirring frequently, 3 minutes or until apple is crisp-tender. Add vinegar, jelly, mustard, and salt, and cook 2 minutes. Remove from heat and swirl in butter. Spoon sauce over chicken.

TO REDUCE THE FAT

Decrease oil to 1 tablespoon and use a nonstick skillet. Increase jelly to 3 tablespoons and omit butter.

Calories 302, Total Fat 5.5g, Saturated Fat 1g, Cholesterol 99mg, Sodium 351mg, Protein 40g, Carbohydrates 21g

Tequila Chicken over Pepper Linguine

Wine is often used as a cooking ingredient, but spirits have their place in the kitchen, too. Penne alla Vodka is a modern classic, and this sophisticated sauté gets a subtly smoky flavor from a "shot" of tequila. If you prefer not to cook with spirits, substitute chicken broth for the tequila in step 2.

- 2 tablespoons cornstarch
- 1 teaspoon salt
- ½ cup chicken broth
- 1 pound skinless, boneless chicken breasts, cut for stir-fry (page 15)
- 3 tablespoons olive oil
- ¼ cup tequila
- 1 red onion, finely chopped
- 2 red bell peppers, cut into ¼-inch dice
- 1 package (10 ounces) frozen corn kernels, thawed
- 2 plum tomatoes, cut into ¼-inch dice
- ½ cup orange juice
- ⅓ cup chopped cilantro
- 10 ounces pepper-flavored linguine or regular linguine

1. In large bowl, stir together cornstarch, ½ teaspoon of salt, and ¼ cup of broth. Add chicken and toss to coat. Cover and refrigerate 1 hour or up to overnight.

2. In large skillet, heat 1 tablespoon of oil over medium heat. Lift chicken from cornstarch mixture, reserving cornstarch mixture. Add chicken to pan and stir-fry 4 minutes or until chicken is golden brown and cooked through. Add tequila to pan and cook 2 minutes to evaporate alcohol. Add remaining ¼ cup broth and bring to a boil. Stir in reserved cornstarch mixture and cook, stirring constantly, 1 minute or until slightly thickened.

3. Meanwhile, in large bowl, stir together onion, bell peppers, corn, tomatoes, orange juice, cilantro, and remaining 2 tablespoons oil and ½ teaspoon salt.

4. In large pot of boiling water, cook linguine according to package directions. Drain and add to bowl with vegetable mixture. Add chicken mixture and toss well.

IN A HURRY?

In step 1, toss chicken with cornstarch mixture but do not marinate 1 hour; go straight to step 2. Omit all sauce ingredients in step 3 except corn. Use 4 cups bottled salsa instead and stir corn into it. Cook pasta and add chicken mixture as directed.

LOW FAT

Prep Time: 10 minutes plus marinating time
Cooking Time: 20 minutes
Makes 4 servings

NUTRITION INFORMATION
Per Serving

Calories 641
Total Fat 14g
Saturated Fat 2g
Cholesterol 66mg
Sodium 803mg
Protein 39g
Carbohydrates 82g

HINTS & TIPS

➤ A visit to a pasta shop—or a well-stocked supermarket—will reveal an array of flavored and colored pastas. Some are tinted with vegetables (tomato, spinach, or beet, for instance), while others are flavored with herbs and spices, such as saffron, basil, or pepper.

➤ Tequila is a fiery Mexican liquor made from the sap of the agave, which you may know as the century plant.

➤ If you have a large bag of frozen corn (rather than a 10-ounce box), measure out 1¼ cups for this recipe.

TEQUILA CHICKEN OVER PEPPER LINGUINE

INDIAN-SPICED CHICKEN & CARROTS

Prep Time: 20 minutes
Cooking Time: 15 minutes
Makes 4 servings

NUTRITION INFORMATION
Per Serving
Calories 323
Total Fat 9g
Saturated Fat 1.5g
Cholesterol 66mg
Sodium 734mg
Protein 30g
Carbohydrates 31g

Indian-Spiced Chicken & Carrots

There's not a grain of curry powder in this dish, but you'll recognize the authentic flavors of cumin, coriander seed, cardamom, and cloves. Indian cooks tend to prepare their own spice mixtures for different dishes, rather than use a packaged blend.

- 2 tablespoons cornstarch
- 1½ teaspoons ground coriander
- ½ teaspoon ground cumin
- ¾ teaspoon salt
- ½ teaspoon freshly ground black pepper
- ¼ teaspoon ground cardamom
- ⅛ teaspoon ground cloves
- ¾ cup chicken broth
- 1 pound skinless, boneless chicken breasts, cut for stir-fry (page 15)
- 2 tablespoons vegetable oil
- 3 carrots, cut into matchsticks
- 1 large onion, halved and thinly sliced
- 1 pound all-purpose potatoes, peeled and cut into ¼-inch chunks
- 3 cloves garlic, slivered
- 1 tablespoon chopped parsley

1. In large bowl, stir together cornstarch, 1 teaspoon of coriander, the cumin, ½ teaspoon of salt, the pepper, cardamom, and cloves. Whisk in ¼ cup of broth until smooth. Add chicken and toss to coat.

2. In large nonstick skillet, heat 1 tablespoon of oil over medium-high heat. Lift chicken from its marinade, reserving marinade. Add chicken to pan and sauté, stirring constantly, 4 minutes or until golden brown and cooked through. With slotted spoon, transfer chicken to plate.

3. Add remaining 1 tablespoon oil to pan along with carrots, onion, potatoes, garlic, remaining ½ teaspoon coriander, and ¼ teaspoon salt, and cook, stirring frequently, 5 minutes or until carrots are crisp-tender. Stir in reserved marinade and remaining ½ cup broth, and bring to a boil. Boil 2 minutes or until potatoes are tender. Return chicken to pan and cook 1 minute or until heated through. Serve chicken and vegetables topped with parsley.

Prep Time: 10 minutes
Cooking Time: 20 minutes
Makes 4 servings

NUTRITION INFORMATION
Per Serving
Calories 674
Total Fat 39g
Saturated Fat 15g
Cholesterol 186mg
Sodium 1433mg
Protein 44g
Carbohydrates 32g

Chicken Cheddarburgers with Bacon

The cheese is on the inside of these burgers: Shreds of Cheddar are mixed into the ground chicken along with crisp bits of bacon and a dollop of mustard for finer flavor. Burgers this good deserve something better than everyday white buns, so they're served on sourdough rolls.

- 4 slices bacon
- 1½ pounds ground chicken
- 2 tablespoons Dijon mustard
- ¾ teaspoon salt
- ½ teaspoon freshly ground black pepper
- ¼ pound medium to sharp Cheddar cheese, shredded (1 cup)
- 4 sourdough sandwich rolls, split
- 4 thin slices red onion
- 4 slices tomato

1. In large skillet, cook bacon over medium-low heat 7 minutes or until crisp. Drain on paper towels and then crumble. Reserve bacon fat in skillet.

2. In medium bowl, combine chicken, mustard, salt, pepper, Cheddar, and crumbled bacon. Mix well; shape into 4 patties.

3. Heat bacon fat in skillet over medium heat. Add patties and cook 6 minutes per side or until browned and cooked through. Place burgers on rolls; top with onion and tomato.

TEX-MEX BURGERS WITH PEPPERJACK CHEESE
Omit bacon. In step 2, substitute pepperjack cheese for Cheddar; add 2 minced pickled jalapeño peppers. In step 3, substitute 2 tablespoons olive oil for bacon fat. Omit red onion and tomato; top each burger with 2 tablespoons mild salsa and slice of avocado.
Calories 595, Total Fat 32g, Saturated Fat 10g, Cholesterol 171mg, Sodium 1289mg, Protein 42g, Carbohydrates 31g

CHICKEN THIGHS WITH SHERRY & APRICOTS

Prep Time: 10 minutes
Cooking Time: 50 minutes
Makes 4 servings

NUTRITION INFORMATION

Per Serving

Calories 401

Total Fat 11g

Saturated Fat 5g

Cholesterol 123mg

Sodium 607mg

Protein 28g

Carbohydrates 48g

HINTS & TIPS

➤ Sherry is a fortified wine made from white grapes. Although it originated in Spain, sherry is now produced elsewhere as well (California, for instance). Choose a dry sherry—one labeled *fino* or *manzanilla*—for this dish. When served as a drink, these dry sherries should be chilled.

➤ Apricots are usually treated with a sulfur compound to preserve their light color, but the darker, unsulfured ones have better flavor. Look for them at health food stores.

Chicken Thighs with Sherry & Apricots

Though festive enough for a dinner party, this entrée can be on the table in just about one hour. For further time-saving, you can poach the apricots (step 1) in advance; refrigerate the apricot mixture in a nonmetal container.

- 1 cup dried apricots
- ½ cup dry sherry
- ½ cup dry red wine
- 4 tablespoons sugar
- 3 strips (2 x ½-inch each) orange zest
- 2 tablespoons butter
- 8 bone-in chicken thighs (about 2 pounds), skin removed
- 2 tablespoons flour
- 2 cups frozen pearl onions, thawed and patted dry
- ½ cup chicken broth
- ½ teaspoon salt
- ½ teaspoon freshly ground black pepper
- 2 tablespoons snipped chives

1. In medium saucepan, combine apricots, sherry, red wine, 3 tablespoons of sugar, and orange zest, and bring to a boil over medium heat. Reduce to a simmer, cover, and cook 20 minutes or until apricots are tender. Remove from heat.

2. In large nonstick skillet, heat butter over medium heat. Dredge chicken in flour, shaking off excess. Add chicken to pan and sauté 4 minutes per side or until golden brown. With slotted spoon, transfer chicken to plate.

3. Add pearl onions to pan, sprinkle with remaining 1 tablespoon sugar, and cook 7 minutes or until lightly golden. Add broth, salt, pepper, and apricot mixture, and bring to a boil.

4. Return chicken to pan, reduce to a simmer, cover, and cook 15 minutes or until chicken is tender. Stir in chives.

CHICKEN THIGHS WITH PRUNES In step 1, substitute 1 cup pitted prunes (about 24) for apricots; omit sherry and increase red wine to 1 cup; use only 1 tablespoon of sugar. Cook for only 15 minutes. Proceed with recipe as above, adding prune mixture to chicken in step 3.

Calories 371, Total Fat 11g, Saturated Fat 5g, Cholesterol 123mg, Sodium 604mg, Protein 28g, Carbohydrates 41g

Chicken Fried Rice

Don't wait for your next trip to a Chinese restaurant—cook up a batch of fried rice at home and enjoy it fresh and sizzling hot. Serve the rice in deep bowls, Asian style, to hold the heat. This recipe lends itself to some simple variations: Replace the asparagus with snow peas, use brown rice instead of white, or add some shrimp. Or, try the jazzy Creole variation below.

2 large eggs

½ small red bell pepper, cut into fine dice

3 tablespoons lower-sodium soy sauce

1½ teaspoons sugar

3 teaspoons plus 2 tablespoons vegetable oil

2 tablespoons minced fresh ginger

2 cloves garlic, minced

1 pound asparagus, cut on the diagonal into ¼-inch-thick slices

6 scallions, cut into 1-inch lengths

3 cups shredded cooked chicken breasts or thighs—leftover or poached (page 17)

3 cups cooked rice

3 tablespoons rice vinegar

1½ cups frozen peas, thawed

1. In small bowl, whisk together eggs, bell pepper, 1 tablespoon of soy sauce, and ½ teaspoon of sugar. In small skillet, heat 2 teaspoons of oil over medium-high heat. Add egg mixture and cook, without stirring, 2 minutes or until set. Transfer egg pancake to work surface and cut into ½-inch-wide strips.

2. In large skillet, heat remaining 1 teaspoon plus 2 tablespoons oil over medium-high heat. Add ginger and garlic, and cook 30 seconds. Stir in asparagus and scallions, and cook 3 minutes or until asparagus are crisp-tender.

3. Add chicken and rice, stirring to coat. In small bowl, stir together vinegar, and remaining 2 tablespoons soy sauce and 1 teaspoon sugar. Pour over rice mixture. Cook, stirring constantly, 7 minutes or until rice is piping hot and slightly crusty. Stir in peas and egg strips, and cook 1 minute or until peas are heated through.

CREOLE FRIED RICE Omit step 1 and egg pancake ingredients (eggs, bell pepper, soy sauce, and sugar). In step 2, heat 2 tablespoons of oil. Add ¼ pound diced fully-cooked chorizo and cook over medium heat 5 minutes or until lightly crisped. Increase garlic to 3 cloves; add as directed. Omit ginger. Substitute 1 large green bell pepper, cut into ½-inch chunks, for asparagus and add along with scallions. Cook, stirring frequently, 5 minutes or until bell pepper is crisp-tender. In step 3, add chicken and rice as directed; omit vinegar, soy sauce, sugar, and peas; but stir in ¼ teaspoon salt, 2 teaspoons turmeric, and 2 teaspoons hot pepper sauce. Cook, stirring frequently, 7 minutes or until rice is piping hot and slightly crusty. Stir in ¼ cup chopped parsley.
Calories 540, Total Fat 22g, Saturated Fat 6g, Cholesterol 114mg, Sodium 644mg, Protein 44g, Carbohydrates 39g

LEFTOVERS

Prep Time: 25 minutes
Cooking Time: 15 minutes
Makes 4 servings

NUTRITION INFORMATION
Per Serving
Calories 574
Total Fat 21g
Saturated Fat 4.5g
Cholesterol 200mg
Sodium 640mg
Protein 44g
Carbohydrates 51g

HINTS & TIPS

This recipe is a great way to use up leftover rice, but if you don't have any, just cook 1 cup of rice according to package directions (this will yield about 3 cups). Spread the cooked rice on a large platter or jelly-roll pan to cool (you can even put it in the freezer for a few minutes). After cooling the rice, fluff it with a fork and it's ready to hit the skillet.

CHICKEN FRIED RICE

CHICKEN WITH ALMONDS & RED PEPPERS

Prep Time: 20 minutes
Cooking Time: 15 minutes
Makes 4 servings

NUTRITION INFORMATION
Per Serving
Calories 525
Total Fat 31g
Saturated Fat 4g
Cholesterol 141mg
Sodium 874mg
Protein 41g
Carbohydrates 22g

Chicken with Almonds & Red Peppers

Sweet, crunchy, glazed whole almonds are the surprising and delicious garnish for this stir-fry. The almonds are pretty irresistible: It's a good idea to move them out of reach while you cook the chicken, or you may find that you have no garnish left when the stir-fry is ready to serve.

- 3 tablespoons plus ½ teaspoon sugar
- ½ teaspoon salt
- 1 cup blanched whole almonds
- 1½ teaspoons cornstarch
- ½ cup chicken broth
- 2 tablespoons lower-sodium soy sauce
- 1 tablespoon dry sherry
- 2 tablespoons vegetable oil
- 2 tablespoons minced fresh ginger
- 2 cloves garlic, minced
- 1½ pounds skinless, boneless chicken thighs, cut into 1-inch chunks
- 2 red bell peppers, cut into 1-inch chunks
- 2 scallions, thinly sliced

1. In large skillet, heat 3 tablespoons of sugar, ¼ teaspoon of salt, and the almonds over medium heat. Stir-fry 3 minutes or until almonds are crisp and glazed. Transfer almonds to plate.

2. In small bowl, whisk together cornstarch, broth, soy sauce, sherry, remaining ½ teaspoon sugar, and ¼ teaspoon salt; set aside. In large skillet, heat oil over medium-high heat. Add ginger and garlic, and cook 30 seconds. Add chicken and stir-fry 5 minutes or until cooked through. Add bell peppers and stir-fry 3 minutes or until crisp-tender.

3. Whisk broth mixture and pour into pan. Bring to a boil and boil 1 minute or until sauce is of coating consistency. To serve, sprinkle with glazed almonds and scallions.

LOW FAT

Prep Time: 15 minutes
Cooking Time: 35 minutes
Makes 4 servings

NUTRITION INFORMATION
Per Serving
Calories 630
Total Fat 20g
Saturated Fat 6g
Cholesterol 157mg
Sodium 1174mg
Protein 47g
Carbohydrates 63g

Spaghetti with Chicken Bolognese Sauce

This hearty Italian pasta sauce—sometimes known simply as "ragú"—is usually made with ground beef and heavy cream and simmered for hours. This interpretation is lighter in calories and easier on your schedule, too. Try it with tagliatelle, rigatoni, or fusilli as a change from spaghetti.

- 1 tablespoon olive oil
- 2 slices bacon, finely chopped
- 1 small onion, finely chopped
- 1 carrot, finely chopped
- 1½ pounds skinless, boneless chicken thighs, cut into chunks
- ⅓ cup dry red wine
- ½ cup chicken broth
- 3 tablespoons tomato paste
- ¾ teaspoon salt
- ½ teaspoon freshly ground black pepper
- 1 cup milk
- 10 ounces spaghetti
  Grated Parmesan cheese (optional)

1. In large skillet, heat oil over medium-low heat. Add bacon, stirring to coat. Add onion and carrot, and cook, stirring frequently, 7 minutes or until vegetables are very tender.

2. In food processor, finely chop chicken. Add chicken to skillet and cook 5 minutes or until no longer pink. Stir in wine and cook 2 minutes to evaporate the alcohol. Stir in broth, tomato paste, salt, and pepper. Cover and simmer 10 minutes or until sauce starts to thicken. Add milk, cover, and simmer 10 minutes longer or until sauce is thick and all milk has been absorbed.

3. Meanwhile, in large pot of boiling water, cook spaghetti according to package directions. Drain and return to cooking pot. Add sauce and toss well. Serve with Parmesan cheese, if you like.

Chicken with Creamy Mushroom Sauce

Sautés are often finished by deglazing the pan—adding wine or stock and stirring up the caramelized meat juices in the skillet to make a sauce. Here, after the chicken and mushrooms are cooked, the pan is deglazed with bourbon (or brandy); add a good splash of cream and the result is a heady, fragrant sauce.

- 2 tablespoons olive oil
- 1 tablespoon butter
- 4 small skinless, boneless chicken breast halves (about 1¼ pounds), pounded to ¼-inch thickness (page 15)
- 2 tablespoons flour
- 1 small onion, finely chopped
- 1 clove garlic, minced
- ½ pound fresh shiitake mushrooms, stems trimmed and caps quartered
- ½ pound button mushrooms, trimmed and quartered
- ¼ cup bourbon or brandy
- ½ cup chicken broth
- ⅓ cup heavy or whipping cream
- ½ teaspoon salt
- ½ teaspoon freshly ground black pepper

1. In large nonstick skillet, heat oil and butter over medium heat. Dredge chicken in flour, shaking off excess. Add chicken to pan and sauté 1½ minutes per side or until golden brown and cooked through. With slotted spoon, transfer chicken to plate.

2. Add onion and garlic to pan and cook, stirring frequently, 5 minutes or until onion is golden brown. Add shiitake and button mushrooms, and cook, stirring frequently, 7 minutes or until mushrooms are tender.

3. Add bourbon to pan and cook 2 minutes to evaporate alcohol. Add broth, bring to a boil, and boil 2 minutes. Add cream, salt, and pepper, and return to a boil. Return chicken to pan and cook 1 minute or just until heated through. Serve topped with mushrooms and sauce.

TO REDUCE THE FAT

Omit step 1 and do not pound chicken or dredge it in flour. In step 2, use nonstick skillet and cook onion and garlic in 2 teaspoons oil. Add chicken, 1½ cups chicken broth, ½ teaspoon salt, and ½ teaspoon black pepper along with mushrooms. Bring to a boil, reduce to a simmer, cover, and cook 15 minutes or until chicken is cooked through and mushrooms are tender. Transfer chicken to dinner plates. In step 3, omit bourbon, broth, and cream (also, do not add salt and pepper here, as they were added along with chicken earlier). Blend 1½ teaspoons cornstarch with 1 tablespoon water. Add cornstarch mixture to pan and cook, stirring, for 1 minute or until sauce is slightly thickened. Spoon over chicken.

Calories 228, Total Fat 5g, Saturated Fat 1g, Cholesterol 82mg, Sodium 779mg, Protein 36g, Carbohydrates 9g

Prep Time: 20 minutes
Cooking Time: 20 minutes
Makes 4 servings

NUTRITION INFORMATION
Per Serving
Calories 399
Total Fat 19g
Saturated Fat 8g
Cholesterol 117mg
Sodium 553mg
Protein 36g
Carbohydrates 11g

HINTS & TIPS

➤ A cook's pantry should include two types of olive oil: an "extra-virgin" and a "pure" olive oil. Extra-virgin olive oil, which is from the first pressing of the olives, has a much deeper, olive-y taste than pure olive oils. Save the more expensive extra-virgin oil for dishes where its flavor can shine through, such as salad dressings. Use a pure olive oil when other flavors (such as the mushrooms, here) need to be prominent.

➤ Another option to the bourbon or brandy called for in this dish is an aged rum, which has a very faint sweetness, like bourbon.

CHICKEN WITH CREAMY MUSHROOM SAUCE

Turmeric-Yogurt Chicken with Tomatoes

The spicy sauce, bright with fresh ginger, scallions, and curry powder, is tamed with a big dollop of yogurt. Don't add the yogurt until the pan is off the heat, or the sauce may curdle.

- 2 tablespoons cornstarch
- 2 teaspoons turmeric
- 1½ teaspoons Madras or other hot curry powder
- ¾ teaspoon salt
- ¾ cup chicken broth
- 1¼ pounds skinless, boneless chicken thighs, cut into 1-inch chunks
- 2 tablespoons vegetable oil
- 3 scallions, thinly sliced
- 2 cloves garlic, minced
- 2 tablespoons minced fresh ginger
- 2 cups canned tomatoes, chopped with their juice
- ¼ cup mango chutney, finely chopped
- ½ cup chopped cilantro
- ¼ cup plain low-fat yogurt

1. In large bowl, stir together cornstarch, turmeric, curry powder, and ¼ teaspoon of salt. Add ¼ cup of broth and stir until smooth. Add chicken and stir to coat. Cover and refrigerate at least 1 hour or up to overnight.

2. In large nonstick skillet, heat oil over medium-high heat. Lift chicken from its marinade, add to pan, and sauté 5 minutes or until golden brown and cooked through. With slotted spoon, transfer chicken to plate.

3. Add scallions, garlic, and ginger to pan. Reduce heat to low and cook 1 minute. Add tomatoes, chutney, remaining ½ cup broth, and ½ teaspoon salt, and bring to a boil. Reduce to a simmer and cook, uncovered, for 4 minutes or until sauce is slightly thickened. Return chicken to pan and simmer 2 minutes or until chicken is heated through. Remove from heat and stir in cilantro and yogurt.

Prep Time: 20 minutes plus marinating time
Cooking Time: 15 minutes
Makes 4 servings

NUTRITION INFORMATION
Per Serving
Calories 357
Total Fat 13g
Saturated Fat 2.5g
Cholesterol 119mg
Sodium 1135mg
Protein 30g
Carbohydrates 27g

Orange-Mustard Chicken with Almond Coating

If you like honey mustard, you'll enjoy the marmalade-mustard marinade used here.

- 4 tablespoons orange juice
- 4 tablespoons orange marmalade
- 6 teaspoons Dijon mustard
- 4 small skinless, boneless chicken breast halves (about 1¼ pounds), pounded to ¼-inch thickness (page 15)
- 2 slices firm-textured white bread (2 ounces)
- ¾ cup natural (unblanched) almonds
- ¼ cup packed parsley leaves
- ½ teaspoon salt
- 4 tablespoons olive oil

1. In shallow glass or ceramic baking dish, stir together 2 tablespoons of orange juice, 2 tablespoons of marmalade, and 4 teaspoons of mustard. Place chicken in orange mixture and spoon over to coat. Let sit while you prepare coating.

2. In food processor, combine bread, almonds, parsley, and salt. Process to fine crumb consistency. Transfer to shallow plate or sheet of waxed paper. Lift chicken from orange mixture (discard any mixture remaining in dish). Dip chicken in almond-crumb mixture, pressing it into chicken. Transfer to baking sheet or platter large enough to hold cutlets in single layer and refrigerate, uncovered, at least 1 hour or up to 8 hours.

3. In small bowl, stir together remaining 2 tablespoons orange juice, 2 tablespoons marmalade, and 2 teaspoons mustard. In large nonstick skillet, heat 2 tablespoons of oil over medium heat. Add 2 cutlets to pan and cook 1½ minutes per side or until golden brown and cooked through. Repeat with remaining cutlets and oil. Slices the cutlets crosswise on the diagonal to serve.

Prep Time: 20 minutes plus chilling time
Cooking Time: 10 minutes
Makes 4 servings

NUTRITION INFORMATION
Per Serving
Calories 523
Total Fat 29g
Saturated Fat 3.5g
Cholesterol 82mg
Sodium 655mg
Protein 39g
Carbohydrates 27g

ORANGE-MUSTARD CHICKEN WITH ALMOND COATING

STEAMED GINGER CHICKEN

Prep Time: 15 minutes
Cooking Time: 20 minutes
Makes 4 servings

NUTRITION INFORMATION

Per Serving

Calories 258

Total Fat 12g

Saturated Fat 2.5g

Cholesterol 498mg

Sodium 775mg

Protein 25g

Carbohydrates 14g

Sautéed Chicken Livers with Balsamic Vinegar

Among the mildest of vinegars—and certainly the richest in flavor—balsamic originated in Italy. It is made from white grape juice aged for years in a succession of barrels made of different woods. The vinegar emerges sweet and mellow, and is almost a sauce in itself.

- 2 tablespoons olive oil
- ⅓ cup minced onion
- 2 pounds spinach, tough stems removed (16 cups)
- 2 teaspoons sugar
- ¾ teaspoon salt
- 1 pound chicken livers, trimmed
- 3 tablespoons balsamic vinegar
- ⅓ cup chicken broth
- 1 tablespoon tomato paste
- ¼ teaspoon dried sage
- ¼ teaspoon freshly ground black pepper

1. In large skillet, heat 1 tablespoon of oil over medium heat. Add onion and cook, stirring frequently, 5 minutes or until onion is tender. Add half of spinach, ½ teaspoon of sugar, and ¼ teaspoon of salt. Cook, stirring frequently, 5 minutes or until spinach is tender. Transfer spinach to 2 serving plates. Repeat with remaining spinach, another ½ teaspoon sugar, and ¼ teaspoon salt. Drain any liquid remaining in pan.

2. Add remaining 1 tablespoon oil to pan and heat over medium-high heat. Add livers and remaining ¼ teaspoon salt, and cook, stirring frequently, 5 minutes or until livers are almost cooked through. Add vinegar and remaining 1 teaspoon sugar, and cook 30 seconds. Add broth, tomato paste, sage, and pepper, and cook 1 minute or until livers are cooked through. Spoon livers and sauce over spinach.

LOW FAT

QUICK TO FIX

Prep Time: 10 minutes
Cooking Time: 15 minutes
Makes 4 servings

NUTRITION INFORMATION

Per Serving

Calories 231

Total Fat 5.5g

Saturated Fat 1g

Cholesterol 99mg

Sodium 413mg

Protein 40g

Carbohydrates 3g

Steamed Ginger Chicken

In order to steam the chicken in a skillet, you'll need a rack (a small cake cooling rack is perfect) and a high, domed lid for the pan. If the lid isn't deep enough, you can invert a large, heatproof bowl over the skillet. Remove it very carefully, using two potholders; watch out for the rising steam.

- 2 tablespoons lower-sodium soy sauce
- ½ teaspoon grated lemon zest
- 2 teaspoons fresh lemon juice
- ½ teaspoon sugar
- 4 skinless, boneless chicken breast halves (about 1½ pounds)
- ¼ cup minced fresh ginger
- 1 tablespoon sesame oil
- 2 scallions, thinly sliced

1. In small bowl, stir together soy sauce, lemon zest, lemon juice, and sugar. Place chicken on heatproof plate that is large enough to hold chicken in single layer, yet small enough to fit in skillet. Spoon soy mixture and ginger over chicken.

2. Place rack in large skillet and pour water to come just below rack. Place plate on rack and bring water to a simmer. Cover and cook, turning chicken over midway, 15 minutes or until chicken is just cooked through.

3. Place chicken on dinner plates. Pour juices and ginger from plate into small bowl. Stir in sesame oil and scallions and spoon over chicken.

STEAMED CHICKEN PRIMAVERA Follow step 1 as directed, but omit soy sauce and ginger. In step 2, cook chicken only 10 minutes, then uncover and add ½ pound trimmed sugar snap peas and ½ pound asparagus, cut into 2-inch lengths. Cover and cook 5 minutes or until chicken is cooked through and vegetables are crisp-tender. In step 3, substitute olive oil for sesame oil.

Calories 258, Total Fat 5.5g, Saturated Fat 1g, Cholesterol 99mg, Sodium 113mg, Protein 43g, Carbohydrates 7g

From Oven to Table: Roast, Bake & Broil

There's no mistaking the tantalizing aroma that fills the house when there's chicken in the oven—whether you're roasting a whole bird with sausage stuffing, baking mustard-crusted drumsticks, or broiling chicken Spanish style, with tomatoes and olives.

Perfect Roasted Chicken with Fresh Herbs & Lemon

Prep Time: 10 minutes
Cooking Time: 50 minutes
Makes 4 servings

A plump, beautifully browned roasted chicken, fragrant with rosemary, thyme, and lemon, is an entrée that's always welcome. The secret to success is an herb-shallot butter rubbed under the skin to keep the bird moist. Be careful not to tear the skin as you rub on the butter mixture (which should be at room temperature). Use your fingers to carefully separate the skin from the flesh.

NUTRITION INFORMATION
Per Serving
Calories 525
Total Fat 35g
Saturated Fat 14g
Cholesterol 185mg
Sodium 1133mg
Protein 48g
Carbohydrates 1g

4	tablespoons butter, at room temperature
1	tablespoon minced fresh rosemary
1	tablespoon minced fresh thyme
1	shallot, minced
1½	teaspoons salt
½	teaspoon freshly ground black pepper
1	whole chicken (about 3½ pounds), giblets removed and reserved for another use
1	large lemon
2	cloves garlic, unpeeled

1. Preheat oven to 400°F. In small bowl, mash together butter, rosemary, thyme, shallot, ½ teaspoon of salt, and the pepper. With your fingers, rub herb butter under skin around legs and breast of chicken.

2. With fork, prick lemon in several places. Rub cavity of chicken with ½ teaspoon of salt and place lemon and garlic in cavity. With kitchen string, tie chicken legs together. Lift wings up toward neck, then fold wing tips under back of chicken so wings stay in place. Sprinkle remaining ½ teaspoon of salt over chicken.

3. Place chicken, breast-side up, on rack in 9 x 13-inch baking pan. Roast for 50 minutes, basting frequently with pan drippings, until chicken is cooked through and richly browned.

4. Transfer chicken to platter or carving board. Pour pan drippings from baking pan into a gravy separator. Pour 1 cup of water or chicken broth into baking pan and stir with whisk to scrape up any browned bits (caramelized meat juices) from bottom and sides of pan (see technique photo, top right). Pour deglazed juices into gravy separator (bottom photo). Pour off fat and serve chicken with degreased pan gravy.

ORANGE-CHILI ROAST CHICKEN In step 1, add 1 tablespoon chili powder and 2 teaspoons grated orange zest to butter mixture. In step 2, substitute 1 navel orange, quartered, for the lemon. Complete steps 2, 3, and 4 as directed.
Calories 533, Total Fat 36g, Saturated Fat 14g, Cholesterol 185mg, Sodium 1152mg, Protein 48g, Carbohydrates 3g

TECHNIQUE

MAKING PAN GRAVY

After pouring the pan drippings into a gravy separator, add liquid (water, broth, or wine) to the roasting pan and, with a whisk, scrape up the caramelized meat juices to deglaze.

Add the deglazed juices to the gravy separator. Let the juices settle until the fat rises to the top, then pour off the juices, leaving the fat in the gravy separator. This pan gravy can be served as is, or reduced slightly to concentrate the flavors.

HINTS & TIPS

➤ Shallots are often used to impart a mild onion flavor in situations where the pungency of a real onion would be too harsh, as in the case of the herb butter used here. However, if you'd prefer, you can substitute chopped scallion instead. Use only the white and tender green parts of the scallion.

➤ Experiment with the fresh herbs used in the herb butter to see if you can come up with some variations that you like. Try a combination of fresh sage and parsley; or crushed cumin and minced cilantro; or oregano and hot paprika.

PERFECT ROASTED CHICKEN WITH FRESH HERBS & LEMON

ROASTED CHICKEN WITH FENNEL BUTTER

Prep Time: 25 minutes
Cooking Time: 55 minutes
Makes 4 servings

NUTRITION INFORMATION
Per Serving

Calories 752

Total Fat 48g

Saturated Fat 21g

Cholesterol 216mg

Sodium 1465mg

Protein 52g

Carbohydrates 30g

HINTS & TIPS

➤ Try this recipe using dill seeds instead of fennel seeds, and add some finely chopped fresh dill as well, if it's available.

➤ Most whole seeds, as well as nuts, benefit from a brief toasting. They can begin to scorch very suddenly, so keep an eye on them and remove them from the heat as soon as they're fragrant.

➤ You don't have to serve the garlic cloves with the chicken; they'll have done a nice job of flavoring even if you don't actually eat them.

Roasted Chicken with Fennel Butter

As a delicious change from the usual roasted potatoes, it's carrots, onions, and garlic that are roasted along with the bird. The chicken and vegetables are lavished with butter that's been infused with toasted fennel seeds. The buttery pan juices are too good to miss, so spoon them over the chicken and vegetables, and provide plenty of bread for mopping up the plates.

1	tablespoon fennel seeds
1	stick (4 ounces) butter, at room temperature
1	teaspoon grated lemon zest
10	carrots, quartered crosswise
8	small onions (about 1 pound), peeled
8	cloves garlic, unpeeled
1¾	teaspoons salt
1	whole chicken (about 3½ pounds), giblets removed and reserved for another use

1. Preheat oven to 400°F. In small ungreased skillet, toast fennel seeds over low heat for 3 minutes or until fragrant and lightly crisped. When cool, transfer to zip-seal plastic bag and lightly crush with flat side of skillet or rolling pin (or crush with mortar and pestle). Transfer to large bowl, add butter and lemon zest, and mix to thoroughly combine. Measure out 4 tablespoons of fennel butter and set aside.

2. Add carrots, onions, garlic, and ¾ teaspoon of salt to bowl and toss to combine. Transfer vegetables to baking or roasting pan large enough to hold vegetables in single layer.

3. With your fingers, rub reserved 4 tablespoons fennel butter under skin around legs and chicken breast. Season cavity and skin of chicken with remaining 1 teaspoon salt. With kitchen string, tie chicken legs together. Lift wings up toward neck, then fold wing tips under back of chicken so wings stay in place.

4. Place chicken, breast-side down, on top of vegetables. Roast for 25 minutes. Stir vegetables, turn chicken breast-side up, and roast for 25 minutes longer or until chicken is cooked through and vegetables are tender.

TO REDUCE THE FAT

In step 1, decrease butter to 4 tablespoons. Blend with half of toasted fennel seeds. Use this fennel butter to put under skin of chicken in step 3. In step 2, toss vegetables with 2 tablespoons olive oil and remaining toasted fennel seeds instead of fennel butter. Roast chicken and vegetables in two separate roasting pans.

Calories 710, Total Fat 43g, Saturated Fat 15g, Cholesterol 185mg, Sodium 1347mg, Protein 51g, Carbohydrates 30g

ROASTED CHICKEN WITH PROVENÇAL VEGETABLES

Cut 1 fennel bulb (about 1 pound) lengthwise into 8 wedges. Chop enough of fennel fronds to measure ½ cup. Make fennel butter as directed in step 1. In step 2, decrease carrots to 6; increase garlic to 12 cloves; add fennel wedges and 8 plum tomatoes, halved lengthwise. Roast vegetables and chicken as directed. Just before serving, sprinkle chopped fennel fronds over vegetables.

Calories 760, Total Fat 48g, Saturated Fat 21g, Cholesterol 216mg, Sodium 1549mg, Protein 53g, Carbohydrates 30g

Orange-Honey Glazed Chicken

Duck à l'orange may not be your idea of a simple family dinner, but you can enjoy similar flavors with far less effort. The sweetness of the honey is adroitly balanced with soy sauce and paprika. Serve the chicken with steamed Brussels sprouts or cabbage, and brown or white rice.

- 1 tablespoon olive oil
- ¼ cup minced onion
- 2 cloves garlic, minced
- ½ cup orange juice
- ¼ cup honey
- 2 tablespoons soy sauce
- 2 teaspoons paprika
- ¾ teaspoon salt
- ¾ teaspoon freshly ground black pepper
- ½ teaspoon ground ginger
- 1 whole chicken (about 3½ pounds), split in half lengthwise (see technique photos, at right)

1. Preheat oven to 375°F. In medium skillet, heat oil over low heat. Add onion and garlic and cook, stirring frequently, 5 minutes or until onion is soft. Increase heat to medium; add orange juice, honey, soy sauce, paprika, salt, pepper, and ginger, and bring to a boil. Boil mixture 3 minutes or until slightly thickened.

2. Place chicken, skin-side up, in roasting pan big enough to hold chicken in single layer. Spoon half of orange mixture over chicken. Bake for 20 minutes.

3. Spoon remaining orange mixture over chicken and bake for 20 minutes longer, basting twice, until cooked through. Pour pan juices into cup or gravy separator. Spoon (or pour) off and discard fat. Serve with degreased pan juices.

JALAPEÑO-JELLY CHICKEN In step 1, sauté onion and garlic as directed. Omit orange juice and honey. Add ⅔ cup jalapeño jelly and 3 tablespoons fresh lime juice when adding remaining sauce ingredients and boil 2 minutes. In steps 2 and 3, use jalapeño-jelly mixture in place of orange mixture.
Calories 601, Total Fat 27g, Saturated Fat 7g, Cholesterol 154mg, Sodium 1108mg, Protein 49g, Carbohydrates 36g

HINTS & TIPS

➤ A split chicken cooks a little faster than a whole one, and the job of carving it may seem less daunting to the inexperienced. You don't really have to carve the chicken at all—just cut each half in half again.

➤ It's a good idea to line the roasting pan with foil for this recipe, because the sugary glaze is likely to burn onto the pan.

➤ For an added depth of flavor, try this recipe with a wildflower honey, such as buckwheat.

Prep Time: 10 minutes
Cooking Time: 50 minutes
Makes 4 servings

NUTRITION INFORMATION
Per Serving

Calories 542
Total Fat 27g
Saturated Fat 7g
Cholesterol 154mg
Sodium 1096mg
Protein 49g
Carbohydrates 24g

TECHNIQUE

SPLITTING CHICKEN

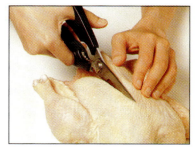

With the chicken breast-side up and starting at the tail end, use poultry shears to cut through the rib bones along one side of the breast bone.

With poultry shears, cut along both sides of the backbone to separate the two halves of the chicken. Discard the backbone or save for making stock.

ORANGE-HONEY GLAZED CHICKEN

ROASTED CHICKEN WITH SHALLOTS & ROSEMARY

Prep Time: 15 minutes
Cooking Time: 55 minutes
Makes 4 servings

Roasted Chicken with Shallots & Rosemary

Like garlic, shallots turn sweeter and sweeter the longer they cook. These whole roasted shallots are irresistible—there are enough for three per person, but you can toss in a few more if you like. You can eat them as a vegetable, or mash them with your fork to spread on bites of chicken or on bread.

3 tablespoons olive oil

12 shallots (about 8 ounces), peeled

3 sprigs fresh rosemary

1 whole chicken (about 3½ pounds), giblets removed and reserved for another use

1½ teaspoons salt

¾ teaspoon freshly ground black pepper

2 tablespoons flour

1. Preheat oven to 400°F. Pour oil into 9 x 13-inch baking pan. Add shallots and rosemary, and toss to coat. Place roasting rack in pan.

2. With your fingers, gently loosen skin from chicken breast and legs. Rub 1¼ teaspoons of salt and ½ teaspoon of pepper under skin, inside cavity, and over skin of chicken. Tie chicken legs with kitchen string. Lift wings up toward neck, then fold wing tips under back of chicken so wings stay in place. Place chicken, breast-side up, on rack in pan. Bake for 50 minutes, basting frequently with pan drippings, until skin is crisp and chicken is cooked through. Transfer chicken and shallots to serving platter. Pour fat from baking pan into small bowl and set aside. Discard rosemary.

3. Pour 1 cup of water into baking pan and scrape up any browned bits from bottom of pan. Spoon 2 tablespoons of reserved fat into small saucepan. Heat over medium heat. Whisk in flour until well combined and cook 2 to 3 minutes or until lightly browned. Pour in deglazed pan juices from baking pan along with remaining ¼ teaspoon salt and ¼ teaspoon pepper and cook over low heat until slightly thickened. Serve gravy with chicken and shallots.

Prep Time: 20 minutes
Cooking Time: 55 minutes
Makes 4 servings

Roasted Chicken with Sun-Dried Tomatoes & Pancetta

Pancetta is an unsmoked Italian bacon that is cured with salt and spices; the bacon slices are rolled together to form a sausage-like log. Unlike American-style bacon, pancetta is mostly used as a flavoring. Here, it's teamed with another typically Italian ingredient, sun-dried tomatoes.

3 tablespoons olive oil

6 ounces sliced pancetta, coarsely chopped

1½ pounds all-purpose potatoes, peeled and cut into ½-inch chunks

⅓ cup oil-packed sun-dried tomatoes, coarsely chopped

1 whole chicken (about 3½ pounds), giblets removed and reserved for another use

½ teaspoon salt

½ teaspoon freshly ground black pepper

½ teaspoon dried rosemary, crumbled

1. Preheat oven to 400°F. In 9 x 13-inch baking pan, combine oil and pancetta and roast 5 minutes or until oil begins to sizzle. Add potatoes and sun-dried tomatoes; toss to combine.

2. Sprinkle chicken inside and out with salt, pepper, and rosemary. Tie legs together with kitchen string. Lift wings up toward neck, then fold wing tips under back of chicken so wings stay in place. Place breast-side up on top of potato mixture and roast 30 minutes.

3. Stir potato mixture, baste chicken with pan juices, and bake 20 minutes or until vegetables are tender and chicken is cooked through.

Chicken with Lemon & Thyme

Served with steamed green beans and boiled new potatoes, this is a perfect springtime dinner.

- ¼ cup fresh lemon juice (about 2 lemons)
- 2 tablespoons olive oil
- 2 tablespoons fresh thyme
  or 1 teaspoon dried
- 1¼ teaspoons salt
- ½ teaspoon crushed red pepper flakes
- 3 cloves garlic, crushed and peeled
- 1 whole chicken (about 3½ pounds),
  cut into 8 serving pieces (page 14), wings
  discarded

1. In large bowl, whisk together lemon juice, oil, thyme, salt, and red pepper flakes until well combined. Stir in garlic. With your fingers, loosen skin of chicken without removing it. Add chicken to bowl and toss to coat, making sure some of the marinade gets under skin. Cover and refrigerate at least 1 hour or up to 4 hours.

2. Preheat broiler. Lift chicken from its marinade and place on broiler pan. Spoon half of marinade over chicken and broil 8 inches from heat for 15 minutes, turning chicken as it colors. Spoon remaining marinade over chicken and broil for 10 minutes or until cooked through and nicely browned.

*Prep Time: 15 minutes plus
  marinating time*
Cooking Time: 25 minutes
Makes 4 servings

NUTRITION INFORMATION
Per Serving
Calories 453
Total Fat 27g
Saturated Fat 7g
Cholesterol 154mg
Sodium 510mg
Protein 48g
Carbohydrates 1g

Herb-Scented Chicken with Sausage Stuffing

If you roast a stuffed bird only on holidays, consider this "everyday" recipe, which is far simpler than preparing a stuffed turkey. If you can't find shiitake mushrooms, just use more button mushrooms.

- 6 cups cubed (1-inch) coarse-textured country bread (about 8 ounces)
- 2 tablespoons olive oil
- ½ pound sweet Italian sausage, casings removed
- 1 large onion, finely chopped
- 10 ounces button mushrooms, thinly sliced
- ½ pound fresh shiitake mushrooms, stems trimmed and caps thinly sliced
- 1 teaspoon salt
- ¼ teaspoon freshly ground black pepper
- ¾ cup chicken broth
- 2 tablespoons butter, at room temperature
- 1 whole chicken (about 3½ pounds), giblets removed and reserved for another use

1. Preheat oven to 375°F. Place bread on baking sheet and bake, shaking pan once, 7 minutes or until golden brown. Transfer to large bowl.

2. In large skillet, heat oil over medium heat. Crumble in sausage and sauté 5 minutes or until just cooked through. Transfer to bowl with bread cubes.

3. Add onion to pan and cook, stirring frequently, 7 minutes or until onion is soft. Add the mushrooms, sprinkle with

¼ teaspoon of salt and the pepper, and cook, stirring frequently, 7 minutes or until mushrooms are tender. Transfer to bowl with bread. Add broth and butter to bowl and stir until butter has melted. Set aside to cool slightly before stuffing chicken.

4. Loosely fill neck cavity and body cavity of chicken with stuffing mixture. (If there is any stuffing left over, spoon into lightly greased pan, cover with foil, and place in oven alongside chicken during final 25 minutes of roasting.) With kitchen string, tie legs together. Lift wings up toward neck, then fold wing tips under back of chicken so wings stay in place. Sprinkle remaining ¾ teaspoon salt over chicken. Place chicken, breast-side up, on rack in 9 x 13-inch baking pan and roast for 20 minutes. Baste with pan drippings and roast for 30 minutes, basting twice more, until chicken is cooked through.

TO REDUCE THE FAT

In step 2, omit olive oil and Italian sausage. In step 3, omit butter and increase broth to 1 cup; stir in ½ pound fully-cooked chicken sausage, coarsely chopped. Stuff and roast as directed. Remove skin before eating.

Calories 483, Total Fat 13g, Saturated Fat 3.5g, Cholesterol 127mg, Sodium 1303mg, Protein 50g, Carbohydrates 40g

Prep Time: 25 minutes
Cooking Time: 1 hour 20 minutes
Makes 4 servings

NUTRITION INFORMATION
Per Serving
Calories 936
Total Fat 57g
Saturated Fat 18g
Cholesterol 213mg
Sodium 1732mg
Protein 65g
Carbohydrates 40g

HERB-SCENTED CHICKEN WITH SAUSAGE STUFFING

MEDITERRANEAN CHICKEN & VEGETABLE ROAST

Prep Time: 20 minutes
Cooking Time: 55 minutes
Makes 4 servings

Puttanesca-Style Chicken

Not for the timid, puttanesca sauce is a bold blend of tomatoes, garlic, anchovies, olives, capers, and hot pepper. Usually spooned over pasta, the sauce is equally delicious with baked chicken. Pasta is the side dish of choice—penne, fettuccine, or whatever you have in the cupboard.

2 tablespoons olive oil

1 small onion, finely chopped

3 cloves garlic, finely chopped

2 teaspoons anchovy paste

1½ cups canned tomatoes, drained and chopped

½ cup Gaeta or Calamata olives, pitted and coarsely chopped

1 tablespoon capers

¼ teaspoon cayenne pepper

3 strips (2 x ½-inch each) orange zest

1 whole chicken (about 3½ pounds), cut into 8 serving pieces (page 14), wings discarded

½ teaspoon salt

1. In small skillet, heat oil over low heat. Add onion and garlic, and cook, stirring frequently, 5 minutes or until onion is soft. Stir in anchovy paste and cook 2 minutes or until melted.

2. Preheat oven to 375°F. In 9 x 13-inch glass baking dish, stir together tomatoes, olives, capers, cayenne, orange zest, and onion mixture. With your fingers, gently loosen skin of chicken and rub salt under skin. Place chicken on top of tomato mixture. Bake, uncovered, for 45 minutes or until chicken is cooked through. Remove chicken from pan. Skim off any fat from surface of sauce.

3. Spoon most of tomato sauce onto dinner plates. Top with chicken and remaining tomato sauce.

Prep Time: 15 minutes
Cooking Time: 35 minutes
Makes 4 servings

Mediterranean Chicken & Vegetable Roast

Herbs grow abundantly in the Mediterranean basin, and the generous use of herbs is a keynote of Mediterranean cuisines. Tapenade, an ingredient in this recipe, is a pungent Provençal condiment made of ripe olives, capers, anchovies, olive oil, and lemon juice.

3 tablespoons olive oil

6 cloves garlic, crushed and peeled

2 packages (9 ounces each) frozen artichoke hearts, thawed

1 pound asparagus, cut into 1-inch lengths

½ teaspoon dried rosemary

1 bay leaf

1 teaspoon salt

¼ cup store-bought tapenade (olive spread)

¼ cup chopped fresh basil leaves

4 bone-in chicken breast halves (about 2½ pounds)

1 tablespoon fresh lemon juice

1. Preheat oven to 400°F. In 9 x 13-inch glass baking dish, combine oil and garlic. Place in oven and heat 5 minutes or until oil begins to sizzle. Stir in artichokes, asparagus, rosemary, bay leaf, and ½ teaspoon of salt. Roast 10 minutes.

2. Meanwhile, in small bowl, stir together tapenade and basil. With your fingers, gently loosen chicken skin without removing it. Spoon tapenade mixture under skin.

3. Place chicken, skin-side up, on top of roasted vegetables. Sprinkle chicken with lemon juice and remaining ½ teaspoon salt. Bake, uncovered, for 25 minutes or until vegetables are tender and chicken is cooked through. Discard bay leaf before serving.

Broiled Cumin Chicken Breasts with Banana Salsa

There's a long list of fruits that partner well with poultry: cranberries, apples, oranges, lemons, apricots—and you can now add bananas to the roster. The sweet-and-spicy Caribbean-inspired banana salsa offers a cooling counterpoint to cumin-rubbed broiled chicken breasts.

- 2 tablespoons fresh lime juice
- 2 tablespoons honey
- 2½ teaspoons ground cumin
- 1 teaspoon salt
- ½ teaspoon hot pepper sauce (red)
- 1 red bell pepper, cut into ¼-inch dice
- ¼ cup chopped cilantro
- 2 firm-ripe bananas (about 1 pound), cut into ½-inch cubes
- 1 teaspoon paprika
- ¼ teaspoon sugar
- 4 small skinless, boneless chicken breast halves (about 1¼ pounds)
- 1 tablespoon olive oil

1. In medium bowl, stir together lime juice, honey, ½ teaspoon of cumin, ½ teaspoon of salt, and the hot pepper sauce.

Add bell pepper and cilantro, and toss to combine. Add banana and gently toss. Cover and refrigerate until serving time.

2. In small bowl, stir together paprika, sugar, and remaining 2 teaspoons cumin and ½ teaspoon salt. Rub spice mixture into both sides of chicken. Sprinkle with olive oil.

3. Preheat broiler. Place chicken on broiler pan and broil 6 inches from heat for 5 minutes per side or until lightly browned and cooked through. Serve with banana salsa.

CHILI-BROILED CHICKEN WITH MANGO SALSA

In step 1, omit cumin. Substitute 1 large mango, peeled and cut into ½-inch chunks for the banana. In step 2, omit paprika, cumin, and salt. Add 2 teaspoons chili powder and ½ teaspoon dried oregano to spice rub. Proceed with recipe as directed.

Calories 273, Total Fat 6g, Saturated Fat 1g, Cholesterol 82mg, Sodium 413mg, Protein 33g, Carbohydrates 23g

LOW FAT
QUICK TO FIX

Prep Time: 15 minutes
Cooking Time: 10 minutes
Makes 4 servings

NUTRITION INFORMATION
Per Serving
Calories 301
Total Fat 6g
Saturated Fat 1g
Cholesterol 82mg
Sodium 695mg
Protein 34g
Carbohydrates 29g

Baked Chicken Breasts with Goat Cheese

The velvety "stuffing," a combination of goat cheese, cream cheese, and sun-dried tomatoes, is an attractive shade of pink and a delightful discovery when you cut into the chicken. You may find it easier to snip the sun-dried tomatoes with kitchen scissors, rather than chopping them with a knife.

- 4 ounces soft goat cheese
- 2 tablespoons cream cheese
- 1 large egg
- ¼ cup oil-packed sun-dried tomatoes, drained and finely chopped
- ¼ cup pecan halves, coarsely chopped
- 1 scallion, thinly sliced
- ¼ teaspoon freshly ground black pepper
- 4 bone-in chicken breast halves, with skin (about 2½ pounds)
- 2 tablespoons fresh lemon juice
- 1 tablespoon olive oil
- ½ teaspoon salt

1. In medium bowl, beat goat cheese and cream cheese until soft and well combined. Beat in egg. Stir in sun-dried tomatoes, pecans, scallion, and pepper.

2. With your fingers, carefully lift chicken skin. Spread goat-cheese mixture under skin and replace skin.

3. Preheat oven to 375°F. Place chicken, stuffed-side up, in baking pan. In small bowl, whisk together lemon juice, oil, and salt. Drizzle lemon-juice mixture over chicken and bake for 30 minutes or until stuffing is set and chicken is cooked through.

Prep Time: 20 minutes
Cooking Time: 30 minutes
Makes 4 servings

NUTRITION INFORMATION
Per Serving
Calories 518
Total Fat 30g
Saturated Fat 10g
Cholesterol 203mg
Sodium 454mg
Protein 55g
Carbohydrates 6g

BROILED CUMIN CHICKEN BREASTS WITH BANANA SALSA

Broiled Chicken Breasts with Pumpkin Seed Sauce

The Mexican "mole verde de pepitos" (green pumpkin-seed sauce) has antecedents that date back to the time of the Mayan empire. Typically used for a slow-cooked whole chicken, this easy version of the sauce is applied to broiled chicken breasts. Serve with baked acorn squash and flour tortillas.

4 tablespoons fresh lime juice (2 to 3 limes)

4 skinless, boneless chicken breast halves (about 1½ pounds)

1½ teaspoons ground coriander

1 teaspoon salt

½ teaspoon sugar

1 tablespoon plus 1 teaspoon olive oil

½ cup hulled pumpkin seeds

1 clove garlic, slivered

⅓ cup chicken broth

¼ cup packed cilantro leaves and tender stems

1. Sprinkle 2 tablespoons of lime juice over chicken. In small bowl, stir together ground coriander, ½ teaspoon of salt, and the sugar. Rub mixture into chicken.

2. In small skillet, heat 1 tablespoon of oil over low heat. Add pumpkin seeds and cook, stirring frequently, 3 minutes or until seeds begin to pop. Transfer to food processor. In same skillet, heat remaining 1 teaspoon oil over low heat. Add garlic and cook 1 minute or until tender. Transfer to food processor. Add broth, cilantro, and remaining 2 tablespoons lime juice and ½ teaspoon salt to processor and process until smooth.

3. Preheat broiler. Place chicken on broiler pan and broil 6 inches from heat for 5 minutes per side or until cooked through. Serve chicken topped with sauce.

LOW FAT

QUICK TO FIX

Prep Time: 10 minutes
Cooking Time: 15 minutes
Makes 4 servings

NUTRITION INFORMATION
Per Serving
Calories 273
Total Fat 8g
Saturated Fat 1.5g
Cholesterol 99mg
Sodium 782mg
Protein 41g
Carbohydrates 7g

Ricotta-Herb Stuffed Chicken Breasts

The seasoned ricotta that's stuffed under the skin of these chicken breasts is something like the cheese filling used in lasagna or cannelloni. The creamy ricotta is mixed with Parmesan, fresh basil, oregano, and rosemary. Pasta, simply tossed with butter or garlicky oil, is the perfect side dish.

1 cup ricotta cheese

¼ cup grated Parmesan cheese

⅓ cup chopped fresh basil leaves

½ teaspoon dried oregano

½ teaspoon salt

¼ teaspoon dried rosemary, crumbled

¼ teaspoon freshly ground black pepper

1 large egg

4 boneless chicken breast halves, with skin (about 1½ pounds)

1. Preheat oven to 375°F. In medium bowl, stir together ricotta, Parmesan, basil, oregano, ¼ teaspoon of salt, the rosemary, and pepper. Stir in egg.

2. With your fingers, carefully lift chicken skin. Spoon ricotta mixture under skin and replace skin. Place chicken, skin-side up, in 7 x 11-inch glass baking dish. Sprinkle with remaining ¼ teaspoon salt. Bake for 25 minutes or until chicken is cooked through.

Prep Time: 15 minutes
Cooking Time: 25 minutes
Makes 4 servings

NUTRITION INFORMATION
Per Serving
Calories 379
Total Fat 20g
Saturated Fat 9g
Cholesterol 186mg
Sodium 533mg
Protein 45g
Carbohydrates 3g

BROILED CHICKEN BREASTS WITH PUMPKIN SEED SAUCE

Chicken Breasts with Sour Cream-Horseradish Coating

Prep Time: 15 minutes
Cooking Time: 25 minutes
Makes 4 servings

To trim some fat from this recipe, use low-fat sour cream and "light" mayonnaise. The assertive flavor of the horseradish will compensate for any reduction in flavor.

3   slices firm-textured white bread (3 ounces)
¾   cup sour cream
¼   cup mayonnaise
4   tablespoons drained white horseradish
½   teaspoon salt
4   skinless, boneless chicken breast halves (about 1½ pounds)
2   tablespoons butter, melted
1   small cucumber, peeled, seeded, and cut into ¼-inch dice
2   tablespoons minced red onion
4   teaspoons fresh lemon juice

1. In food processor, process bread to fine crumbs; set aside. In shallow bowl or pie plate, stir together ¼ cup of sour cream, the mayonnaise, 3 tablespoons of horseradish, and the salt. Coat chicken with sour-cream mixture. In large bowl, toss bread crumbs with butter. Dip chicken into bread crumb mixture, patting gently into chicken.

2. Preheat oven to 375°F. Lightly grease baking sheet. Place pan in oven for 5 minutes. Place coated chicken on preheated pan and bake for 10 minutes. Turn chicken over and bake for 10 to 15 minutes or until coating is crisp and chicken is cooked through.

3. Meanwhile, in small bowl, stir together cucumber, onion, lemon juice, and remaining ½ cup sour cream and 1 tablespoon horseradish. Serve sauce with chicken.

SOUR CREAM-COATED CHICKEN WITH PEARS

In step 1, omit horseradish. Coat and bake chicken as directed. In step 3, omit cucumber, onion, and horseradish. Combine sour cream and lemon juice as directed and stir in 2 ripe pears (peeled and cut into 1-inch-thick wedges), 1 tablespoon honey, and 1 tablespoon snipped chives.

Calories 562, Total Fat 30g, Saturated Fat 12g, Cholesterol 142mg, Sodium 674mg, Protein 43g, Carbohydrates 30g

NUTRITION INFORMATION
Per Serving
Calories 510
Total Fat 30g
Saturated Fat 12g
Cholesterol 142mg
Sodium 691mg
Protein 43g
Carbohydrates 16g

Roasted Chicken Breasts with Parsley-Butter Stuffing

Prep Time: 15 minutes
Cooking Time: 50 minutes
Makes 4 servings

You don't need stale bread to make stuffing; drying it in the oven does the trick.

3   slices firm-textured white bread (3 ounces)
4   tablespoons butter
2   shallots, minced
2   cloves garlic, minced
½   cup chopped parsley
⅓   cup chicken broth
4   bone-in chicken breast halves, with skin (about 2½ pounds)
½   teaspoon salt
¼   teaspoon freshly ground black pepper

1. Preheat oven to 375°F. Cut bread into ½-inch cubes, spread on baking sheet, and bake 7 minutes or until golden brown.

2. Meanwhile, in small skillet, melt butter over medium heat. Add shallots and garlic, and cook, stirring frequently, 5 minutes or until shallots are soft. Transfer to large bowl. Add parsley, broth, and toasted bread cubes.

3. With your fingers, carefully lift chicken skin. Rub salt and pepper under skin. Spoon bread mixture under skin, pulling skin to cover bread. Place chicken, skin-side up, on baking sheet and bake for 35 minutes or until cooked through.

TO REDUCE THE FAT

In step 2, reduce butter to 1 tablespoon and increase broth to ½ cup.

Calories 484, Total Fat 25g, Saturated Fat 8g, Cholesterol 153mg, Sodium 710mg, Protein 50g, Carbohydrates 12g

NUTRITION INFORMATION
Per Serving
Calories 559
Total Fat 33g
Saturated Fat 13g
Cholesterol 177mg
Sodium 754mg
Protein 50g
Carbohydrates 12g

CHICKEN BREASTS WITH SOUR CREAM-HORSERADISH COATING

CHICKEN WITH POTATOES & VEGETABLES IN A PACKET

Prep Time: 25 minutes
Cooking Time: 25 minutes
Makes 4 servings

NUTRITION INFORMATION

Per Serving

Calories 415

Total Fat 14g

Saturated Fat 7.5g

Cholesterol 113mg

Sodium 816mg

Protein 37g

Carbohydrates 34g

TECHNIQUE

HOW TO FOLD A FOIL PACKET

Fold the rectangle of foil crosswise in half to make a center line. Open up the foil and place the ingredients on one half.

Fold the foil over the food. Starting at one long side, make several small folds in the foil to seal. Do not fold the foil all the way up to the food; it needs some steaming room. Fold the two short ends over in the same manner.

Chicken with Potatoes & Vegetables in a Packet

The French call this oven-poaching technique "en papillote" and traditionally use kitchen parchment for the packets. Sealing the paper packets is a tricky and tedious job, but if you substitute aluminum foil, you can just fold and crimp the edges together. Either way, everything cooked en papillote turns out moist and tender, cooked in a cloud of its own fragrant steam.

1¼ pounds small red-skinned potatoes, thinly sliced

½ pound sugar snap peas, strings removed

2 carrots, cut into matchsticks

1 teaspoon grated lemon zest

1 teaspoon salt

4 tablespoons butter, at room temperature

2 shallots, minced, or 2 scallions, thinly sliced

4 small skinless, boneless chicken breast halves (about 1¼ pounds)

½ teaspoon dried tarragon

1. In large pot of boiling salted water, blanch potatoes for 3 minutes. Drain and transfer to large bowl. Add sugar snap peas, carrots, lemon zest, and ¾ teaspoon of salt to bowl and toss to combine.

2. Preheat oven to 400°F. In small bowl, stir together butter and shallots until well combined. Tear off four 15-inch lengths of foil. Place potato mixture on one half of each sheet. Place chicken breast half on top of vegetables (see technique photo, top left). Sprinkle with tarragon and remaining ¼ teaspoon salt. Divide butter mixture evenly among packets, placing mixture on chicken breasts.

3. Fold sheet of foil over chicken and vegetables and fold edges over to tightly seal (bottom left). Place packets on baking sheet and bake for 25 minutes or until chicken and vegetables are cooked through. (To test, unfold end of one packet.) Serve chicken and vegetables in packets.

TO REDUCE THE FAT

Omit the butter. Toss shallots with 2 tablespoons olive oil. Assemble and bake packets as directed.

Calories 373, Total Fat 9g, Saturated Fat 1g, Cholesterol 82mg, Sodium 699mg, Protein 37g, Carbohydrates 34g

MOROCCAN CHICKEN WITH COUSCOUS In large
bowl, combine 1⅓ cups couscous (8 ounces), 1 teaspoon ground coriander, ¾ teaspoon salt, ½ teaspoon ground cinnamon, ¼ teaspoon ground black pepper, and 1 teaspoon grated lemon zest. Add 2¼ cups boiling water, cover, and let stand 5 minutes or until couscous is tender and liquid has been absorbed. Stir in 1½ cups rinsed and drained garbanzos (chick-peas), ½ cup raisins, and ⅓ cup chopped cilantro. In step 1, omit potatoes and sugar snap peas. Increase carrots to 4 and shred instead of cutting into matchsticks; do not toss with lemon zest and salt. Stir carrots into couscous mixture. In step 2, prepare shallot butter as directed. Tear off foil as directed and divide couscous mixture (instead of potato mixture) among sheets of foil. Top with chicken; omit tarragon and sprinkle chicken with 2 tablespoons lemon juice, ¼ teaspoon salt, and shallot butter. Seal and bake as in step 3.

Calories 638, Total Fat 16g, Saturated Fat 8g, Cholesterol 113mg, Sodium 945mg, Protein 46g, Carbohydrates 78g

Baked Chicken Breasts Reuben

You know the classic Reuben sandwich: corned beef, Swiss cheese, and sauerkraut on rye. This reinterpretation of the Reuben transforms the sandwich into a satisfying main dish, enhanced with the addition of bacon and apples. Caraway seeds provide a hint of "rye" flavor.

- 2 teaspoons olive oil
- 2 slices bacon
- 1 small onion, finely chopped
- 1 Granny Smith apple, peeled and cut into ½-inch cubes
- 1 McIntosh apple, peeled and cut into ½-inch cubes
- 1 bag (1 pound) sauerkraut, rinsed and drained
- ½ cup chicken broth
- 1 tablespoon Dijon mustard
- ½ teaspoon caraway seeds
- 4 small skinless, boneless chicken breast halves (about 1¼ pounds)
- 2 ounces Swiss cheese, grated

1. In large skillet, heat oil over medium heat. Add bacon and cook 5 minutes or until crisp. With slotted spoon, transfer bacon to paper towels to drain.

2. Add onion to skillet and cook 5 minutes or until crisp-tender. Add apples and cook, stirring, 4 minutes or until apples are crisp-tender. Remove pan from heat and stir in sauerkraut, broth, mustard, and caraway seeds. Crumble bacon and add to pan.

3. Preheat oven to 400°F. Spoon half of sauerkraut mixture into bottom of 7 x 11-inch glass baking dish. Top with chicken breasts. Spoon remaining sauerkraut mixture over chicken. Bake for 25 minutes. Sprinkle cheese over chicken and bake for 3 minutes or until cheese has melted and chicken is cooked through.

TO REDUCE THE FAT

Omit bacon and step 1. In step 2, in large nonstick skillet, heat 2 teaspoons olive oil. Complete recipe as directed.
Calories 303, Total Fat 8g, Saturated Fat 3.5g, Cholesterol 95mg, Sodium 1032mg, Protein 37g, Carbohydrates 16g

Prep Time: 15 minutes
Cooking Time: 45 minutes
Makes 4 servings

NUTRITION INFORMATION

Per Serving

Calories 366
Total Fat 15g
Saturated Fat 6g
Cholesterol 103mg
Sodium 1110mg
Protein 38g
Carbohydrates 16g

Broiled Lemon Chicken

Complete the meal with a toss of brown and wild rice, diced tomato, and scallions. This recipe can easily be doubled—worth doing because the "planned-overs" make great sandwiches: Spread Italian rolls with a little of the lemon sauce, then tuck in the chicken and some torn arugula.

- ¼ cup fresh lemon juice (about 2 lemons)
- 2 tablespoons olive oil
- 2 tablespoons soy sauce
- 1½ teaspoons sugar
- ¼ teaspoon salt
- 2 cloves garlic, crushed and peeled
- 2 scallions, thinly sliced
- 4 small skinless, boneless chicken breast halves (about 1¼ pounds)
- 1¼ teaspoons cornstarch
- ⅓ cup chicken broth
- 2 tablespoons chopped parsley

1. In small bowl, stir together lemon juice, oil, soy sauce, sugar, and salt. Measure out ¼ cup of mixture and set aside. Transfer remaining mixture to zip-seal plastic bag along with garlic and scallions. Add chicken and toss to coat. Refrigerate at least 30 minutes or up to 1 hour.

2. Preheat broiler. Place chicken on broiler pan. Spoon marinade over chicken and broil 6 inches from heat for 5 minutes per side or until cooked through.

3. In small bowl, stir together cornstarch and broth until well combined. Pour into small saucepan along with reserved lemon-juice mixture. Bring to a boil over medium heat and cook, stirring constantly, 1 minute or until slightly thickened. Stir in parsley. Spoon sauce over chicken.

Prep Time: 15 minutes plus marinating time
Cooking Time: 15 minutes
Makes 4 servings

NUTRITION INFORMATION

Per Serving

Calories 241
Total Fat 8.5g
Saturated Fat 1.5g
Cholesterol 82mg
Sodium 839mg
Protein 34g
Carbohydrates 6g

BROILED LEMON CHICKEN

BAKED CHICKEN BREASTS WITH CAPONATA & MOZZARELLA

Prep Time: 15 minutes
Cooking Time: 20 minutes
Makes 4 servings

NUTRITION INFORMATION

Per Serving
Calories 251
Total Fat 5.5g
Saturated Fat 1g
Cholesterol 82mg
Sodium 1137mg
Protein 36g
Carbohydrates 12g

Chicken, Black Beans & Peppers in a Packet

Canned beans are a real timesaver and the start of many substantial meals, but they need a little nudge in terms of seasoning. Here, salsa, diced bell pepper, and fresh cilantro flavor the beans in sassy Mexican style. Warm some tortillas in the oven during the last few minutes of baking.

1 can (10 ounces) black beans, rinsed and drained

1 cup medium-hot salsa

1 small green bell pepper, cut into ¼-inch dice

⅓ cup chopped cilantro

4 small skinless, boneless chicken breast halves (about 1¼ pounds)

2 tablespoons fresh lime juice

1 tablespoon olive oil

½ teaspoon salt

1. Preheat oven to 400°F. In large bowl, stir together beans, salsa, bell pepper, and cilantro. Tear off four 15-inch lengths of foil. Place bean mixture on one half of each sheet. Place chicken breast half on top of beans. Sprinkle with lime juice, oil, and salt.

2. Fold sheet of foil over chicken and beans and fold edges over to tightly seal (see technique photos, page 223). Place packets on baking sheet and bake for 20 minutes or until chicken is cooked through and beans are piping hot. (To test, unfold end of one packet.) Serve chicken and beans in packets.

CONFETTI CHICKEN In step 1, use 1 can (10 ounces) red beans instead of black beans; use 2 finely chopped pickled jalapeño peppers instead of green bell pepper; increase cilantro to ½ cup; and add 1½ cups thawed frozen corn kernels and 1½ teaspoons chili powder. Assemble and bake as directed.

Calories 306, Total Fat 6g, Saturated Fat 1g, Cholesterol 82mg, Sodium 1258mg, Protein 37g, Carbohydrates 25g

Prep Time: 10 minutes
Cooking Time: 40 minutes
Makes 4 servings

NUTRITION INFORMATION

Per Serving
Calories 305
Total Fat 12g
Saturated Fat 4g
Cholesterol 104mg
Sodium 686mg
Protein 39g
Carbohydrates 7g

Baked Chicken Breasts with Caponata & Mozzarella

Look in the Italian-foods aisle of your supermarket for jars or cans of caponata, a tasty Sicilian appetizer made from vegetables—usually eggplant, onions, celery, and tomatoes—flavored with capers and vinegar. Keep a jar or two on your shelf to serve as an "instant" first course or sandwich filling.

1 can (7½ ounces) caponata

½ cup canned tomatoes, chopped with their juice

¼ cup chicken broth

¼ cup orange juice

4 tablespoons chopped fresh basil leaves

4 small skinless, boneless chicken breast halves (about 1¼ pounds)

¼ teaspoon salt

1 cup shredded mozzarella cheese (4 ounces)

1. Preheat oven to 350°F. In medium bowl, stir together caponata, tomatoes, broth, and orange juice. Stir in 2 table-spoons of basil. Place chicken in 7 x 11-inch glass baking dish. Sprinkle chicken with salt.

2. Spoon caponata mixture over chicken and bake for 35 minutes. Sprinkle mozzarella over chicken and bake for 5 minutes or until chicken is cooked through. Sprinkle remaining 2 tablespoons basil over chicken just before serving.

BAKED CHICKEN & MOZZARELLA SALAD Sprinkle chicken with ¼ cup orange juice and ¼ teaspoon salt and bake in 350°F. oven for 5 minutes or until cooked through. When cool, cut crosswise into ¼-inch-thick slices. In large bowl, whisk together ¼ cup orange juice and 2 tablespoons olive oil. Stir in 1 can (7½ ounces) caponata, 2 diced fresh tomatoes, 1 cup (4 ounces) diced mozzarella, sliced chicken, and ¼ cup chopped fresh basil. Serve over mixed greens.

Calories 377, Total Fat 18g, Saturated Fat 5g, Cholesterol 104mg, Sodium 577mg, Protein 39g, Carbohydrates 11g

Chicken Breasts Stuffed with Spinach, Fontina & Raisins

Prep Time: 25 minutes
Cooking Time: 30 minutes
Makes 4 servings

Party-perfect in just an hour, these filled, rolled chicken breasts are handsome when sliced crosswise for a colorful pinwheel effect. Creamy scalloped potatoes make an elegant accompaniment. To avoid watering down the filling, squeeze the spinach really dry: After thawing, drain it well in a sieve or colander. Then squeeze the rest of the excess liquid from the spinach with your hands.

NUTRITION INFORMATION
Per Serving

Calories 498

Total Fat 26g

Saturated Fat 8g

Cholesterol 170mg

Sodium 801mg

Protein 47g

Carbohydrates 19g

- 4 small skinless, boneless chicken breast halves (about 1¼ pounds), pounded to ¼-inch thickness (page 15)
- ½ teaspoon salt
- 1 package (10 ounces) spinach leaves, thawed and squeezed dry
- 4 ounces Fontina cheese, sliced
- ⅓ cup pecans, finely chopped
- ¼ cup raisins
- ½ teaspoon dried sage
- 2 slices firm-textured white bread (2 ounces)
- 2 tablespoons grated Parmesan cheese
- 1 large egg
- 2 tablespoons olive oil

1. Sprinkle chicken on both sides with ¼ teaspoon of salt. Dividing evenly, spread spinach over chicken breasts. Top with Fontina. Sprinkle pecans, raisins, and sage on top. Roll chicken breasts up from one short end. Secure with toothpicks.

2. Preheat oven to 375°F. In food processor, process bread to fine crumbs. Add Parmesan and remaining ¼ teaspoon salt and process to combine. Transfer to plate or sheet of waxed paper. In shallow pie plate, beat egg with 1 teaspoon of water. Dip chicken into egg mixture, then into bread crumbs, patting crumbs in.

3. Place chicken on baking sheet, drizzle with oil, and bake for 25 to 30 minutes or until crust is golden brown and chicken is cooked through. Remove toothpicks before serving.

PEPPERJACK-STUFFED CHICKEN WITH BROCCOLI
In step 1, substitute 1 cup frozen chopped broccoli, thawed and patted dry, for spinach; substitute 1 cup (4 ounces) shredded pepperjack for Fontina; substitute walnuts for pecans; substitute minced sun-dried tomatoes for raisins. Omit sage. In step 2, omit Parmesan. Proceed as directed.
Calories 486, Total Fat 27g, Saturated Fat 7.5g, Cholesterol 166mg, Sodium 730mg, Protein 45g, Carbohydrates 15g

---

HINTS & TIPS

➤ Fontina, a buttery, semisoft cheese, originated in the Aosta Valley in northern Italy. The finest Fontina, labeled Fontina Val d'Aosta, comes from this region. But Fontina from other parts of Italy is nearly as good, and quite a bit less expensive.

➤ The pepperjack cheese used in the variation is Monterey Jack laced with bits of jalapeño pepper.

➤ Though the inspiration for this dish is decidedly Italian, the use of pecans gives it a slight American twist. Purists might want to replace the pecans with pine nuts or almonds.

CHICKEN BREASTS STUFFED WITH SPINACH, FONTINA & RAISINS

POTATO-CRUSTED BAKED CHICKEN

Prep Time: 15 minutes
Cooking Time: 25 minutes
Makes 4 servings

NUTRITION INFORMATION
Per Serving
Calories 351
Total Fat 14g
Saturated Fat 4g
Cholesterol 210mg
Sodium 563mg
Protein 46g
Carbohydrates 7g

Potato-Crusted Baked Chicken

*Here's a brilliant use for instant mashed potatoes. As a breading for baked chicken,
the dried potatoes create a delicately crunchy crust. Serve with fresh tomatoes, or with canned
tomatoes cooked with green beans or zucchini.*

⅓ cup grated Parmesan cheese

½ teaspoon salt

½ teaspoon freshly ground black pepper

½ teaspoon dried sage

2 large eggs

4 skinless, boneless chicken breast halves
(about 1½ pounds)

⅔ cup dried instant mashed potatoes

2 tablespoons olive oil

1. Preheat oven to 375°F. In shallow bowl or pie plate, stir
together Parmesan, salt, pepper, and sage. In another shallow
bowl, beat eggs with 1 tablespoon of water. Dip chicken into
Parmesan mixture, pressing it into chicken. Dip chicken into
egg mixture, then into potatoes, pressing them into chicken.

2. Lightly grease baking sheet. Place baking sheet in oven
to heat for 5 minutes. Place chicken on preheated baking
sheet; drizzle olive oil over chicken. Bake for 10 minutes,
turn chicken over, and bake for 10 to 15 minutes longer
or until coating is crusty and golden brown and chicken is
cooked through.

DEVILED-POTATO CHICKEN In step 1, omit Parmesan
and sage. In shallow bowl or pie plate, stir together ¼ cup
Dijon mustard, 1½ teaspoons hot pepper sauce (red),
1 teaspoon freshly ground black pepper, and ½ teaspoon
salt. Omit egg mixture. Dredge chicken in mustard mixture,
then coat with potatoes and bake as directed.

*Calories 300, Total Fat 10g, Saturated Fat 1.5g, Cholesterol 99mg,
Sodium 818mg, Protein 40g, Carbohydrates 6g*

QUICK TO FIX

Prep Time: 15 minutes
Cooking Time: 15 minutes
Makes 4 servings

NUTRITION INFORMATION
Per Serving
Calories 340
Total Fat 17g
Saturated Fat 2.5g
Cholesterol 99mg
Sodium 1240mg
Protein 41g
Carbohydrates 6g

Broiled Spanish Chicken
with Olives & Tomatoes

*For a tempting dinner in no time flat, plan ahead: Prepare the six-spice mixture in advance (store
it in a small freezer bag) and you'll be ready to start cooking the chicken as soon as you walk in the
door. Put a pot of water on to boil and cook some rice while the chicken is under the broiler.*

1½ teaspoons ground coriander

1½ teaspoons paprika

1 teaspoon dried oregano

¾ teaspoon salt

¼ teaspoon cayenne pepper

½ teaspoon anise or fennel seed

4 skinless, boneless chicken breast halves
(about 1½ pounds)

2 tablespoons olive oil

2 tomatoes, peeled, seeded, and
coarsely chopped

½ cup Gaeta or Calamata olives, pitted
and coarsely chopped

1 tablespoon capers

1 tablespoon slivered almonds, toasted

1. In small bowl, stir together coriander, paprika, oregano,
salt, and cayenne. Place anise in small bag and with rolling
pin or heavy skillet, press on seeds until finely ground (or
crush with mortar and pestle). Stir into spice mixture.
Measure out 1½ teaspoons of spice mixture and set aside.
Rub remaining spice mixture into both sides of chicken.
Drizzle 1 tablespoon of oil over chicken.

2. Preheat broiler. Place chicken on broiler pan and
broil 8 inches from heat for 5 minutes per side or until
cooked through.

3. Meanwhile, in small skillet, heat remaining 1 tablespoon
oil over low heat. Add reserved 1½ teaspoons spice mixture and
cook 1 minute or until fragrant. Transfer to medium bowl, stir
in tomatoes, olives, capers, and almonds. Serve chicken with
tomato mixture on top.

BAKED CHICKEN WITH CORN & RED CHILI SAUCE

Prep Time: 10 minutes
Cooking Time: 50 minutes
Makes 4 servings

NUTRITION INFORMATION

Per Serving
Calories 371
Total Fat 10g
Saturated Fat 1.5g
Cholesterol 107mg
Sodium 840mg
Protein 46g
Carbohydrates 24g

HINTS & TIPS

➤ You can use slightly stale tortillas for this recipe, since they'll soften in cooking. There is actually a whole category of Mexican recipes based on using up stale tortillas. They provide substance to casseroles and, in this case, thicken the sauce.

➤ Be sure to use corn tortillas for this recipe. Flour tortillas would make the sauce gummy.

➤ If you should happen to have any leftovers, remove the chicken from the bone, shred it, and reheat it in the sauce. Use this as the filling for a barbecue-style sandwich.

Baked Chicken with Corn & Red Chili Sauce

You will happily recognize the authentic Mexican flavors in this hearty baked chicken dish. The sauce, which is made in a novel way, is a purée of canned tomatoes, chipotle peppers, bell peppers, and corn tortillas. Coleslaw and corn bread are ideal side dishes for the saucy chicken.

- 2 tablespoons olive oil
- 1 red bell pepper, finely chopped
- 1 tablespoon chili powder
- 2 corn tortillas (6-inch diameter), torn into large pieces
- 1½ cups canned tomatoes, chopped with their juice
- 2 tablespoons tomato paste
- 1 chipotle pepper in adobo sauce
- ¾ teaspoon salt
- 1 cup frozen corn kernels, thawed
- 4 bone-in chicken breast halves (about 2½ pounds), skin removed
- 8 lime wedges

1. In large skillet, heat oil over medium heat. Add bell pepper and cook, stirring frequently, 5 minutes or until tender. Stir in chili powder and tortillas, and cook 2 minutes or until tortillas soften. Stir in tomatoes, tomato paste, chipotle, and salt, and bring to a boil. Reduce to a simmer, cover, and cook 10 minutes to develop flavors. Transfer to food processor and process until smooth.

2. Preheat oven to 375°F. Spoon sauce into 9 x 13-inch glass baking dish. Stir in corn. Place chicken in pan in single layer and top with half of sauce. Bake, uncovered, for 30 minutes or until chicken is cooked through. Serve chicken topped with sauce and with lime wedges.

GREEN CHILI CHICKEN In step 1, substitute 2 green peppers for red pepper and cook as directed. Add chili powder and tortillas as directed. Omit tomatoes, tomato paste, and chipotle. Transfer mixture to food processor and add 1½ cups (packed) cilantro leaves and stems, 1 cup chicken broth, 2 pickled jalapeño peppers, and ¾ teaspoon salt, and process until smooth. Layer and bake as directed in step 2.
Calories 358, Total Fat 11g, Saturated Fat 1.5g, Cholesterol 107mg, Sodium 973mg, Protein 46g, Carbohydrates 20g

Baked Rosemary Chicken Breasts with Roasted Garlic

With 45 minutes to savor the aroma of roasting garlic, you'll be more than ready to sit down to dinner when the chicken is done. The garlic cloves are not a garnish—squeeze them out of their skins and spread the sweet roasted garlic on bread, or serve with pasta or potatoes.

- 2 tablespoons chopped fresh rosemary or 2 teaspoons dried, crumbled
- 1¼ teaspoons salt
- ½ teaspoon freshly ground black pepper
- 4 bone-in chicken breast halves, with skin (about 2½ pounds)
- ¼ cup olive oil
- 16 cloves garlic, unpeeled

1. In small bowl, stir together rosemary, salt, and pepper. With your fingers, carefully loosen chicken skin without removing it. Rub rosemary mixture under skin.

2. Preheat oven to 375°F. Place olive oil and garlic in 9 x 13-inch metal baking pan. Toss to coat garlic with oil. Heat in oven for 5 minutes or until oil begins to sizzle.

3. Add chicken to pan, skin-side down, and bake for 20 minutes. Turn chicken skin-side up and bake for 20 minutes longer or until chicken is cooked through. Serve chicken topped with pan juices and roasted garlic.

Prep Time: 10 minutes
Cooking Time: 45 minutes
Makes 4 servings

NUTRITION INFORMATION
Per Serving
Calories 529
Total Fat 35g
Saturated Fat 8g
Cholesterol 145mg
Sodium 871mg
Protein 48g
Carbohydrates 4g

Oven-Poached Chicken Breasts with Sesame Sauce

Tahini is sometimes referred to as the "butter" of the Middle East. With its soft, rich texture and nutlike flavor, it's a delicious sauce or spread. Stir tahini before using to reincorporate the oil.

- 1 cup chicken broth, canned or homemade (page 45)
- 8 cloves garlic, crushed and peeled
- 1 teaspoon grated lemon zest
- 4 skinless, boneless chicken breast halves (about 1½ pounds)
- ¼ cup tahini (sesame paste), stirred well
- 2 teaspoons fresh lemon juice
- ½ teaspoon salt
- ¼ teaspoon cayenne pepper
- 3 tablespoons plain low-fat yogurt
- 3 tablespoons chopped fresh mint or 1 teaspoon dried
- 1 tablespoon sesame seeds

1. Preheat oven to 350°F. In 9 x 13-inch glass baking dish, stir together broth, garlic, and lemon zest. Place chicken in pan in single layer, cover with foil, and bake for 15 to 20 minutes or until chicken is just cooked through. Remove chicken from its poaching liquid and cover chicken with foil to keep warm. Reserve poaching liquid and 6 cloves of garlic (discard remaining 2 cloves garlic).

2. In food processor, combine tahini, lemon juice, salt, cayenne, ⅓ cup of reserved poaching liquid, and reserved garlic cloves, and process until smooth. Transfer to bowl and stir in yogurt and mint.

3. In small ungreased skillet, toast sesame seeds over low heat 2 minutes or until fragrant. Place chicken on 4 serving plates, spoon sauce on top, and sprinkle with sesame seeds.

CHICKEN PITAS In step 1, oven-poach chicken as directed. When cool enough to handle, shred chicken. Make sesame sauce as directed in step 2. In medium bowl, combine shredded chicken with 2 cups shredded lettuce, 2 chopped tomatoes, and sesame sauce. Spoon chicken mixture into 4 large pita breads. Omit step 3 and sesame seeds.
Calories 553, Total Fat 12g, Saturated Fat 2g, Cholesterol 99mg, Sodium 1154mg, Protein 52g, Carbohydrates 58g

Prep Time: 15 minutes
Cooking Time: 25 minutes
Makes 4 servings

NUTRITION INFORMATION
Per Serving
Calories 314
Total Fat 12g
Saturated Fat 2g
Cholesterol 99mg
Sodium 690mg
Protein 44g
Carbohydrates 7g

BAKED ROSEMARY CHICKEN BREASTS WITH ROASTED GARLIC

Chicken Rolls Stuffed with Asparagus & Black Forest Ham

Saltimbocca—rolled veal scallops filled with prosciutto and fresh sage leaves—is the inspiration for this sophisticated dinner dish. The pounded chicken breasts are rolled around a heady sage-scented Gorgonzola-pecan spread and a slice of delicate Black Forest ham (sold at most deli counters). Halved cherry tomatoes, sautéed in olive oil and tossed with snipped chives, is an ideal side dish.

Prep Time: 25 minutes
Cooking Time: 25 minutes
Makes 4 servings

NUTRITION INFORMATION
Per Serving

Calories 649

Total Fat 37g

Saturated Fat 14g

Cholesterol 201mg

Sodium 1712mg

Protein 57g

Carbohydrates 23g

- 12 thin stalks asparagus
- 6 ounces Gorgonzola or other blue cheese
- 2 tablespoons cream cheese
- ⅓ cup pecan halves, finely chopped
- ½ teaspoon freshly ground black pepper
- ⅛ teaspoon dried sage
- 4 small skinless, boneless chicken breast halves (about 1¼ pounds), pounded to ¼-inch thickness (page 15)
- ¼ pound thinly sliced Black Forest ham
- 1 large egg
- 1 cup plain dried bread crumbs
- 2 tablespoons olive oil

1. In medium pot of boiling water, blanch asparagus for 2 minutes. Drain and rinse under cold water.

2. In medium bowl, with electric mixer, beat Gorgonzola and cream cheese until well combined. Stir in pecans, pepper, and sage.

3. Place chicken cutlets on work surface, smooth-side (skinned-side) down, with one short end facing you. Cover entire surface of chicken with ham. Spread cheese mixture to within ½ inch of each short end (see technique photo, top right). Place 3 asparagus crosswise and roll chicken up from one short end (bottom photo). Secure with toothpicks.

4. Preheat oven to 400°F. In shallow bowl or pie plate, beat egg with 1 tablespoon of water. In another shallow bowl, toss together bread crumbs and oil. Dip each chicken roll first in egg mixture, then in bread crumb mixture, patting crumbs in.

5. Place chicken rolls, seam-side down, on lightly greased baking sheet and bake for 25 minutes or until topping is golden and chicken is firm to the touch. Remove toothpicks before serving.

TO REDUCE THE FAT

In step 2, reduce Gorgonzola to 3 ounces; use 4 tablespoons reduced-fat cream cheese (Neufchâtel) instead of regular cream cheese; reduce pecans to ¼ cup. In step 4, omit oil. In step 5, spray chicken rolls lightly with nonstick cooking spray before baking.

Calories 513, Total Fat 23g, Saturated Fat 9g, Cholesterol 184mg, Sodium 1459mg, Protein 53g, Carbohydrates 23g

TECHNIQUE

MAKING CHICKEN ROLLS

With the skinned side of the chicken down, cover the pounded chicken cutlet with ham and then with the Gorgonzola mixture. Be sure the mixture does not go all the way to the edges of the cutlet; leave a border of about ½ inch.

Place the asparagus on the chicken cutlet and roll up. Secure the roll with 2 or 3 toothpicks.

CHICKEN ROLLS STUFFED WITH ASPARAGUS & BLACK FOREST HAM

Ginger-Fennel Chicken Breasts

Here's a no-shopping-trip special: For all its enticingly spicy flavor, this recipe is made with ingredients that are probably on your kitchen shelves right now. Do make sure the herbs and spices are fresh, though. Rub a little of each between your fingers and sniff to be sure it's still potent.

2 teaspoons fennel seeds

1 teaspoon dried sage

1 teaspoon ground ginger

¾ teaspoon salt

½ teaspoon freshly ground black pepper

½ teaspoon sugar

1 large egg

4 skinless, boneless chicken breast halves (about 1½ pounds)

2 tablespoons butter, melted

4 lemon wedges

1. Preheat oven to 350°F. Place fennel seeds in small bag and with rolling pin or flat side of skillet, lightly crush without pulverizing (or crush with mortar and pestle). Transfer to shallow bowl or pie plate and stir in sage, ginger, salt, pepper, and sugar. In separate shallow bowl or pie plate, beat egg with 1 tablespoon of water.

2. Dip chicken in egg mixture, then in fennel mixture, pressing seeds into chicken. Place on lightly greased baking sheet. Drizzle butter over chicken and bake for 20 minutes or until cooked through. Serve with lemon wedges.

QUICK TO FIX

Prep Time: 10 minutes
Cooking Time: 20 minutes
Makes 4 servings

NUTRITION INFORMATION
Per Serving
Calories 277
Total Fat 10g
Saturated Fat 5g
Cholesterol 167mg
Sodium 622mg
Protein 41g
Carbohydrates 3g

Baked Tortilla-Crusted Chicken Legs

Breadcrumbs and cracker crumbs are old hat: Why not try tortilla crumbs for breading chicken? The crumbs are seasoned with chili powder, coriander, and cayenne, so they don't just stand there—they really do something for the chicken! Serve with a colorful toss of corn, tomatoes, and scallions.

2 cups buttermilk

½ teaspoon grated lime zest

4 whole chicken legs (about 2½ pounds), split into drumsticks and thighs (page 14), skin removed

8 corn tortillas (6-inch diameter), torn into pieces

1 tablespoon chili powder

1 teaspoon ground coriander

1 teaspoon salt

¼ teaspoon cayenne pepper

2 tablespoons olive oil

2 tablespoons fresh lime juice

Lime wedges (optional)

1. In large bowl, whisk together buttermilk and lime zest. Add chicken and toss to coat. Cover and refrigerate at least 1 hour or up to overnight.

2. Preheat oven to 350°F. In food processor, combine tortillas, chili powder, coriander, salt, and cayenne. Process to fine crumbs.

3. Lift chicken from buttermilk mixture. Dredge in tortilla mixture, pressing mixture into chicken. Place on lightly greased baking sheet and drizzle with oil. Bake 30 minutes, turning chicken pieces over midway, until crisp and golden brown. Sprinkle with lime juice and serve with lime wedges, if desired.

TO REDUCE THE FAT

Substitute bone-in chicken breast halves, skin removed, for the chicken legs. Omit the oil in step 3; instead spray the chicken with nonstick cooking spray before baking.

Calories 361, Total Fat 6g, Saturated Fat 1.5g, Cholesterol 110mg, Sodium 867mg, Protein 48g, Carbohydrates 28g

Prep Time: 10 minutes plus marinating time
Cooking Time: 30 minutes
Makes 4 servings

NUTRITION INFORMATION
Per Serving
Calories 408
Total Fat 16g
Saturated Fat 3.5g
Cholesterol 132mg
Sodium 886mg
Protein 38g
Carbohydrates 28g

BAKED TORTILLA-CRUSTED CHICKEN LEGS

ASIAN BREADED CHICKEN WITH LIME

Prep Time: 10 minutes
Cooking Time: 30 minutes
Makes 4 servings

Mustard-Crusted Drumsticks

One definition of "deviled" is baked or broiled with a mustard-crumb coating; these drumsticks are coated with a honey-mustard mixture before they're breaded. When you're planning your next picnic, consider these devilish drumsticks. Bring along potato salad, and beefsteak tomatoes for slicing.

NUTRITION INFORMATION
Per Serving
Calories 361
Total Fat 14g
Saturated Fat 2.5g
Cholesterol 118mg
Sodium 851mg
Protein 34g
Carbohydrates 21g

4 slices firm-textured white bread (4 ounces)

¼ cup packed parsley

3 tablespoons Dijon mustard

1 tablespoon honey

½ teaspoon dried rosemary, crumbled

½ teaspoon salt

½ teaspoon freshly ground black pepper

8 chicken drumsticks (about 2½ pounds), skin removed

2 tablespoons olive oil

4 lemon wedges

1. Preheat oven to 400°F. In food processor, combine bread and parsley, and process to form fine crumbs. Transfer to shallow bowl. In shallow bowl or pie plate, stir together mustard, honey, rosemary, salt, and pepper. Dip chicken in mustard mixture, coating it well. Dip chicken into bread-crumb mixture, pressing crumbs into chicken.

2. Transfer chicken to greased jelly-roll pan and drizzle chicken with oil. Bake for 30 minutes or until coating is golden brown and chicken is cooked through. Serve with lemon wedges.

Asian Breaded Chicken with Lime

The sesame oil called for here is the dark Asian-style oil sold in small bottles. Made from toasted sesame seeds, it has an intense flavor and is mostly used as a seasoning, not a cooking oil. Try a little of it in salad dressings or as a final fillip when stir-frying.

Prep Time: 15 minutes
Cooking Time: 25 minutes
Makes 4 servings

NUTRITION INFORMATION
Per Serving
Calories 464
Total Fat 24g
Saturated Fat 4g
Cholesterol 118mg
Sodium 957mg
Protein 41g
Carbohydrates 22g

3 slices firm-textured white bread (3 ounces)

½ cup salted peanuts

½ cup cilantro leaves and tender stems

1 tablespoon sesame seeds

1 teaspoon grated lime zest

2 tablespoons sesame oil

2 egg whites

8 chicken drumsticks (about 2½ pounds), skin removed

½ cup fresh lime juice

¼ cup lower-sodium soy sauce

2 teaspoons sugar

2 scallions, thinly sliced

1. In food processor, combine bread, peanuts, cilantro, sesame seeds, and lime zest, and process to fine crumbs. Divide mixture between 2 shallow bowls and add 1 tablespoon sesame oil to each bowl. Toss each to combine. (Coating is done in 2 batches so that it doesn't get too mushy, which would make it difficult to coat chicken.)

2. Preheat oven to 375°F. In shallow bowl or pie plate, lightly beat egg whites with 1 tablespoon of water. Dip chicken first in egg-white mixture, then in bread-crumb mixture, pressing it onto chicken. Transfer chicken to lightly greased baking sheet. Bake for 25 minutes or until coating is crisp and golden, and chicken is cooked through.

3. Meanwhile, in small saucepan, combine lime juice, soy sauce, and sugar, and heat over low heat 30 seconds or until sugar has dissolved. Remove from heat and divide among 4 small bowls. Divide scallions among bowls of dipping sauce. Serve each person a bowl of dipping sauce with the chicken.

DRUMSTICKS WITH HONEY-BROILED PEARS

Prep Time: 15 minutes
Cooking Time: 15 minutes
Makes 4 servings

NUTRITION INFORMATION
Per Serving
Calories 473
Total Fat 19g
Saturated Fat 4.5g
Cholesterol 122mg
Sodium 848mg
Protein 37g
Carbohydrates 40g

Drumsticks with Honey-Broiled Pears

Pears usually need some ripening time after you bring them home from the store. For this recipe, they should be ripe enough to be sweetly fragrant, but not so soft that they turn to mush when cooked.

    3   teaspoons mild curry powder
 1¼   teaspoons salt
    ¾   teaspoon ground ginger
    ¼   teaspoon cayenne pepper
    ⅛   teaspoon ground cardamom
    8   chicken drumsticks (about 2½ pounds)
    1   tablespoon olive oil
    3   tablespoons honey
    1   tablespoon fresh lemon juice
    4   firm-ripe pears, peeled and cut
        into 1-inch cubes

1. In large bowl, stir together 1½ teaspoons of curry powder, 1 teaspoon of salt, the ginger, cayenne, and cardamom. Add drumsticks and toss well to coat. Add oil and toss again.

2. In separate bowl, stir together honey, lemon juice, remaining 1½ teaspoons curry powder, and remaining ¼ teaspoon salt. Add pears and toss to coat.

3. Preheat broiler. Place chicken on one end of broiler pan. Broil 6 inches from heat for 5 minutes. Lift pears from honey mixture, reserving mixture, and spread pears out at other end of broiler pan. Broil chicken and pears 10 minutes, turning both after 5 minutes and spooning half of reserved honey mixture over pears.

4. Place chicken on 4 serving plates. Toss pears with the remaining honey mixture and spoon alongside chicken.

CHICKEN WITH RUM-GLAZED PINEAPPLE Marinate drumsticks as directed in step 1. Omit step 2 and pears. In small saucepan, stir together ¼ cup packed dark brown sugar, ¼ cup dark rum, and 2 tablespoons fresh lime juice. Bring to a boil, reduce to a simmer, and cook 7 to 10 minutes or until syrupy. Stir in 1½ teaspoons curry powder and ¼ teaspoon salt. Cool to room temperature. Add eight ¾-inch-thick rounds of fresh pineapple to rum syrup. Cook chicken and pineapple (instead of pears) as directed in steps 3 and 4.
Calories 422, Total Fat 19g, Saturated Fat 4.5g, Cholesterol 122mg, Sodium 853mg, Protein 37g, Carbohydrates 18g

---

Prep Time: 15 minutes
Cooking Time: 30 minutes
Makes 4 servings

NUTRITION INFORMATION
Per Serving
Calories 397
Total Fat 27g
Saturated Fat 8.5g
Cholesterol 141mg
Sodium 708mg
Protein 33g
Carbohydrates 4g

Cajun Drumsticks

The Creole mustard used on these drumsticks is a spicy-hot, coarse-grained mustard made with brown mustard seeds (instead of yellow seeds) and can be found in many supermarkets and most gourmet stores.

    2   teaspoons dried thyme
 1½   teaspoons dried oregano
    ¾   teaspoon salt
    ½   teaspoon garlic powder
    ½   teaspoon onion powder
    ½   teaspoon ground white pepper
    ½   teaspoon freshly ground black pepper
    ½   teaspoon cayenne pepper
    8   chicken drumsticks (about 2½ pounds),
        skin removed
    2   tablespoons olive oil
    ¾   cup sour cream
    2   tablespoons mayonnaise
    2   teaspoons Creole mustard
    2   teaspoons Worcestershire sauce
    ½   teaspoon hot pepper sauce (red)

1. In large bowl, stir together thyme, oregano, salt, garlic powder, onion powder, white pepper, black pepper, and cayenne. Add chicken and toss well to coat.

2. Preheat oven to 350°F. Add olive oil to bowl with chicken and toss to coat. Transfer chicken to jelly-roll pan and bake for 30 minutes or until cooked through.

3. Meanwhile, in medium bowl, stir together sour cream, mayonnaise, mustard, Worcestershire, and hot pepper sauce. Serve with chicken.

IN A HURRY?
Substitute ⅔ cup bottled ranch dressing for sauce made in step 3.

Crispy Oven "Fried" Chicken

Many health-conscious people do not fry chicken anymore, but choose the lower-fat oven option and bake breaded chicken instead. A drizzle of olive oil keeps the chicken moist as it bakes, but there's only 3 tablespoons of oil in the recipe, rather than the cup or more needed for frying.

- 2 egg whites
- 2 tablespoons honey
- 1 teaspoon salt
- ⅔ cup flour
- ⅓ cup grated Parmesan cheese
- 4 whole chicken legs (about 2½ pounds), split into drumsticks and thighs (page 14), skin removed
- 3 tablespoons olive oil

1. In shallow bowl or pie plate, stir together egg whites, honey, and ¼ teaspoon of salt. In separate shallow bowl or pie plate, stir together flour, Parmesan, and remaining ¾ teaspoon salt.

2. Preheat oven to 400°F. Dip chicken pieces first in egg-white mixture, then in flour mixture, coating chicken well. Place chicken on greased jelly-roll pan. Drizzle olive oil over chicken and bake 35 to 40 minutes, carefully turning chicken over midway, or until cooked through.

SPICY HERBED CHICKEN Stir ½ teaspoon cayenne pepper and 2 teaspoons dried basil, tarragon, or thyme into flour-Parmesan mixture in step 1.

Calories 439, Total Fat 20g, Saturated Fat 4.5g, Cholesterol 134mg, Sodium 872mg, Protein 39g, Carbohydrates 25g

Prep Time: 15 minutes
Cooking Time: 40 minutes
Makes 4 servings

NUTRITION INFORMATION
Per Serving
Calories 439
Total Fat 20g
Saturated Fat 4.5g
Cholesterol 134mg
Sodium 872mg
Protein 39g
Carbohydrates 25g

Baked Chicken Legs with Basil-Lemon Garnish

Baked tomatoes make a quick and easy side dish for the chicken: Halve two or more tomatoes, sprinkle the cut sides with a mixture of breadcrumbs and Parmesan, and slip them under the broiler for a few minutes, until the tomatoes are hot and the topping is golden.

- 2 tablespoons olive oil
- 1 clove garlic, peeled
- ½ teaspoon dried tarragon
- ¼ teaspoon crushed red pepper flakes
- 4 whole chicken legs (about 2½ pounds), split into drumsticks and thighs (page 14)
- 1 teaspoon salt
- ⅔ cup chopped fresh basil leaves
- 1½ teaspoons grated lemon zest
- 2 tablespoons fresh lemon juice

1. In small skillet, heat oil over low heat. Add garlic, tarragon, and red pepper flakes, and cook very slowly, turning garlic as it colors, 5 minutes or until oil is fragrant and garlic is golden brown. Discard garlic. Transfer herb oil to large bowl and cool to room temperature.

2. With your fingers, carefully loosen chicken skin without removing it. Add chicken legs to bowl with oil mixture and toss to coat, making sure some marinade gets under the skin.

3. Preheat broiler. Place chicken legs on broiler pan and sprinkle with ¾ teaspoon of salt. Broil 8 inches from heat for 20 minutes, turning pieces as they color, until cooked through.

4. Meanwhile, in small bowl, stir together basil, lemon zest, and remaining ¼ teaspoon salt. To serve, sprinkle lemon juice and then basil mixture over chicken.

Prep Time: 15 minutes
Cooking Time: 25 minutes
Makes 4 servings

NUTRITION INFORMATION
Per Serving
Calories 392
Total Fat 26g
Saturated Fat 6g
Cholesterol 128mg
Sodium 705mg
Protein 37g
Carbohydrates 2g

BAKED CHICKEN LEGS WITH BASIL-LEMON GARNISH

BROILED CITRUS DRUMSTICKS

Prep Time: 10 minutes
Cooking Time: 30 minutes
Makes 4 servings

Brown-Sugared Drumsticks

Though brown sugar may seem more appropriate for mixing into cookie dough, plenty of grilling sauces use sweetness as a counterpoint to a salty or tart taste. In the luscious coating for this chicken, the balance shifts a bit, letting the sugar play a starring role, with salty soy sauce and pungent black pepper as the balancing flavors.

- 4 tablespoons butter, melted
- 1 tablespoon soy sauce
- ⅔ cup packed dark brown sugar
- ¼ cup all-purpose flour
- ½ teaspoon salt
- ½ teaspoon freshly ground black pepper
- 8 chicken drumsticks (about 2½ pounds), skin removed

1. Preheat oven to 375°F. In shallow bowl or pie plate, stir together butter and soy sauce. In separate shallow bowl or pie plate, stir together brown sugar, flour, salt, and pepper. Coat chicken with butter mixture, then dredge in brown-sugar mixture, patting it on until well coated.

2. Generously grease jelly-roll pan. Place chicken on pan and bake for 15 minutes or until coating is set. Carefully turn chicken over and bake for 15 minutes longer or until coating is crisp and chicken is cooked through.

LOW FAT

Prep Time: 20 minutes plus
   marinating time
Cooking Time: 20 minutes
Makes 4 servings

Broiled Citrus Drumsticks

Separating grapefruit segments from the membranes takes some time and care. If you want to speed things up, halve each fruit crosswise (as if you were serving it on a plate), then carefully scoop out the half-segments with a serrated grapefruit spoon. Squeeze the juice from the grapefruit shells and measure it as directed.

- 1 large pink or white grapefruit
- 2 navel oranges
- 3 tablespoons honey
- 1¼ teaspoons salt
- 1 red bell pepper, cut into ¼-inch dice
- ¼ cup minced red onion
- 4 cloves garlic, crushed and peeled
- ¼ teaspoon cayenne pepper
- 8 chicken drumsticks (about 2½ pounds), skin removed
- 2 tablespoons olive oil

1. With paring knife, cut off and discard skin, white pith, and outer membrane of grapefruit. Working over bowl to catch juices, section grapefruit: Use paring knife to cut along both sides of each dividing membrane to release segments. Cut segments into ½-inch pieces and transfer to medium bowl. Squeeze any juice left in membranes into bowl. Pour grapefruit juice into measuring cup; you should have ½ cup (if not, supplement with orange juice in next step).

2. Repeat segmenting procedure for oranges; add orange segments to bowl with grapefruit. (If necessary, add orange juice to get ½ cup of citrus juice.) Stir 2 tablespoons of honey, ¼ teaspoon of salt, the bell pepper, and onion into bowl with citrus fruit. Cover citrus relish and refrigerate.

3. In medium bowl, stir together grapefruit juice, garlic, cayenne, and remaining 1 tablespoon honey and 1 teaspoon salt. Transfer to zip-seal plastic bag. Add chicken, seal bag, and shake to distribute marinade. Refrigerate at least 2 hours or up to 4 hours.

4. Preheat broiler. Add oil to bag with chicken and shake to combine. Place chicken on broiler pan and broil 6 inches from heat for 20 minutes, turning chicken as it colors, until cooked through. Serve with citrus relish.

BROILED LIME-MARINATED CHICKEN WITH OREGANO

Broiled Lime-Marinated Chicken with Oregano

Prep Time: 10 minutes plus
   marinating time
Cooking Time: 10 minutes
Makes 4 servings

NUTRITION INFORMATION
Per Serving
Calories 431
Total Fat 26g
Saturated Fat 7g
Cholesterol 136mg
Sodium 414mg
Protein 37g
Carbohydrates 11g

This marinade works equally well on chicken breasts or legs. For a light supper, team the broiled chicken with a tossed salad and skinny, crisp breadsticks. For a more substantial meal, round out the dish with buttered rice, couscous, or pasta, and a cooked vegetable such as sautéed summer squash or steamed asparagus.

- 3 tablespoons fresh lime juice
- 2 tablespoons honey
- 1 tablespoon olive oil
- 2 scallions, thinly sliced
- 1 tablespoon fresh oregano, finely chopped, or ½ teaspoon dried
- ½ teaspoon freshly ground black pepper
- ½ teaspoon salt
- ⅛ teaspoon ground nutmeg
- 8 chicken thighs (about 2½ pounds), skin on, boned (page 10)

1. In medium bowl, stir together lime juice, honey, oil, scallions, oregano, pepper, salt, and nutmeg. With your fingers, carefully loosen skin of chicken without removing it. Transfer lime mixture to large zip-seal plastic bag. Add chicken and toss to coat, making sure some marinade gets under the skin. Refrigerate at least 1 hour or up to 4 hours, turning bag occasionally to distribute marinade over chicken.

2. Preheat broiler. Lift chicken from its marinade and place skin-side down on broiler pan. Spoon marinade on top. Broil 8 inches from heat for 5 minutes. Turn skin-side up and broil for 3 to 5 minutes or until chicken is lightly browned and cooked through.

Jamaican Jerk Chicken

Prep Time: 15 minutes plus
   marinating time
Cooking Time: 25 minutes
Makes 4 servings

NUTRITION INFORMATION
Per Serving
Calories 538
Total Fat 31g
Saturated Fat 8g
Cholesterol 186mg
Sodium 1120mg
Protein 53g
Carbohydrates 10g

Nobody's absolutely positive why this lively Caribbean spice blend—and the foods cooked with it, primarily chicken and pork—are called "jerk." Call it something else if you don't like the name, but do try it—there's nothing quite like its singular mingling of sweetness, spice, and heat. Serve the chicken with a tropical salsa made with pineapple, banana, mango, or papaya and lime juice.

- 6 scallions, thinly sliced
- ⅓ cup red wine vinegar
- 2 tablespoons packed dark brown sugar
- 1 tablespoon olive oil
- 1¼ teaspoons ground allspice
- 1½ teaspoons salt
- 1 teaspoon freshly ground black pepper
- 2 teaspoons hot pepper sauce (red)
- 2½ pounds bone-in chicken thighs and drumsticks

1. In large bowl, stir together scallions, vinegar, brown sugar, oil, allspice, salt, and pepper. With your fingers, carefully loosen skin of chicken without removing it. Add chicken to bowl and toss to coat, making sure some marinade gets under the skin. Cover and refrigerate at least 4 hours or up to overnight.

2. Preheat broiler. Place chicken on broiler pan and broil 8 inches from heat, turning pieces often as they brown, for 25 minutes or until chicken is cooked through.

Greek Baked Chicken with Feta & Dill

The chicken thighs (or breasts, if you prefer) are stuffed under the skin with a mixture of spinach and feta, flavored with lemon and fresh dill. Orzo, the pasta shape most associated with Greece, is a natural choice to serve on the side.

- 1 tablespoon olive oil
- ¼ cup minced onion
- 2 cloves garlic, minced
- 1 package (10 ounces) frozen chopped spinach, thawed and squeezed dry
- 6 ounces feta cheese, crumbled
- ¼ cup snipped fresh dill
- ½ teaspoon grated lemon zest
- 8 bone-in chicken thighs, with skin (about 2 pounds)
- 2 tablespoons fresh lemon juice
- ½ teaspoon salt

1. In small skillet, heat oil over low heat. Add onion and garlic, and cook, stirring frequently, 5 minutes or until tender. Add spinach and cook, stirring frequently, 2 minutes or until dry. Transfer spinach mixture to large bowl. Stir in feta, dill, and lemon zest.

2. Preheat oven to 375°F. With your fingers, carefully loosen skin of chicken without removing it. Push cheese mixture under skin, then press skin to seal. Place chicken in 7 x 11-inch baking dish and sprinkle with lemon juice and salt. Bake for 40 minutes or until chicken is cooked through.

Prep Time: 20 minutes
Cooking Time: 50 minutes
Makes 4 servings

NUTRITION INFORMATION
Per Serving
Calories 456
Total Fat 31g
Saturated Fat 12g
Cholesterol 147mg
Sodium 916mg
Protein 38g
Carbohydrates 7g

Maple Syrup-Baked Chicken Thighs with Sweet Potatoes

A tangy blend of maple syrup, ketchup, vinegar, and spices flavors both the chicken and the sweet potatoes. The potatoes need more cooking time than the chicken, so they bake for 20 minutes before the chicken is added to the pan. For a side salad, try romaine lettuce and sweet red onion.

- ⅓ cup maple syrup
- ¼ cup ketchup
- 2 tablespoons cider vinegar
- 1 tablespoon butter
- 2 cloves garlic, minced
- 1 teaspoon ground ginger
- ¾ teaspoon salt
- ½ teaspoon freshly ground black pepper
- ¼ teaspoon cayenne pepper
- 2 tablespoons olive oil
- 2 pounds sweet potatoes, peeled and cut into ½-inch cubes
- 8 bone-in chicken thighs (about 2 pounds), skin removed

1. Preheat oven to 375°F. In small saucepan, stir together maple syrup, ketchup, vinegar, butter, garlic, ginger, salt, black pepper, and cayenne. Bring to a simmer over low heat and cook 10 minutes to melt butter and develop flavors.

2. Meanwhile, pour oil into 9 x 13-inch broilerproof baking pan. Add sweet potatoes, toss to coat, and bake for 20 minutes. Place chicken on top of potatoes and spoon maple syrup mixture on top. Bake for 25 minutes or until chicken is cooked through and potatoes are tender.

3. Preheat broiler. Broil 8 inches from heat for 1 to 2 minutes or until chicken is caramelized.

IN A HURRY?
Substitute 1 cup bottled tomato-based barbecue sauce for sauce made in step 1.

LOW FAT

Prep Time: 15 minutes
Cooking Time: 1 hour
Makes 4 servings

NUTRITION INFORMATION
Per Serving
Calories 500
Total Fat 15g
Saturated Fat 4g
Cholesterol 115mg
Sodium 779mg
Protein 29g
Carbohydrates 63g

MAPLE SYRUP-BAKED CHICKEN THIGHS WITH SWEET POTATOES

Baked Chicken Thighs
with Avocado Relish

An unripe avocado is just not worth bothering with—and a ripe one can be hard to find in the supermarket. So shop a few days ahead of time, selecting a firm, unbruised avocado, then place it in a loosely closed paper bag and leave it at room temperature until it yields to thumb pressure.

1½   teaspoons ground cumin
1   teaspoon ground coriander
1   teaspoon chili powder
¾   teaspoon dried oregano
1¼   teaspoons salt
8   bone-in chicken thighs (about 2 pounds), skin removed
1   pound plum tomatoes, coarsely chopped
1   avocado, cut into ½-inch cubes
⅓   cup chopped cilantro
¼   cup minced red onion
2   tablespoons red wine vinegar

1. Preheat oven to 350°F. In small bowl, stir together cumin, ground coriander, chili powder, oregano, and ½ teaspoon of salt. Rub mixture into both sides of chicken. Place on baking sheet and bake 25 minutes or until cooked through.

2. Meanwhile, in large bowl, stir together tomatoes, avocado, cilantro, onion, vinegar, and remaining ¾ teaspoon salt. Serve chicken with avocado relish on top.

Prep Time: 15 minutes
Cooking Time: 25 minutes
Makes 4 servings

NUTRITION INFORMATION
Per Serving
Calories 270
Total Fat 13g
Saturated Fat 2.5g
Cholesterol 107mg
Sodium 861mg
Protein 28g
Carbohydrates 11g

Broiled Chicken Thighs
with Red Onion Marmalade

The slow-cooked, orange-flavored onion relish is the real star of this recipe, and you might want to make an extra batch: The sweet-and-sour "marmalade" can be served over any plain roasted, baked, or broiled chicken (turkey, too). And it makes a great topping for a chicken or turkey burger.

3   cloves garlic, minced
½   teaspoon plus 2 tablespoons sugar
1   teaspoon dried thyme
1   teaspoon salt
½   teaspoon freshly ground black pepper
½   teaspoon ground ginger
8   skinless, boneless chicken thighs (about 1½ pounds)
3   tablespoons olive oil
1½   pounds red onions, halved and thinly sliced
2   tablespoons thinly slivered orange zest
⅓   cup orange juice
2   tablespoons balsamic vinegar
1   tablespoon tomato paste

1. In large bowl, stir together garlic, ½ teaspoon of sugar, the thyme, ½ teaspoon of salt, the pepper, and ginger. Add chicken and toss well to coat. Add 1 tablespoon of oil and toss again. Cover and refrigerate at least 30 minutes or up to overnight.

2. In large skillet, heat remaining 2 tablespoons oil over medium heat. Add onions and remaining 2 tablespoons sugar and cook, stirring frequently, 20 minutes or until onions are lightly browned. Add orange zest, orange juice, vinegar, tomato paste, and remaining ½ teaspoon salt, and cook, stirring frequently, 15 minutes or until onions are very soft, glossy, and flavorful.

3. Preheat broiler. Place chicken on broiler pan and broil 6 inches from heat for 5 minutes per side or until cooked through. Serve chicken with red onion marmalade spooned on top.

Prep Time: 20 minutes plus marinating time
Cooking Time: 45 minutes
Makes 4 servings

NUTRITION INFORMATION
Per Serving
Calories 410
Total Fat 17g
Saturated Fat 3g
Cholesterol 141mg
Sodium 781mg
Protein 37g
Carbohydrates 28g

BAKED CHICKEN THIGHS WITH AVOCADO RELISH

BROILED CHICKEN THIGHS TERIYAKI

Prep Time: 10 minutes plus
    marinating time
Cooking Time: 15 minutes
Makes 4 servings

NUTRITION INFORMATION

Per Serving
Calories 322
Total Fat 9g
Saturated Fat 2.5g
Cholesterol 188mg
Sodium 802mg
Protein 46g
Carbohydrates 8g

Broiled Chicken Thighs Teriyaki

You can buy bottled teriyaki marinade, but making the sauce from scratch (in just minutes) is bound to be more rewarding. The teriyaki sauce also works well with chicken kabobs and drumsticks. Rice is a must with this meal; add crisp-tender vegetables or a salad and you're set.

½   cup lower-sodium soy sauce
½   cup dry sherry
2   tablespoons light brown sugar
1   tablespoon light corn syrup
1   clove garlic, crushed and peeled
8   skinless, boneless chicken thighs
    (about 2 pounds)
2   scallions, thinly sliced

1. In small saucepan, stir together soy sauce, sherry, brown sugar, corn syrup, and garlic. Bring to a boil over medium heat and cook 1 minute or until sugar has dissolved. Cool to room temperature. Transfer mixture to zip-seal plastic bag, add chicken, close bag, and shake to distribute marinade. Refrigerate at least 4 hours or up to overnight.

2. Preheat broiler. Place chicken on broiler pan. Spoon half of marinade over chicken and broil 6 inches from heat for 5 minutes. Turn chicken over, spoon remaining marinade on top, and broil 5 minutes longer or until chicken is cooked through. Serve chicken sprinkled with scallions.

Prep Time: 20 minutes
Cooking Time: 10 minutes
Makes 4 servings

NUTRITION INFORMATION

Per Serving
Calories 320
Total Fat 17g
Saturated Fat 3g
Cholesterol 141mg
Sodium 830mg
Protein 34g
Carbohydrates 6g

Broiled Chicken Thighs with Tomato-Olive Spread

For a head start on dinner, make the tomato-olive spread the night before; refrigerate it in a covered container. The next day, you'll need just 10 minutes from start to finish. Don't overlook the luscious variation: a round of chewy focaccia topped with the tomato-olive spread, chicken, and mozzarella.

2   tablespoons olive oil
2   cloves garlic, minced
¼   cup Calamata olives, pitted and
    coarsely chopped
4   oil-packed sun-dried tomato halves, drained
2   tablespoons chopped fresh basil leaves
2   tablespoons tomato paste
¼   teaspoon grated orange zest
2   tablespoons orange juice
1¼ teaspoons dried rosemary, crumbled
¾   teaspoon salt
8   skinless, boneless chicken thighs
    (about 1½ pounds)

1. In small skillet, heat 1 tablespoon of oil over low heat. Add garlic and cook 30 seconds or until soft. Transfer to food processor. Add olives, sun-dried tomatoes, basil, tomato paste, orange zest, and orange juice, and process until mixture is of spreadlike consistency.

2. In small bowl, stir together rosemary, remaining 1 tablespoon oil, and salt. Rub on both sides of chicken.

3. Preheat broiler. Place chicken on broiler pan and broil 6 inches from heat for 5 minutes per side or until cooked through. Spread hot chicken with some of the olive mixture and serve.

CHICKEN FOCACCIA Reduce chicken to 1 pound. Make olive mixture as directed in step 1. In step 2, omit oil and rub chicken with ¾ teaspoon rosemary, crumbled, and ¼ teaspoon salt. Broil chicken as directed in step 3 and when cool enough to handle, cut into ½-inch chunks. Preheat oven to 450°F. Brush 9-inch-round store-bought focaccia bread with 1 tablespoon olive oil. Bake for 10 minutes. Spread olive mixture over focaccia and top with chicken and 4 ounces shredded mozzarella cheese. Bake for 5 minutes or until cheese has melted.

Calories 437, Total Fat 26g, Saturated Fat 7g, Cholesterol 118mg, Sodium 740mg, Protein 32g, Carbohydrates 19g

Yogurt Chicken
with Hazelnut Coating

With a natural sweetness no other nut can match, hazelnuts (or filberts) are prized for cooking and baking. After shelling, they're still clad in a papery brown skin, which is slightly bitter. To remove it, toast (or blanch) the nut; after this treatment, most of the skin will rub right off.

1 cup plain low-fat yogurt

3 tablespoons finely chopped mango chutney

½ teaspoon grated lime zest

1 tablespoon fresh lime juice

¾ teaspoon salt

¼ teaspoon cayenne pepper

1¼ cups hazelnuts

2 tablespoons butter, melted

1 large egg

8 skinless, boneless chicken thighs (about 1½ pounds)

1. In medium bowl, stir together yogurt, chutney, lime zest, lime juice, ¼ teaspoon of salt, and the cayenne until well combined. Cover and refrigerate until serving time.

2. Preheat oven to 375°F. Toast hazelnuts in oven for 10 minutes or until their skins begin to pop. Transfer to kitchen towel and rub until skins come off (some skin will remain; do not worry). Return nuts to oven and bake for 5 minutes or until lightly browned. Cool to room temperature, transfer to food processor, and process until finely ground. Transfer ground nuts to shallow pan or pie plate. Add melted butter and remaining ½ teaspoon salt, and toss to combine.

3. In shallow bowl, beat egg with 1 tablespoon of water. Dip chicken first in egg mixture, then in nuts, patting them into chicken. Transfer to lightly greased baking sheet. Bake for 25 minutes or until chicken is cooked through and nuts are golden brown. Serve yogurt sauce alongside.

Prep Time: 15 minutes
Cooking Time: 40 minutes
Makes 4 servings

NUTRITION INFORMATION
Per Serving
Calories 591
Total Fat 38g
Saturated Fat 8g
Cholesterol 213mg
Sodium 825mg
Protein 43g
Carbohydrates 21g

Apricot-Glazed Thighs

Those jars of jam and preserves in your refrigerator door—apricot, plum, cherry, marmalade—can do double duty at dinner time as glazes for meat and poultry. All they need is a touch of tartness or heat to balance their sweetness. This glaze has both, in the form of lemon, mustard, and ginger.

1 cup apricot jam

¾ teaspoon grated lemon zest

3 tablespoons fresh lemon juice

1 tablespoon spicy brown mustard

2 teaspoons olive oil

½ teaspoon ground ginger

1½ teaspoons chili powder

1 teaspoon ground cumin

1 teaspoon salt

8 bone-in chicken thighs (about 2 pounds), skin removed

1. Preheat broiler. In small saucepan, melt jam over low heat. Push through fine-meshed sieve into medium bowl. Stir in lemon zest, lemon juice, mustard, oil, and ginger.

2. In large bowl, stir together chili powder, cumin, and salt. Add chicken and toss well to coat. Place chicken on broiler pan and brush with half of apricot mixture. Broil 8 inches from heat for 10 minutes. Turn chicken over and brush with remaining apricot mixture. Broil for 6 minutes or until chicken is cooked through.

LOW FAT
QUICK TO FIX

Prep Time: 10 minutes
Cooking Time: 20 minutes
Makes 4 servings

NUTRITION INFORMATION
Per Serving
Calories 380
Total Fat 8g
Saturated Fat 1.5g
Cholesterol 107mg
Sodium 781mg
Protein 26g
Carbohydrates 53g

YOGURT CHICKEN WITH HAZELNUT COATING

Three-Mushroom Loaf

You can substitute button mushrooms for the fresh shiitakes, but the dried shiitakes are a necessity.

- 1 package (.35 ounce) dried shiitake mushrooms
- ½ cup boiling water
- 1 tablespoon olive oil
- ½ pound sweet Italian sausage, casings removed
- 2 shallots, minced, or 2 scallions, thinly sliced
- ½ pound fresh shiitake mushrooms, stems trimmed and caps finely chopped
- ½ pound button mushrooms, finely chopped
- ⅓ cup dry red wine
- 1 teaspoon salt
- ¾ teaspoon dried rosemary, crumbled
- 2 slices firm-textured white bread (2 ounces), crumbled
- ¼ cup heavy or whipping cream
- 1 pound ground chicken
- ¾ teaspoon freshly ground black pepper

1. In small bowl, soak dried shiitakes in boiling water. Let stand 20 minutes or until mushrooms are soft. With slotted spoon, scoop mushrooms from soaking liquid, reserving liquid. Rinse mushrooms and finely chop. Strain liquid through paper towel-lined sieve; set aside.

2. In large skillet, heat oil over medium heat. Add sausage and cook 2 minutes. Add shallots and cook, stirring frequently, 5 minutes or until shallots are soft. Add fresh shiitakes, button mushrooms, and soaked shiitake mushrooms, and cook, stirring frequently, 5 minutes or until fresh mushrooms are soft.

3. Add mushroom soaking liquid to pan, increase heat to high, and cook 3 minutes or until evaporated. Add wine, ¼ teaspoon of salt, and the rosemary, and cook, stirring frequently, 5 minutes or until liquid has evaporated and mushrooms are very tender. Transfer to large bowl.

4. Preheat oven to 350°F. Add bread crumbs and cream, and stir to combine. Add chicken, pepper, and remaining ¾ teaspoon salt, and mix well. Pack mixture into 8½ x 4½-inch loaf pan. Bake for 45 minutes or until juices run clear when meatloaf is pierced with knife. Cool 10 minutes before slicing.

TO REDUCE THE FAT

In step 1, increase dried shiitake mushrooms to 2 packages and boiling water to ¾ cup. In step 2, omit sausage and use large nonstick skillet to cook shallots and mushrooms as directed. In step 3, increase wine to ½ cup and salt to 1¼ teaspoons. In step 4, substitute milk for cream. Cut 1 pound skinless, boneless chicken breast into large chunks and process in food processor until finely ground. Substitute this for ground chicken. Bake as directed.

Calories 270, Total Fat 6g, Saturated Fat 1.5g, Cholesterol 68mg, Sodium 888mg, Protein 31g, Carbohydrates 18g

Prep Time: 20 minutes plus mushroom soaking time
Cooking Time: 1 hour 5 minutes
Makes 4 servings

NUTRITION INFORMATION
Per Serving
Calories 544
Total Fat 37g
Saturated Fat 13g
Cholesterol 158mg
Sodium 1176mg
Protein 32g
Carbohydrates 16g

Chicken Meatloaf with Apricots

This may be the most delicate meatloaf ever. You'll love the leftovers, too, on a roll with mustard.

- 1 tablespoon olive oil
- 1 small onion, finely chopped
- 2 cloves garlic, minced
- 2 slices firm-textured white bread, crumbled
- ¼ cup milk
- 1 pound ground chicken
- 1 large egg plus 1 egg yolk
- ½ cup chopped cilantro
- ½ cup dried apricots, finely chopped
- 1½ teaspoons ground cumin
- 1 teaspoon ground coriander
- 1 teaspoon salt
- ½ teaspoon freshly ground black pepper

1. Preheat oven to 350°F. In small skillet, heat oil over low heat. Add onion and garlic, and cook, stirring frequently, 7 minutes or until onion is soft. Transfer to large bowl. Add bread and milk, and stir to combine. Add chicken, whole egg, egg yolk, cilantro, apricots, cumin, coriander, salt, and pepper, and mix well.

2. Pack mixture into 8½ x 4½-inch loaf pan, smoothing top. Bake for 45 minutes or until top is firm to the touch and juices run clear when meatloaf is pierced with knife. Cool 10 minutes before slicing.

Prep Time: 20 minutes
Cooking Time: 55 minutes
Makes 4 servings

NUTRITION INFORMATION
Per Serving
Calories 341
Total Fat 17g
Saturated Fat 4g
Cholesterol 203mg
Sodium 781mg
Protein 25g
Carbohydrates 21g

CHICKEN MEATLOAF WITH APRICOTS

Barbecues
& Picnics

The classic picnic basket packed to the brim with fried chicken and all the fixings is just one of many options for eating al fresco. If grilling is your thing, go beyond burgers with skewered chicken and shrimp, Mexican-style fajitas, or even chicken-topped pizzas cooked over the coals.

Chicken Salad-Stuffed Deviled Eggs

Here, two picnic favorites turn up in tandem. Instead of bottled mayonnaise, the salad is dressed with olive oil, lemon juice, and Dijon mustard—the basic ingredients of mayonnaise, but fresher.

Prep Time: 15 minutes
Cooking Time: 20 minutes
Makes 12 stuffed egg halves

NUTRITION INFORMATION
Per Egg Half
Calories 90
Total Fat 6g
Saturated Fat 1.5g
Cholesterol 116mg
Sodium 167mg
Protein 7g
Carbohydrates 1g

6   large eggs
3   tablespoons olive oil
3   tablespoons fresh lemon juice
1   tablespoon Dijon mustard
½   teaspoon salt
¼   teaspoon freshly ground black pepper
1   cup finely chopped cooked chicken breasts or thighs—leftover or poached (page 17)
¼   cup minced red bell pepper
¼   cup minced onion

1. Place eggs in large pot of cold water. Bring to a boil. Boil 2 minutes, turn off heat, cover, and let stand 17 minutes. Drain, run under cold water, and peel. Halve eggs lengthwise and scoop yolks into large bowl.

2. Add oil, lemon juice, mustard, salt, and black pepper to yolks and stir until smooth. Stir in chicken, bell pepper, and onion. Mound chicken mixture into egg whites. Cover and refrigerate until serving time.

Caribbean Chicken with Banana Chutney

Before baking, these chicken thighs are rubbed with a hot and sweet curry-pepper mixture.

Prep Time: 20 minutes plus marinating time
Cooking Time: 1 hour
Makes 4 servings

NUTRITION INFORMATION
Per Serving
Calories 499
Total Fat 11g
Saturated Fat 2.5g
Cholesterol 141mg
Sodium 1177mg
Protein 36g
Carbohydrates 67g

BANANA CHUTNEY:
1   tablespoon olive oil
1   large onion, finely chopped
2   cloves garlic, finely chopped
1   red bell pepper, cut into ¼-inch dice
⅓   cup packed light brown sugar
⅓   cup red wine vinegar
1   teaspoon freshly ground black pepper
1   teaspoon curry powder
½   teaspoon ground ginger
½   teaspoon salt
⅓   cup raisins
1½ pounds ripe bananas, cut into ½-inch-thick slices

CARIBBEAN SPICE-RUBBED CHICKEN:
2½ teaspoons freshly ground black pepper
2½ teaspoons curry powder
1   tablespoon light brown sugar
2½ teaspoons ground ginger
1¼ teaspoons salt
8   skinless, boneless chicken thighs (about 1½ pounds)

1. Prepare Banana Chutney: In large skillet, heat oil over medium heat. Add onion and garlic, and cook, stirring frequently, 7 minutes or until onion is soft. Stir in bell pepper and cook 5 minutes or until crisp-tender. Stir in brown sugar, vinegar, black pepper, curry powder, ginger, and salt, and bring to a boil. Add raisins and bananas, and cook, stirring occasionally, 15 minutes or until chutney is thick and fully flavored. Cool chutney to room temperature, cover, and refrigerate.

2. Meanwhile, make Caribbean Spice-Rubbed Chicken: In large bowl, stir together black pepper, curry powder, brown sugar, ginger, and salt. Add chicken, toss well to coat, cover, and refrigerate at least 1 hour or up to overnight.

3. Preheat oven to 400°F. Place chicken on baking sheet and bake for 30 minutes or until crisp and cooked through. Cool to room temperature before packing for a picnic. Pack chutney and chicken separately.

HOT WINGS WITH DIPPING SAUCE In step 1, make chutney as directed, but when cool, process in food processor or blender to coarse puree. Stir ⅓ cup plain low-fat yogurt into purée, refrigerate, and serve as a dipping sauce with baked wings. Substitute 4 pounds chicken wings (wing tips discarded) for thighs. Marinate and bake chicken as directed.
Makes 8 servings: Calories 402, Total Fat 19g, Saturated Fat 5g, Cholesterol 72mg, Sodium 592mg, Protein 25g, Carbohydrates 34g

CARIBBEAN CHICKEN WITH BANANA CHUTNEY

Grilled Chicken & Corn Pizza

Suffused with great smoky flavor, this summer-special pizza is cooked over the fire and topped with grilled chicken and vegetables. The Sausage, Mushroom & Red Onion Pizzas (page 41) can also be cooked this way.

- 1 tablespoon olive oil
- 1 tablespoon fresh lemon juice
- 1½ teaspoons dried oregano
- ¾ teaspoon ground cumin
- ½ teaspoon salt
- ¾ pound skinless, boneless chicken breasts
- 1 ear of corn, shucked
- 1 medium red onion, cut into 4 thick slices
- 1 pound store-bought pizza or bread dough
- 2 cups mozzarella cheese, shredded (8 ounces)
- 2 large tomatoes, seeded and finely chopped

1. Preheat grill to medium-high. In large bowl, stir together oil, lemon juice, oregano, cumin, and salt. Add chicken and toss until well coated. Rinse corn to wet it.

2. Place chicken, corn, and onion on grill, and grill 6 inches from heat for following amounts of time: Grill corn 15 minutes or until lightly charred all over. Grill onion 4 minutes per side or until lightly charred. Grill chicken 3 minutes per side or until cooked through. When ingredients are cool, separate onion into rings, then use a sharp paring knife to cut corn from cob and cut chicken into 1-inch chunks.

3. Shape dough into 12-inch round. Lightly oil grill rack. Place dough on rack and grill 6 inches from heat for 3 minutes or until dough begins to puff. Watch dough carefully and give it a couple of quarter-turns to be sure it isn't sticking to grill. Turn dough over (see technique photo, at right) and top with mozzarella, tomatoes, corn, onion, and chicken. Grill pizza for 10 to 15 minutes or until dough is crispy, rotating it occasionally so it cooks evenly. Use tongs to slide pizza off grill and onto a serving platter.

GRILLED SALSA & PEPPERJACK PIZZA Marinate chicken as directed in step 1. Omit corn. In step 2, grill chicken and onion as directed. In step 3, shape, grill, and top pizza as directed, but omit tomatoes and use ½ pound shredded pepperjack cheese instead of mozzarella. Just before serving, top grilled pizza with ½ cup bottled mild or medium-hot salsa and ⅓ cup chopped cilantro.

Calories 660, Total Fat 26g, Saturated Fat 11g, Cholesterol 109mg, Sodium 2166mg, Protein 46g, Carbohydrates 64g

---

LOW FAT

Prep Time: 20 minutes
Cooking Time: 30 minutes
Makes 4 servings

NUTRITION INFORMATION
Per Serving
Calories 620
Total Fat 21g
Saturated Fat 8.5g
Cholesterol 94mg
Sodium 1682mg
Protein 44g
Carbohydrates 68g

TECHNIQUE

GRILLING PIZZA DOUGH

After grilling the pizza dough on the first side, carefully turn the dough over with tongs, getting the tongs as close to the center of the pizza round as possible. After turning the dough, use the tongs to slide it back to the middle of the grill before topping the pizza and browning the second side.

HINTS & TIPS

➤ Remove the grill rack from the fire after cooking the chicken and vegetables. Let the rack cool and oil it before grilling the round of dough, either by brushing it with oil or spraying it with nonstick cooking spray. **If using cooking spray, apply it at a good distance from the fire to avoid flare-ups.**

➤ Sturdy, long-handled barbecue tongs are always good to have on hand when you're grilling, but they are actually a necessity for flipping over a round of pizza dough.

➤ To remove corn from the cob, stand the ear of corn on end and slice off the kernels with downward strokes of a paring knife.

GRILLED CHICKEN & CORN PIZZA

Orange Maple-Glazed Chicken Breasts

This sweet marinade is liable to burn and stick to the grill rack, so you'll want to start soaking the rack as soon as the chicken is served. An easy way to accomplish this is by dampening several thicknesses of newspaper with the garden hose, then wrapping the rack in the paper.

- ⅓ cup orange juice
- 2 tablespoons maple syrup
- ½ teaspoon salt
- ½ teaspoon dried rosemary, crumbled
- ½ teaspoon freshly ground black pepper
- ⅛ teaspoon ground allspice
- 1 clove garlic, crushed and peeled
- 4 skinless, boneless chicken breast halves (about 1½ pounds)
- 4 teaspoons olive oil

1. In medium bowl, stir together orange juice, maple syrup, salt, rosemary, pepper, allspice, and garlic. Add chicken, transfer to zip-seal plastic bag, seal, and refrigerate 30 minutes or up to overnight.

2. Preheat grill to medium-high. Lift chicken from marinade. Place chicken on grill and brush with half of marinade and half of oil. Grill 6 inches from heat for 4 minutes. Turn chicken over, brush with remaining marinade and oil, and grill for 3 to 4 minutes or until chicken is cooked through.

LOW FAT

Prep Time: 5 minutes plus marinating time
Cooking Time: 10 minutes
Makes 4 servings

NUTRITION INFORMATION
Per Serving
Calories 265
Total Fat 7g
Saturated Fat 1g
Cholesterol 99mg
Sodium 402mg
Protein 40g
Carbohydrates 9g

Chicken & Roasted Pepper Pinwheels

For an extremely up-to-date picnic, bring chicken-cheese "wraps" made with lahvash (a soft Middle-Eastern bread sold in large rounds or rectangles). The easiest way is to carry the foil-wrapped rolls to the picnic whole, then cut them once you've settled in your picnic spot.

- 1 clove garlic, peeled
- 2 packages (3 ounces each) cream cheese, at room temperature
- ⅔ cup bottled roasted red peppers, rinsed and drained
- ¼ cup fresh basil leaves
- ½ teaspoon salt
- 2 round lahvash bread sheets for wraps (12-inch diameter, 4 ounces each)
- 3 cups shredded cooked chicken breasts or thighs—leftover or poached (page 17)
- ¼ pound Monterey Jack cheese, shredded (1 cup)
- ½ cup Calamata olives, pitted and coarsely chopped

1. In small pot of boiling water, blanch garlic 2 minutes. Drain. In food processor, combine cream cheese, roasted peppers, basil, salt, and garlic, and process until smooth. Spread mixture onto one side of each lahvash.

2. Sprinkle chicken, cheese, and olives on top. Tightly roll each lahvash up. Wrap in foil and refrigerate at least 4 hours. Unwrap and cut each roll into 8 pinwheels.

GREEK-STYLE PINWHEELS WITH FETA, MINT & DILL In step 1, blanch garlic as directed. In food processor, combine garlic with cream cheese (increase to 8 ounces), 4 ounces crumbled feta cheese, ¼ cup fresh mint, 1 teaspoon grated lemon zest, 1 tablespoon fresh lemon juice, and ½ teaspoon salt; omit roasted pepper and basil; process until smooth. Spread on lahvash as directed. In step 2, omit Monterey Jack cheese. Sprinkle chicken, olives, and ½ cup snipped fresh dill over cream-cheese mixture. Roll up, refrigerate, and cut as directed.
Calories 173, Total Fat 8.5g, Saturated Fat 4.5g, Cholesterol 44mg, Sodium 335mg, Protein 12g, Carbohydrates 11g

LEFTOVERS

Prep Time: 15 minutes plus chilling time
Cooking Time: 2 minutes
Makes 16 pieces

NUTRITION INFORMATION
Per Piece
Calories 169
Total Fat 8g
Saturated Fat 4g
Cholesterol 42mg
Sodium 293mg
Protein 12g
Carbohydrates 11g

ORANGE MAPLE-GLAZED CHICKEN BREASTS

PERFECT PICNIC CHICKEN

Prep Time: 15 minutes plus
    marinating time
Cooking Time: 45 minutes
Makes 8 servings

NUTRITION INFORMATION

Per Serving

Calories 524

Total Fat 26g

Saturated Fat 7.5g

Cholesterol 156mg

Sodium 756mg

Protein 52g

Carbohydrates 17g

HINTS & TIPS

➤ Although yellow and white cornmeal are nutritionally pretty much equal, yellow cornmeal will give the chicken a more appetizing golden color.

➤ When placing the chicken pieces on the baking pans, don't crowd them together, or they will steam instead of developing a crispy, baked coating.

➤ Wrap these chicken pieces individually in foil or, for a homey, old-fashioned air, in waxed paper. Place the wrapped chicken pieces in a cooler for transporting to a picnic.

Perfect Picnic Chicken

This oven-baked chicken, breaded with a mixture of flour and cornmeal, is delicious cold, and the coating is sturdy enough to stand up to a little off-road travel. For a real camp-style meal, you could make some on-the-spot accompaniments over an open fire, such as corn on the cob, grilled vegetable packets, or roasted potatoes. And, of course, toasted marshmallows for dessert.

1½ cups plain low-fat yogurt

2 tablespoons cider vinegar

2 teaspoons salt

2 whole chickens (about 3½ pounds each), cut into 10 pieces each (page 14)

1½ cups flour

⅔ cup yellow cornmeal

1 teaspoon freshly ground black pepper

1. In large bowl, stir together yogurt, vinegar, and ¾ teaspoon of salt until well combined. Add chicken, cover, and refrigerate 1 hour or up to 4 hours.

2. Preheat oven to 425°F. On plate or sheet of waxed paper, combine flour, cornmeal, pepper, and 1 teaspoon of salt. Dredge chicken in flour mixture, shaking off excess. Generously grease 2 jelly-roll pans.

3. Place half of chicken on each pan. Bake for 20 minutes or until bottom crust is set. Turn pieces over and bake for 20 to 25 minutes longer or until cooked through. Sprinkle remaining ¼ teaspoon salt over chicken. Cool to room temperature before wrapping or refrigerating.

CHILI-SPICED PICNIC CHICKEN Marinate chicken as directed in step 1. In step 2, add 1½ teaspoons chili powder, 1 teaspoon ground cumin, and 1 teaspoon ground coriander to flour-cornmeal mixture. Dredge and bake chicken as directed.

Calories 524, Total Fat 26g, Saturated Fat 7.5g, Cholesterol 156mg, Sodium 756mg, Protein 52g, Carbohydrates 17g

HONEY-CITRUS PICNIC CHICKEN In step 1, substitute 2 tablespoons fresh lemon juice for vinegar. Add 3 tablespoons honey, 1 teaspoon grated lime zest, and 1 teaspoon grated lemon zest to yogurt mixture. Marinate, dredge, and bake chicken as directed.

Calories 549, Total Fat 26g, Saturated Fat 7.5g, Cholesterol 156mg, Sodium 756mg, Protein 52g, Carbohydrates 24g

MOROCCAN-STYLE PICNIC CHICKEN In step 1, substitute 2 tablespoons fresh lemon juice for vinegar. Marinate chicken as directed. In step 2, add 2 teaspoons paprika, 1½ teaspoons turmeric, 1 teaspoon ground coriander, and 1 teaspoon ground ginger to flour-cornmeal mixture. Dredge and bake chicken as directed.

Calories 524, Total Fat 26g, Saturated Fat 7.5g, Cholesterol 156mg, Sodium 756mg, Protein 52g, Carbohydrates 17g

Indonesian Coconut Chicken Legs

Crunchy and slightly sweet, shredded coconut gives these spiced chicken legs a very special texture. Hidden underneath the coconut is a curry-like coating—a mixture of coriander, turmeric, ginger, and cumin. Partner the chicken with a salad of blanched green beans dressed with sesame oil and balsamic vinegar, or a new potato salad tossed with the same dressing.

Prep Time: 15 minutes plus
   chilling time
Cooking Time: 30 minutes
Makes 4 servings

NUTRITION INFORMATION
Per Serving
Calories 531
Total Fat 33g
Saturated Fat 16g
Cholesterol 130mg
Sodium 870mg
Protein 36g
Carbohydrates 24g

- 2 teaspoons ground coriander
- 2 teaspoons turmeric
- 1 teaspoon ground ginger
- 1 teaspoon ground cumin
- 1 teaspoon salt
- ½ teaspoon freshly ground black pepper
- 2 egg whites
- 2½ cups shredded coconut
- 4 whole chicken legs (about 2½ pounds), split into drumsticks and thighs (page 14), skin removed
- 3 tablespoons vegetable oil

1. In shallow bowl or pie plate, stir together coriander, turmeric, ginger, cumin, salt, and pepper. In another shallow bowl, beat egg whites with 1 tablespoon of water. Place coconut on plate or sheet of waxed paper. Dip chicken first in egg mixture, then in curry mixture, and then in coconut. Place on plate and refrigerate, uncovered, at least 1 hour or up to 8 hours for coating to set.

2. Preheat oven to 400°F. Place chicken on lightly greased jelly-roll pan. Drizzle oil over chicken. Bake 30 minutes, turning chicken over midway, until chicken is cooked through and coating is crisp. Let cool to room temperature before packing.

Marinated Chicken Legs with Plums

Here's a fine centerpiece for an upscale picnic—a tailgate dinner before an open-air concert, perhaps. Carry the plums in a separate container and spoon them on at serving time. If you can't find Chinese hoisin sauce, substitute plum jam. The marinade is also great on chicken kabobs.

LOW FAT

Prep Time: 15 minutes plus
   marinating time
Cooking Time: 25 minutes
Makes 4 servings

NUTRITION INFORMATION
Per Serving
Calories 373
Total Fat 11g
Saturated Fat 3g
Cholesterol 135mg
Sodium 1026mg
Protein 34g
Carbohydrates 31g

- ⅓ cup hoisin sauce
- 3 tablespoons lower-sodium soy sauce
- 1 tablespoon fresh lemon juice
- 2 teaspoons vegetable oil
- ¾ teaspoon freshly ground black pepper
- ½ teaspoon ground cinnamon
- 4 whole chicken legs (about 2½ pounds), split into drumsticks and thighs (page 14), skin removed
- 2 teaspoons butter
- 1 pound plums, cut into ½-inch chunks
- 1 tablespoon sugar
- 1 scallion, thinly sliced

1. In large bowl, whisk together hoisin sauce, soy sauce, lemon juice, oil, ½ teaspoon of pepper, and the cinnamon. Add chicken and toss to coat. Cover and refrigerate at least 1 hour or up to overnight.

2. Preheat oven to 400°F. Place chicken and its marinade on jelly-roll pan and bake for 25 minutes or until cooked through.

3. Meanwhile, in large skillet, heat butter over medium heat. Add plums, sugar, and remaining ¼ teaspoon pepper, and cook, stirring frequently, 10 minutes or until plums are tender. Add scallion and toss to combine.

4. Let chicken cool to room temperature before packing. Pack chicken and plum sauce separately.

MARINATED CHICKEN LEGS WITH PLUMS

Chicken Calzones with Two Cheeses

Calzones could be described as pizza turnovers: They're circles of dough, stuffed with pizza-like fillings and folded to make half-rounds. These hefty calzones contain shredded chicken, spinach, fresh basil, and lots of melty cheese. If you have access to a grill on your picnic, you could reheat the calzones for 1 or 2 minutes to re-melt the cheese.

- 1 tablespoon olive oil
- 1 small onion, finely chopped
- 2 cloves garlic, finely chopped
- 1 red bell pepper, finely chopped
- 1 package (10 ounces) frozen chopped spinach, thawed and squeezed dry
- ¾ teaspoon salt
- 2 cups shredded cooked chicken thighs or breasts—leftover or poached (page 17)
- ¼ pound Fontina cheese, shredded (1 cup)
- ¼ pound mozzarella cheese, shredded (1 cup)
- ⅓ cup chopped fresh basil leaves
- 1 pound store-bought pizza or bread dough, cut into 4 pieces
- 1 large egg

1. In large skillet, heat oil over medium heat. Add onion and garlic, and stir-fry 7 minutes or until onion is tender. Add bell pepper and cook 5 minutes or until crisp-tender. Add spinach and salt, and cook 2 minutes or until spinach is heated through. Transfer to large bowl and cool to room temperature. Stir in chicken, Fontina, mozzarella, and basil.

2. Preheat oven to 425°F. On lightly floured surface, roll each piece of dough out to an 8-inch round. Mound chicken mixture on bottom half of each round, leaving ½-inch border. Brush bottom half with water along edge. Fold top half over chicken mixture and press edges to seal (see technique photo, top right).

3. Make two small slashes in top of each calzone (bottom photo). Lightly grease a large baking sheet. In small bowl, beat together egg and 1 tablespoon of water. Place calzones on prepared baking sheet; brush with egg mixture. Bake for 15 minutes or until top is crispy and golden brown.

CHICKEN & BROCCOLI CALZONES WITH SMOKED MOZZARELLA In step 1, sauté onion and garlic as directed, but increase garlic to 3 cloves; omit bell pepper; substitute 1 package (10 ounces) thawed frozen chopped broccoli for the spinach and cook 5 minutes or until tender. Sprinkle ½ teaspoon sage over broccoli as it cooks. Substitute ½ pound smoked mozzarella for the Fontina and regular mozzarella. Omit basil. Add ⅓ cup golden raisins to the chicken mixture. Assemble, brush with glaze, and bake as directed.

Calories 696, Total Fat 29g, Saturated Fat 11g, Cholesterol 165mg, Sodium 1850mg, Protein 44g, Carbohydrates 68g

LEFTOVERS

Prep Time: 30 minutes
Cooking Time: 30 minutes
Makes 4 servings

NUTRITION INFORMATION
Per Serving
Calories 694
Total Fat 32g
Saturated Fat 12g
Cholesterol 175mg
Sodium 2006mg
Protein 46g
Carbohydrates 59g

TECHNIQUE

MAKING CALZONES

After folding the calzone dough over the filling, press with the edge of your thumb to seal the dough (and give the calzone a decorative border).

With a sharp paring knife, make two short slashes in the top of the calzone for steam to escape. Do not cut through to the bottom dough.

CHICKEN CALZONES WITH TWO CHEESES

GRILLED CHICKEN & RED PEPPER SALAD

Prep Time: 10 minutes
Cooking Time: 20 minutes
Makes 4 servings

NUTRITION INFORMATION

Per Serving
Calories 539
Total Fat 20g
Saturated Fat 3g
Cholesterol 99mg
Sodium 1191mg
Protein 47g
Carbohydrates 43g

Grilled Chicken & Red Pepper Salad

Add a loaf of bread, cold drinks, and fresh fruit for dessert, and you're really celebrating summer with this grilled chicken salad. For a change, make the salad with different small pasta shapes such as tubettini, ditalini, or tiny shells.

- 1 cup orzo
- 5 tablespoons balsamic vinegar
- 4 tablespoons olive oil
- 1½ teaspoons salt
- ⅓ cup Calamata olives, pitted and coarsely chopped
- 4 skinless, boneless chicken breast halves (about 1½ pounds)
- 1 zucchini (8 ounces), quartered lengthwise
- 1 yellow squash (8 ounces), quartered lengthwise
- 4 red bell peppers, cut lengthwise into flat panels

1. In large pot of boiling water, cook orzo according to package directions. Drain and set aside. In large bowl, whisk together vinegar, 2 tablespoons of oil, and ¾ teaspoon of salt. Stir in olives. On plate, stir together 1 tablespoon of oil and remaining ¾ teaspoon salt. Add chicken, turning to coat; cover and refrigerate while you preheat grill.

2. Preheat grill to medium-high. Brush zucchini and yellow squash with remaining 1 tablespoon oil. Grill chicken and squash 6 inches from heat for 3 to 4 minutes per side or until chicken is just done and squash is tender. When cool enough to handle, cut chicken crosswise into ½-inch chunks and cut squash into 1-inch lengths.

3. Grill bell pepper pieces, skin-side down, for 10 minutes or until skin is blackened. When cool enough to handle, peel and cut into ½-inch-wide strips.

4. Add chicken, squash, peppers, and orzo to bowl of dressing and olives, and toss well. Serve warm, at room temperature, or chilled.

FROM THE FRIDGE

Substitute 3½ cups shredded cooked chicken breast for the grilled chicken. Toss chicken with 1 tablespoon balsamic vinegar and ¼ teaspoon salt. (Omit oil and salt used to marinate uncooked chicken.)

Prep Time: 10 minutes
Cooking Time: 30 minutes
Makes 4 servings

NUTRITION INFORMATION

Per Serving
Calories 495
Total Fat 32g
Saturated Fat 8g
Cholesterol 154mg
Sodium 1016mg
Protein 48g
Carbohydrates 0g

Grilled Rosemary Chicken

To bring out the full flavor of rosemary, the pine needle-like leaves of this aromatic herb should be chopped or crushed before being added to a dish.

- 5 tablespoons olive oil
- ¼ cup coarsely chopped fresh rosemary, or 4 teaspoons dried, crumbled
- 3 strips (2 x ¼-inch each) orange zest
- ¾ teaspoon freshly ground black pepper
- 1 whole chicken (about 3½ pounds), halved lengthwise (see technique photos, page 206)
- 1½ teaspoons salt

1. In small skillet, heat oil over low heat. Add rosemary, orange zest, and pepper, and cook 5 minutes or until oil is fragrant and flavorful. Cool to room temperature, then strain through fine-meshed sieve set over small bowl. Measure out 2 tablespoons of rosemary oil and set aside.

2. With your fingers, gently loosen chicken skin. Rub salt under and over skin. Rub remaining (3 tablespoons) rosemary oil under skin.

3. Preheat grill to medium. Grill chicken, skin-side up, 6 inches from heat for 12 minutes or until nicely browned. Turn chicken over and grill for 12 minutes longer or until cooked through. To serve, cut each chicken half crosswise. Brush with reserved rosemary oil before serving.

Spicy Skewered Chicken & Shrimp

Long, flat metal skewers with handles (or a loop at one end) are best for grilling—food is less likely to slip than when you use round skewers. Have a pot of rice at hand when the grilled goodies are ready, and slide each portion of chicken, shrimp, and vegetables off the skewers onto a bed of rice.

  2   teaspoons paprika
1½   teaspoons dried oregano
  1   teaspoon chili powder
  1   teaspoon sugar
  ¾   teaspoon salt
  ½   teaspoon cayenne pepper
  ½   teaspoon garlic powder
  ¾   pound skinless, boneless chicken breasts,
       cut into 32 chunks
 16   large shrimp (about 1 pound),
       shelled and deveined
  1   yellow bell pepper, cut into 16 chunks
  1   red bell pepper, cut into 16 chunks
  1   red onion, cut into 16 chunks
  2   tablespoons olive oil

1. Preheat grill to medium-high. In large bowl, stir together paprika, oregano, chili powder, sugar, salt, cayenne, and garlic powder. Add chicken and shrimp, and toss well to coat.

2. In separate bowl, gently toss bell peppers and onion with oil. Alternately thread chicken, shrimp, bell peppers, and onion onto eight 10-inch skewers. Grill skewers 6 inches from heat for 5 minutes, turning them over midway, until chicken and shrimp are cooked through.

LOW FAT
QUICK TO FIX

Prep Time: 25 minutes
Cooking Time: 5 minutes
Makes 4 servings

NUTRITION INFORMATION
Per Serving
Calories 291
Total Fat 10g
Saturated Fat 1.5g
Cholesterol 189mg
Sodium 640mg
Protein 40g
Carbohydrates 10g

Honey Mustard
Grilled Chicken with Apple

An early-autumn barbecue is the ideal setting for grilled chicken with tangy glazed apple slices. Keep the grilled fruit idea in mind for other fire-cooked meals: Grilled peaches, nectarines, or pineapple are all delicious with chicken, and skewers of grilled fruits are a classic barbecue dessert.

  ½   cup honey mustard
  4   tablespoons cider vinegar
  ¾   teaspoon freshly ground black pepper
  1   whole chicken (about 3½ pounds),
       cut into 8 serving pieces (page 14)
1½   teaspoons salt
  ⅓   cup apple jelly
  4   Granny Smith or Golden Delicious apples,
       cut horizontally into 4 thick slices each

1. In large bowl, whisk together honey mustard, 2 tablespoons of vinegar, and the pepper. With your fingers, gently loosen skin of chicken. Rub salt over and under chicken skin. Rub mustard mixture under chicken skin.

2. In small saucepan, melt jelly over low heat with remaining 2 tablespoons vinegar. Place apple slices in medium bowl, pour melted jelly over them, and toss to coat well.

3. Preheat grill to medium-high. Grill chicken and apples 6 inches from heat for the following amounts of time: Grill chicken, turning often, for 20 minutes or until cooked through; grill apples for 10 minutes, turning several times, until tender.

Prep Time: 15 minutes
Cooking Time: 20 minutes
Makes 4 servings

NUTRITION INFORMATION
Per Serving
Calories 660
Total Fat 27g
Saturated Fat 6.5g
Cholesterol 154mg
Sodium 1475mg
Protein 48g
Carbohydrates 52g

HONEY MUSTARD GRILLED CHICKEN WITH APPLE

LEMON CHICKEN & VEGETABLE KABOBS

Prep Time: 20 minutes
Cooking Time: 5 minutes
Makes 4 servings

NUTRITION INFORMATION

Per Serving

Calories 249

Total Fat 12g

Saturated Fat 2g

Cholesterol 66mg

Sodium 662mg

Protein 28g

Carbohydrates 8g

Lemon Chicken & Vegetable Kabobs

Fresh lemon is such an engaging flavor, and its sparkling tartness is particularly welcome in hot weather (think lemonade). Grill these colorful kabobs on a warm summer evening when turning on the oven is out of the question. Serve them over rice (add a little lemon juice to the cooking water).

- 3 tablespoons olive oil
- ½ teaspoon grated lemon zest
- 3 tablespoons fresh lemon juice
- 1 teaspoon salt
- ½ teaspoon freshly ground black pepper
- 8 mushrooms, trimmed
- 1 yellow bell pepper, cut into 12 chunks
- 1 red bell pepper, cut into 12 chunks
- ½ large red onion, cut into 1-inch chunks
- 1 pound skinless, boneless chicken breasts, cut into 24 pieces

1. In large bowl, stir together oil, lemon zest, lemon juice, salt, and black pepper. Add mushrooms and bell peppers, and toss well. Add onion and toss gently. Thread mushrooms on one 10-inch skewer, bell peppers (alternating colors) on two 10-inch skewers, and onion on one 10-inch skewer.

2. Add chicken to mixture remaining in bowl and toss well. Thread chicken on two 10-inch skewers. Preheat grill to medium-high. Place all skewers on grill and grill 6 inches from heat for 5 minutes, turning chicken and vegetables as they color, until cooked through. Remove chicken and vegetables from skewers and arrange on serving platter.

Prep Time: 25 minutes
Cooking Time: 10 minutes
Makes 4 servings

NUTRITION INFORMATION

Per Serving

Calories 380

Total Fat 14g

Saturated Fat 4g

Cholesterol 109mg

Sodium 1538mg

Protein 29g

Carbohydrates 37g

Chicken, Pineapple & Bacon Skewers

Inspired by a classic appetizer served on a toothpick, this timeless combination makes a terrific main dish. Bacon wrapped around the chunks of chicken helps keep them moist; a touch of rosemary updates the marinade and balances the sweetness of the pineapple.

- 1 cup ketchup
- ¼ cup unsweetened pineapple juice
- 3 tablespoons strained apricot jam
- 2 tablespoons balsamic vinegar
- ¾ teaspoon salt
- ½ teaspoon freshly ground black pepper
- ½ teaspoon dried rosemary, crumbled
- 1 pound skinless, boneless chicken thighs, cut into 24 pieces
- 12 slices bacon (about 9 ounces), halved crosswise
- 1 large red bell pepper, cut into 24 chunks
- 24 canned pineapple chunks

1. In medium bowl, stir together ketchup, pineapple juice, jam, vinegar, salt, black pepper, and rosemary. Add chicken and toss to coat. Lift chicken out of marinade, reserving marinade. Wrap a bacon strip around each chicken piece.

2. Preheat grill to medium. Alternating ingredients, thread bell pepper, pineapple, and bacon-wrapped chicken onto twelve 10-inch skewers. (Be sure to thread the skewer through the overlap in the bacon so it does not come unwrapped.)

3. Lightly oil grill rack. Place skewers on grill and brush with half of reserved marinade. Grill 5 to 7 minutes, turning skewers midway and brushing with remaining marinade, until chicken is cooked through and bacon is crisp.

Grilled Chicken Kabobs with Mango

Not so long ago the only hot sauce on supermarket shelves was the red Louisiana-style sauce. But these days the options are many, from the fiery, yellow Caribbean hot sauces made with habañero peppers to the tamer green hot sauce used here, made with fresh green jalapeños.

LOW FAT
QUICK TO FIX

Prep Time: 20 minutes
Cooking Time: 5 minutes
Makes 4 servings

2 tablespoons hot pepper sauce (green)

2 tablespoons olive oil

1 tablespoon fresh lime juice

1 tablespoon light brown sugar

¾ teaspoon salt

¾ teaspoon ground ginger

¼ teaspoon ground allspice

1 pound skinless, boneless chicken breasts, cut into 32 chunks

24 cherry tomatoes

8 scallions, cut into fourths

1 large mango (15 ounces), peeled and cut into 24 chunks (see technique photos, page 65)

1. Preheat grill to medium-high. In large bowl, whisk together hot sauce, oil, lime juice, brown sugar, salt, ginger, and allspice. Add chicken, tomatoes, scallions, and mango, and toss well to coat.

2. Alternately thread all ingredients onto eight 10-inch skewers. Grill 6 inches from heat for 5 minutes or until chicken is cooked through and tomatoes and mango are piping hot.

NUTRITION INFORMATION
Per Serving
Calories 271
Total Fat 8.5g
Saturated Fat 1.5g
Cholesterol 66mg
Sodium 720mg
Protein 28g
Carbohydrates 21g

Tex-Mex Chicken & Vegetable Grill

Both the chicken and vegetables are seasoned with a lively blend of chili powder, cumin, coriander, and oregano. For a clear, true flavor, use pure chili powder, which doesn't have other spices already added. While the chicken grills, pop some thickly sliced bread on the grill. That's "Texas toast."

Prep Time: 15 minutes
Cooking Time: 30 minutes
Makes 4 servings

TEX-MEX SPICE RUB:

1 tablespoon ground cumin

2 teaspoons ground coriander

1½ teaspoons dried oregano

1½ teaspoons chili powder

1 teaspoon salt

¾ teaspoon freshly ground black pepper

CHICKEN & VEGETABLES:

4 bone-in chicken breast halves (about 2½ pounds), with skin

2 ears of corn, shucked and halved crosswise

1 zucchini (8 ounces), halved lengthwise and crosswise

1 yellow squash (8 ounces), halved lengthwise and crosswise

1 Spanish onion (about 1 pound), cut into 4 thick rounds

2 tablespoons olive oil

Lime wedges

1. Make Tex-Mex Spice Rub: In large bowl, stir together cumin, coriander, oregano, chili powder, salt, and pepper. Measure out 4½ teaspoons of spice mixture to use as a rub.

2. Prepare Chicken & Vegetables: Rub reserved spice mixture under and over skin of chicken. Add corn, zucchini, squash, and onion to large bowl with remaining spice mixture and toss gently to coat. Add oil and toss again.

3. Preheat grill to medium-high. Grill vegetables 6 inches from heat for 10 minutes, turning as they color, until zucchini, squash, and onion are crisp-tender and corn is lightly charred and hot. Transfer to platter and cover with foil to keep warm.

4. Grill chicken, skin-side up, for 10 minutes. Turn chicken skin-side down and grill for 5 to 7 minutes or until chicken is cooked through. Serve chicken and vegetables with lime wedges.

NUTRITION INFORMATION
Per Serving
Calories 500
Total Fat 20g
Saturated Fat 4.5g
Cholesterol 129mg
Sodium 730mg
Protein 52g
Carbohydrates 30g

GRILLED CHICKEN KABOBS WITH MANGO

GRILLED CHICKEN BREASTS WITH ROASTED-CORN SALSA

Prep Time: 20 minutes plus
  marinating time
Cooking Time: 10 minutes
Makes 4 servings

NUTRITION INFORMATION
Per Serving
Calories 224
Total Fat 3.5g
Saturated Fat 1g
Cholesterol 87mg
Sodium 587mg
Protein 38g
Carbohydrates 10g

Middle Eastern Chicken

A nice accompaniment for this Middle Eastern-style yogurt-marinated chicken would be couscous, tossed with a little bit of olive oil and fresh lemon juice. Serve the couscous chilled or at room temperature.

1	tablespoon paprika
1½	teaspoons ground coriander
1¼	cups plain low-fat yogurt
½	teaspoon grated lemon zest
¾	teaspoon salt
½	teaspoon freshly ground black pepper
½	cup snipped fresh dill
¼	cup chopped fresh mint or 1 tablespoon dried
2	scallions, thinly sliced
4	small skinless, boneless chicken breast halves (about 1¼ pounds), pounded to ½-inch thickness (page 15)
1	large tomato, diced

1. In small ungreased skillet, heat paprika and coriander over low heat for 1 minute or until fragrant. Transfer to large bowl and stir in yogurt, lemon zest, salt, and pepper. Stir in dill, mint, and scallions. Measure out ½ cup of yogurt sauce, cover, and refrigerate.

2. Add chicken to yogurt mixture remaining in large bowl and turn to coat chicken with mixture. Cover and refrigerate at least 30 minutes or up to 4 hours.

3. Preheat grill to medium-high. Grill chicken 6 inches from heat for 3 minutes per side or until cooked through. Stir tomato into reserved yogurt sauce and serve with chicken.

Prep Time: 15 minutes
Cooking Time: 25 minutes
Makes 4 servings

NUTRITION INFORMATION
Per Serving
Calories 427
Total Fat 15g
Saturated Fat 2g
Cholesterol 99mg
Sodium 747mg
Protein 45g
Carbohydrates 33g

Grilled Chicken Breasts with Roasted-Corn Salsa

No matter how you're planning to cook corn on the cob, it should be as fresh as you can possibly get it. Many roadside stands and farmers' markets offer corn picked that same morning. To preserve its natural sweetness, keep the corn refrigerated until you're ready to cook it.

4	ears of corn, shucked
3	tablespoons olive oil
2	tablespoons red wine vinegar
4	teaspoons chili powder
1	large tomato, halved, seeded, and cut into ½-inch chunks
⅓	cup chopped cilantro
⅓	cup minced red onion
1	teaspoon salt
4	skinless, boneless chicken breast halves (about 1½ pounds)

1. Preheat grill to medium. Grill corn 6 inches from heat, turning it frequently, for 15 minutes or until golden brown. When cool enough to handle, use sharp paring knife to scrape kernels into large bowl.

2. Add 1 tablespoon of oil, the vinegar, 2 teaspoons of chili powder, the tomato, cilantro, onion, and ½ teaspoon of salt to corn. Toss and refrigerate until serving time.

3. Toss chicken with remaining 2 tablespoons oil, 2 teaspoons chili powder, and ½ teaspoon salt. Grill chicken 6 inches from heat for 3 minutes per side or until cooked through. Serve chicken with corn salsa.

IN A HURRY?
Use 2 cups frozen corn kernels, thawed, in place of the roasted corn.

Grilled Chicken Sausage with Green Chili Sauce

It's easier to grill peppers if you cut them vertically into flat pieces before cooking them (instead of the more traditional method of grilling a whole, uncut pepper). This method also makes the grilled pepper significantly easier to peel.

- 1 green bell pepper, cut lengthwise into flat panels
- 1 cup packed cilantro leaves and stems
- 1 can (4½ ounces) chopped mild green chilies
- 2 pickled jalapeño peppers
- 2 tablespoons fresh lime juice
- ¼ cup sliced onion
- ½ teaspoon salt
- ¼ teaspoon cayenne pepper
- 1½ pounds fresh chicken sausage
- 4 hard rolls, split

1. Preheat the grill. Grill pepper pieces, skin-side down, 6 inches from heat for 10 minutes or until skin is blackened. When peppers are cool enough to handle, peel them, and transfer to food processor along with cilantro, mild green chilies, jalapeños, lime juice, onion, salt, and cayenne. Process until smooth.

2. Grill sausage, turning them as they cook, 6 inches from heat for 10 minutes or until cooked through. Toast rolls, cut-side down, on grill until lightly toasted. Place sausage in rolls and top with sauce.

LOW FAT
QUICK TO FIX

Prep Time: 10 minutes
Cooking Time: 20 minutes
Makes 4 servings

NUTRITION INFORMATION
Per Serving
Calories 419
Total Fat 13g
Saturated Fat 3g
Cholesterol 101mg
Sodium 1783mg
Protein 38g
Carbohydrates 35g

Fajita-Style Grilled Chicken with Goat Cheese

Fajitas have come a long way from the original strips of grilled steak. Here, lime-marinated chicken and sweetly spiced onions are grilled with bell peppers and served with tangy goat cheese.

- 1 pound skinless, boneless chicken breasts, pounded to ½-inch thickness (page 15)
- 4 tablespoons fresh lime juice
- 1½ teaspoons salt
- 1 Spanish onion, cut into 4 thick rounds
- 1½ teaspoons sugar
- ½ teaspoon cinnamon
- ½ teaspoon ground cumin
- ¼ teaspoon ground cloves
- 3 tablespoons olive oil
- 2 green bell peppers, cut lengthwise into flat panels
- 2 red bell peppers, cut lengthwise into flat panels
- 4 burrito-size flour tortillas (10-inch diameter)
- 1 cup crumbled mild goat or feta cheese

1. Place chicken on plate and sprinkle with 3 tablespoons of lime juice and ½ teaspoon of salt. Cover and refrigerate 30 minutes or up to 1 hour.

2. Preheat grill to medium-high. In medium bowl, gently toss onion with sugar, cinnamon, cumin, cloves, and ½ teaspoon of salt. Add 1 tablespoon of oil and toss again.

3. Toss chicken with 1 tablespoon of oil and place on grill along with onion and peppers. Grill 6 inches from heat for following amounts of time: Grill chicken 3 minutes per side or until cooked through; grill onion 4 minutes per side or until lightly browned and crisp-tender; grill peppers, skin-side down, 10 minutes or until skin is blackened.

4. When ingredients are cool enough to handle: Cut chicken lengthwise into ½-inch-wide strips; cut onions in half; peel peppers and cut into ½-inch-wide strips. Transfer to bowl, add remaining 1 tablespoon oil, 1 tablespoon lime juice, and ½ teaspoon salt. Toss well. Divide evenly among tortillas. Sprinkle with goat cheese and roll up like cone.

Prep Time: 15 minutes plus marinating time
Cooking Time: 10 minutes
Makes 4 servings

NUTRITION INFORMATION
Per Serving
Calories 562
Total Fat 26g
Saturated Fat 9.5g
Cholesterol 93mg
Sodium 1390mg
Protein 40g
Carbohydrates 43g

FAJITA-STYLE GRILLED CHICKEN WITH GOAT CHEESE

Barbecued Chicken for a Crowd

Outdoor entertaining just doesn't get any easier. You can make the barbecue sauce a day in advance, and the same goes for the traditional side dishes—coleslaw, potato salad, and corn bread. Even iced tea can brew in the refrigerator overnight. The barbecue chef can then perform unharried by last-minute details. For a surefire dessert hit, set up a self-service sundae bar on a table in the shade.

Prep Time: 10 minutes
Cooking Time: 50 minutes
Makes 8 servings

NUTRITION INFORMATION
Per Serving
Calories 559
Total Fat 29g
Saturated Fat 7.5g
Cholesterol 154mg
Sodium 841mg
Protein 49g
Carbohydrates 23g

SWEET TOMATO BBQ GLAZE:

- 3 tablespoons vegetable oil
- 2 onions, finely chopped
- 6 cloves garlic, finely chopped
- 1 can (28 ounces) crushed tomatoes
- ½ cup packed dark brown sugar
- ½ cup distilled white vinegar
- 1 tablespoon Worcestershire sauce
- 1¼ teaspoons salt
- 1 teaspoon ground ginger
- ½ teaspoon cayenne pepper

CHICKENS:

- 2 whole chickens (3½ pounds each), cut into 10 pieces each (page 14)
- ½ teaspoon salt

1. Make Sweet Tomato BBQ Glaze: In large skillet, heat oil over medium heat. Add onions and garlic, and cook, stirring frequently, 10 minutes or until onion is tender. Add tomatoes, brown sugar, vinegar, Worcestershire, salt, ginger, and cayenne, and bring to a boil. Reduce to a simmer, cover, and cook 15 minutes or until richly flavored and reduced to 4 cups.

Transfer to food processor and process until smooth. Measure out 2 cups of barbecue sauce to use as a glaze. Set aside remaining barbecue sauce to serve with chicken.

2. Cook Chickens: Preheat grill to medium. Sprinkle salt over chicken. Grill chicken 6 inches from heat for 15 minutes, turning chicken often, until browned all over. Brush chicken with 1 cup of glaze, turn chicken over, brush with remaining cup of glaze and grill, without turning, for 5 to 7 minutes or until chicken is cooked through. Serve reserved barbecue sauce with the grilled chicken.

SWEET & SOUR ASIAN-STYLE BARBECUE Omit step 1 and all glaze ingredients. Instead, in large saucepan, combine 2 cups ketchup, ⅓ cup lower-sodium soy sauce, ½ cup packed light brown sugar, ½ cup rice vinegar, 1 tablespoon Worcestershire, 1 tablespoon sesame oil, 1 teaspoon ground ginger, and 2 minced garlic cloves. Bring to a boil over medium heat, reduce to a simmer, and cook 10 minutes or until sauce is reduced to 3 cups. Grill chicken as directed in step 2, using 2 cups of sauce as a glaze and serving remaining 1 cup sauce at the table.
Calories 557, Total Fat 26g, Saturated Fat 7g, Cholesterol 154mg, Sodium 1422mg, Protein 49g, Carbohydrates 32g

HINTS & TIPS

➤ Discard any unused glaze that remains after the chicken is cooked. Don't add it to the sauce you're serving at the table, because the glaze has been in contact with raw chicken via the basting brush.

➤ Apple cider vinegar makes a fine substitute for distilled white vinegar in this recipe.

➤ Cut-up whole chickens are a good choice for a crowd because there's something to please everyone. As you're grilling, be sure to check white-meat portions first for doneness, as they cook more quickly than dark meat.

➤ If you do a lot of barbecuing, you might consider making a double or triple batch of this glaze. Cook the sauce in a Dutch oven or flameproof casserole instead of a skillet and store in the refrigerator, where it will keep for a couple of weeks.

BARBECUED CHICKEN FOR A CROWD

Dinner Party Dishes

Whether it's an extended-family celebration, a pool party for hungry teens, or an elegant dinner to honor a very special person, chicken is always your best choice. Please the folks with a homey coq au vin; fill up those teenagers with chicken burritos; and wow the honored guest with chicken Marsala.

Chicken Marsala over Noodles

Marsala is a Sicilian wine sweetened with unfermented grape juice and grape syrup and then aged. It adds a deep, dark, almost nutty flavor to this rich sauce.

- 3 tablespoons butter
- 2 tablespoons olive oil
- 8 skinless, boneless chicken breast halves (about 3 pounds), pounded to ½-inch thickness (page 15) and cut crosswise into 6 pieces each
- ⅓ cup flour
- 1 cup dry Marsala
- ⅔ cup chicken broth, canned or homemade (page 45)
- ½ teaspoon salt
- ¼ teaspoon freshly ground black pepper
- 1½ teaspoons cornstarch blended with 1 tablespoon water
- 16 ounces medium egg noodles
- 2 tablespoons snipped chives

1. In large skillet, heat 1 tablespoon of butter and the oil until foam subsides. Dredge chicken in flour, shaking off excess. Add half of chicken to pan and sauté 6 minutes or until golden brown and cooked through. Transfer chicken to platter. Repeat with remaining chicken.

2. Pour off any fat remaining in skillet. Add Marsala to pan, scraping up any browned bits that cling to bottom of pan. Bring to a boil over high heat and cook 2 minutes. Add broth, salt, and pepper; return to a boil and boil 1 minute. Stir in cornstarch mixture and cook, stirring constantly, 1 minute or until sauce is slightly thickened. Remove from heat and swirl in 1 tablespoon of butter.

3. Meanwhile, in large pot of boiling water, cook noodles according to package directions; drain, reserving ½ cup cooking water.

4. Return hot noodles to cooking pot and toss with reserved cooking water and remaining 1 tablespoon butter. Place chicken on top of noodles and spoon sauce over chicken. Sprinkle chives on top.

LOW FAT

QUICK TO FIX

Prep Time: 10 minutes
Cooking Time: 20 minutes
Makes 8 servings

NUTRITION INFORMATION
Per Serving
Calories 540
Total Fat 12g
Saturated Fat 4g
Cholesterol 164mg
Sodium 596mg
Protein 48g
Carbohydrates 48g

Jasmine Rice Salad with Chicken & Pine Nuts

Jasmine rice is named for the mild flowery fragrance it sends forth as it cooks. Native to Thailand, this soft, delicate rice is similar in flavor to Indian basmati rice, but it is considerably less expensive.

- 6 tablespoons olive oil
- 2 onions, finely chopped
- 1 teaspoon sugar
- 2 cups jasmine or basmati rice
- 1½ cups chicken broth, canned or homemade (page 45)
- 1½ teaspoons salt
- ½ cup rice vinegar
- 4 cups shredded cooked chicken breasts—leftover or poached (page 17)
- 2 cups seedless grapes, red and green, halved
- ⅓ cup chopped cilantro
- ½ cup pine nuts, toasted

1. In large saucepan, heat 2 tablespoons of oil over medium-low heat. Add onions and sugar, and cook, stirring frequently, 7 minutes or until onions are soft. Stir in rice, broth, ½ teaspoon of salt, and 1½ cups of water. Bring to a boil, reduce to a simmer, cover, and cook 17 minutes or until rice is tender.

2. Meanwhile, in large bowl, whisk together vinegar and remaining 4 tablespoons oil and 1 teaspoon salt. Add rice to bowl and toss with fork to combine. Add chicken, grapes, cilantro, and pine nuts, and toss with fork. Serve at room temperature or chilled.

LEFTOVERS

Prep Time: 15 minutes
Cooking Time: 25 minutes
Makes 8 servings

NUTRITION INFORMATION
Per Serving
Calories 470
Total Fat 20g
Saturated Fat 3.5g
Cholesterol 62mg
Sodium 696mg
Protein 26g
Carbohydrates 47g

JASMINE RICE SALAD WITH CHICKEN & PINE NUTS

CHICKEN WITH ORANGE-RAISIN SAUCE

Prep Time: 15 minutes
Cooking Time: 45 minutes
Makes 8 servings

NUTRITION INFORMATION
Per Serving
Calories 372
Total Fat 11g
Saturated Fat 6g
Cholesterol 122mg
Sodium 391mg
Protein 41g
Carbohydrates 26g

HINTS & TIPS

➤ All raisins are made from white grapes, but golden raisins are dried with artificial heat (rather than in sunlight) and treated with sulphur dioxide to preserve their light color.

➤ Shallots are mild-flavored members of the onion family. Like garlic, shallots grow in "heads" composed of several cloves, each wrapped in a papery skin.

➤ Adding butter to a sauce just before serving is called "mounting" the sauce. The pure butter flavor comes shining through, and this process also renders the sauce glossy. The butter should be chilled (which keeps the butter from separating when it's heated), so after using the 4 tablespoons of butter in step 2, return the remaining 2 tablespoons to the refrigerator.

Chicken with Orange-Raisin Sauce

A sauce with a golden glow makes this recipe a particularly good choice for a festive dinner. Golden raisins, butter, orange juice and zest, caramelized shallots, and Dijon mustard all contribute to its appealing color. To complement the sauce, serve the chicken with buttery couscous and steamed asparagus or baby green beans. Although this dish is already relatively low in fat (only 27% of its calories are from fat), the reduced-fat version below takes it to a mere 6% calories from fat!

- 1 cup golden raisins
- 6 tablespoons butter
- 8 skinless, boneless chicken breast halves (about 3 pounds)
- ⅓ cup flour
- 3 shallots, finely chopped
- 2 tablespoons sugar
- ⅓ cup red wine vinegar
- ¼ cup finely slivered orange zest (about 1 orange)
- 1 cup orange juice
- 1 tablespoon Dijon mustard
- ½ teaspoon salt

1. In small bowl, combine raisins and ½ cup of hot water. Let stand 20 minutes or until softened. Drain.

2. Meanwhile, in 4- to 5-quart flameproof casserole or Dutch oven, heat 2 tablespoons of butter over medium heat. Dredge chicken in flour, shaking off excess. Add half of chicken to pan and sauté 4 minutes per side or until golden brown. Transfer to platter. Add 2 tablespoons of butter to pan and sauté remaining chicken, transferring to platter when done.

3. Add shallots to pan, reduce heat to low, and cook 4 minutes or until tender. Sprinkle sugar over shallots, increase heat to medium-high, and cook 2 minutes or until shallots have

caramelized. Add vinegar to pan and cook 1 minute. Add orange zest, orange juice, mustard, salt, and raisins; bring to a boil and cook 5 minutes.

4. Return chicken to pan and bring to a boil. Reduce to a simmer, cover, and cook 15 minutes or until chicken is cooked through.

5. Transfer chicken to dinner plates. Return sauce to a boil and cook 2 minutes or until slightly reduced. Remove sauce from heat and swirl in remaining 2 tablespoons butter. Spoon sauce over chicken.

TO REDUCE THE FAT

In step 2, use nonstick Dutch oven or casserole. Substitute 3 tablespoons olive oil for the butter and sauté chicken in batches as directed, using half of oil for each batch. Follow steps 3 and 4 as directed. In step 5, reduce sauce as directed, but omit butter. Instead, blend 1 teaspoon cornstarch in 1 tablespoon of water; add to pan, bring to a boil, and cook, stirring constantly, 1 minute or until slightly thickened.

Calories 297, Total Fat 2g, Saturated Fat 0.5g, Cholesterol 99mg, Sodium 304mg, Protein 41g, Carbohydrates 27g

Apricot-Glazed Roast Chicken with Corn Bread-Pecan Stuffing

You may feel that carving a whole bird in the kitchen is the easy way to go. And no matter how you serve this stuffed chicken, it will taste sensational. But carving at the table definitely adds a note of drama to a dinner party. The technique photos below will help you carry it off.

Prep Time: 15 minutes
Cooking Time: 1 hour 45 minutes
Makes 8 servings

- 7 tablespoons butter
- 1 large onion, finely chopped
- 2 stalks celery, quartered lengthwise and thinly sliced
- 1 bag (7 ounces) corn bread stuffing
- 1 cup chicken broth, canned or homemade (page 45)
- ½ cup pecans, coarsely chopped
- ½ cup chopped parsley
- ½ cup dried apricots, finely chopped
- 1 whole roaster chicken (about 6 pounds), giblets removed and reserved for another use
- 1 teaspoon salt
- ½ cup apricot jam
- 1 tablespoon fresh lemon juice

1. Preheat oven to 400°F. In large skillet, melt 2 tablespoons of butter over medium heat. Add onion and cook, stirring frequently, 7 minutes or until soft. Stir in celery and cook 5 minutes or until celery is crisp-tender. Transfer to large bowl; add corn bread stuffing, broth, pecans, parsley, and apricots. In small saucepan, melt remaining 5 tablespoons butter and add to bowl. Stir until well combined.

2. Rub chicken inside and out with salt. Loosely spoon stuffing into neck and body cavities of chicken. Spoon remaining stuffing into small baking pan; cover with foil. Tie chicken legs together with kitchen string. Lift wings up toward neck, then fold wing tips under back of chicken so wings stay in place.

3. Place chicken breast-side up on rack in 15 x 11-inch roasting pan. Roast chicken for 1 hour. Meanwhile, in small bowl, stir together jam and lemon juice.

4. Place pan of stuffing alongside chicken in oven. Brush half of apricot mixture on chicken and roast for 10 minutes. Brush remaining apricot mixture on chicken and roast for 20 minutes or until chicken is cooked through and glazed. Serve with stuffing.

CURRANT-GLAZED CHICKEN WITH CRANBERRY & ALMOND STUFFING

In preheated oven, toast ⅔ cup natural (unblanched) almonds for 7 minutes or until fragrant and crisp. When cool enough to handle, coarsely chop. In step 1, prepare stuffing mixture as directed, but substitute the toasted almonds for the pecans and ⅔ cup dried cranberries for the apricots. Prepare and stuff chicken as directed in steps 2 and 3, but substitute ½ cup red currant jelly for apricot jam-lemon juice mixture. Roast and baste as directed.

Calories 740, Total Fat 41g, Saturated Fat 13g, Cholesterol 161mg, Sodium 952mg, Protein 48g, Carbohydrates 46g

NUTRITION INFORMATION

Per Serving

Calories 707

Total Fat 39g

Saturated Fat 13g

Cholesterol 161mg

Sodium 953mg

Protein 46g

Carbohydrates 42g

TECHNIQUE

CARVING FOR COMPANY

To carve a whole roast chicken, start by cutting off the wings. Then cut off the legs at the thigh joint (and cut the thighs and drumsticks apart).

Slice the breast meat off the chicken at a slight angle (following the natural slope of the breast). Keep slices about ⅓ inch thick.

APRICOT-GLAZED ROAST CHICKEN WITH CORN BREAD-PECAN STUFFING

Chicken Baked with 40 Cloves of Garlic

Treat your garlic-loving friends to this modern-day classic, redolent of sweet roasted garlic. Even those who normally shy away from garlic may be quite happy with this meal, as the garlic's bite is tamed by the slow cooking. If you prefer, serve plain French bread rather than the sautéed bread.

- 10 tablespoons olive oil
- 2 whole chickens (about 3½ pounds each), each cut into 8 serving pieces (page 14), skin removed
- ⅓ cup flour
- 40 cloves garlic, unpeeled
- 3 stalks celery, halved lengthwise and cut crosswise into 1-inch lengths
- 4 sprigs fresh rosemary or ¾ teaspoon dried
- 3 sprigs fresh thyme or ½ teaspoon dried
- ¾ cup dry vermouth or white wine
- ¾ cup chicken broth
- 1½ teaspoons salt
- 8 slices (½-inch-thick) peasant bread

1. Preheat oven to 350°F. In large skillet, heat 2 tablespoons of oil over medium heat. Dredge chicken in flour, shaking off excess. Add one-third of chicken to pan and sauté 4 minutes per side or until golden brown. Transfer to 10 x 14-inch roasting pan. Repeat sautéing in two more batches, using 2 tablespoons of oil per batch, cooking until golden brown and transferring to roasting pan.

2. Add garlic, celery, rosemary, and thyme to skillet, and cook 1 minute. Add vermouth, increase heat to high, bring to a boil, and cook 2 minutes to evaporate alcohol. Add broth and salt to skillet, and bring to a boil. Pour vegetables and cooking liquid over chicken in roasting pan.

3. Cover pan with foil, place in oven, and bake 45 minutes or until chicken is cooked through and garlic is meltingly tender.

4. Meanwhile, in large skillet, heat remaining 4 tablespoons oil over medium heat. Add bread slices and sauté 1 minute per side or until golden brown. Cut each piece in half. Spoon chicken and garlic onto dinner plates. Serve with sautéed bread for spreading garlic.

Prep Time: 25 minutes
Cooking Time: 1 hour 15 minutes
Makes 8 servings

NUTRITION INFORMATION
Per Serving
Calories 753
Total Fat 30g
Saturated Fat 5.5g
Cholesterol 278mg
Sodium 1033mg
Protein 89g
Carbohydrates 25g

Moroccan Chicken with Almonds

For a Moroccan-style presentation, spoon couscous onto a large round platter and place the chicken pieces and sauce on top. Garnish with sprigs of cilantro. Serve with tall glasses of iced mint tea.

- 3 tablespoons olive oil
- 1½ teaspoons ground cumin
- 1 teaspoon paprika
- 1 teaspoon turmeric
- ¼ teaspoon ground allspice
- 8 whole chicken legs (about 4 pounds), split into drumsticks and thighs (page 14), skin removed
- 1 large onion, finely chopped
- 4 cloves garlic, finely chopped
- 1 cup dried apricots
- ½ cup chopped cilantro
- 1 teaspoon salt
- ½ cup slivered almonds

1. In large skillet, heat oil over medium heat. Add cumin, paprika, turmeric, and allspice, and cook 1 minute. Working in batches, add chicken and cook 4 minutes per side or until golden brown. As chicken browns, transfer to 7- to 8-quart casserole.

2. Add onion and garlic to skillet, and cook 10 minutes or until golden brown and tender. Transfer to casserole with chicken.

3. Add 1½ cups of water to skillet and bring to a boil. Add apricots, ¼ cup of cilantro, and the salt to skillet, and return to a boil. Pour apricot mixture into casserole with chicken. Bring to a boil, reduce to a simmer, cover, and cook 30 minutes or until chicken is tender. Stir in almonds and remaining ¼ cup cilantro.

Prep Time: 15 minutes
Cooking Time: 1 hour
Makes 8 servings

NUTRITION INFORMATION
Per Serving
Calories 305
Total Fat 15g
Saturated Fat 2.5g
Cholesterol 104mg
Sodium 407mg
Protein 29g
Carbohydrates 15g

CHICKEN BAKED WITH 40 CLOVES OF GARLIC

COUNTRY CAPTAIN

Prep Time: 20 minutes
Cooking Time: 1 hour 5 minutes
Makes 8 servings

NUTRITION INFORMATION

Per Serving

Calories 453

Total Fat 20g

Saturated Fat 3g

Cholesterol 133mg

Sodium 644mg

Protein 45g

Carbohydrates 24g

Country Captain

Although it still seems quite exotic, Indian food is no recent arrival to our shores: This dish dates back to the nineteenth century. Perhaps, as the name implies, the recipe was brought back by a ship's captain or a military officer, but it's possible that residents of a port city (Savannah, Georgia, often gets the credit) simply made creative use of the new spices that the sailing ships brought home.

½ cup dried currants or raisins

½ cup slivered almonds

⅓ cup olive oil

2 whole chickens (about 3½ pounds each), each cut into 10 pieces (page 14), skin removed from all but wings

½ cup flour

1 large onion, finely chopped

3 cloves garlic, finely chopped

1 red bell pepper, cut into ¼-inch dice

4 teaspoons curry powder

1 teaspoon dried thyme

1 teaspoon salt

1 can (35 ounces) tomatoes, chopped with their juice

1. Preheat oven to 350°F. In small bowl, combine currants and ½ cup of hot water. Let stand 10 minutes or until softened.

2. Meanwhile, place almonds on baking sheet and bake for 5 minutes or until golden brown. When cool enough to handle, coarsely chop.

3. In large skillet, heat oil over medium heat. Dredge chicken in flour, shaking off excess. Working in batches, add chicken to skillet and cook 4 minutes per side or until golden brown. As it browns, transfer chicken to 10 x 14-inch roasting pan.

4. Add onion and garlic to skillet, and cook 5 minutes or until onion is tender. Add bell pepper and cook 4 minutes or until crisp-tender. Stir in curry powder, thyme, and salt, and cook 1 minute. Add tomatoes and currants and their soaking liquid, and bring to a boil. Pour sauce over chicken in roasting pan. Cover with foil, place in oven, and bake for 30 minutes or until chicken is cooked through. Serve chicken sprinkled with toasted almonds.

PASTA WITH SPICY CHICKEN & TOMATO SAUCE

Follow steps 1 and 2. Omit flour and step 3. Substitute 2 pounds skinless, boneless chicken thighs (cut into bite-size pieces) for whole cut-up chickens, and cook in step 4 after sautéing bell pepper. Add ½ teaspoon cayenne pepper when adding curry powder. Simmer chicken in sauce, uncovered, 20 minutes or until chicken is cooked through and sauce is slightly thickened. Meanwhile, in large pot of boiling water, cook 1½ pounds of fusilli pasta according to package directions. Drain and toss with chicken sauce.

Calories 649, Total Fat 20g, Saturated Fat 3g, Cholesterol 94mg, Sodium 891mg, Protein 37g, Carbohydrates 81g

Chicken Phyllo Pie

The inspiration for this offbeat dish is a Moroccan extravaganza called b'steeya. The original is an oversized "pie" enclosed in paper-thin leaves of a homemade pastry called warka. The filling is shredded squab, scrambled eggs, and sweetened ground almonds. In this more modestly scaled version, butter-brushed phyllo dough takes the place of warka, and chicken is used instead of squab.

- ½ cup whole natural (unblanched) almonds
- ¼ cup confectioners' sugar
- 1 teaspoon ground cinnamon
- 1 cup chicken broth, canned or homemade (page 45)
- 3 cloves garlic, finely chopped
- ½ cup chopped parsley
- ½ cup chopped cilantro
- ¼ cup fresh lemon juice
- ½ teaspoon salt
- 6 eggs, lightly beaten
- ½ cup (1 stick) butter, melted
- 10 sheets (11 x 17-inch) phyllo dough
- 6 cups shredded cooked chicken thighs or breasts—leftover or poached (page 17)

1. Preheat oven to 350°F. Place almonds on baking sheet and cook 7 minutes or until lightly crisped and fragrant. Transfer almonds to food processor. Add confectioners' sugar and cinnamon, and process until finely ground.

2. In medium saucepan, bring broth and garlic to a boil over medium heat. Stir in parsley, cilantro, lemon juice, and salt. Stirring constantly, whisk in eggs. Reduce heat to low and cook 7 minutes or until mixture is thick and eggs are softly set. Drain any liquid remaining.

3. Brush 9-inch springform pan with some of the melted butter. Line with 6 overlapping sheets of phyllo (see technique photo, top right), brushing each sheet with melted butter (entire bottom and sides should be covered with phyllo). Scatter chicken over bottom of pan. Spoon egg mixture over.

4. Fold overlap of phyllo over top of pie. Place 2 sheets of phyllo on top, brushing each with butter. Sprinkle almond mixture over and top with remaining 2 sheets phyllo, brushing each with butter. Trim overhang of phyllo and tuck between edge of pan and pie to seal pie (bottom photo). Brush top with remaining butter. Place springform on jelly-roll pan (to catch any butter that leaks out) and bake for 35 minutes or until phyllo is crisp and golden brown. Release sides of springform pan and serve hot.

MOROCCAN CHICKEN TURNOVERS WITH CURRY BUTTER Omit step 1, but preheat oven to 350°F. In step 2, omit broth and lemon juice. Instead, in large skillet, sauté garlic in 1 tablespoon butter over low heat until tender. In medium bowl, whisk together parsley, cilantro, salt, eggs, and 1 teaspoon grated lemon zest. Add egg mixture and shredded chicken (reduce chicken to 3 cups) to skillet and cook, stirring constantly, 3 to 4 minutes or until eggs are creamy and set. Cool to room temperature. In small saucepan, melt 7 tablespoons butter, 2 teaspoons curry powder, and ½ teaspoon ground ginger over low heat. Omit steps 3 and 4. Using a total of 8 sheets of phyllo, make 2 stacks of 4 sheets each, brushing each sheet with some curry butter before placing the next sheet on top. Cut each stack crosswise into four 4¼ x 11-inch strips for total of 8 strips. Divide chicken mixture evenly among strips, placing mixture on top right hand side of each strip. Fold each strip up like a flag (see technique photos, page 30). Transfer to ungreased baking sheet and brush phyllo packets with remaining butter. Bake 25 minutes or until crisp and golden brown.

Calories 449, Total Fat 28g, Saturated Fat 12g, Cholesterol 291mg, Sodium 497mg, Protein 34g, Carbohydrates 13g

LEFTOVERS

Prep Time: 30 minutes
Cooking Time: 50 minutes
Makes 8 servings

NUTRITION INFORMATION
Per Serving
Calories 522
Total Fat 33g
Saturated Fat 12g
Cholesterol 291mg
Sodium 652mg
Protein 36g
Carbohydrates 20g

TECHNIQUE

MAKING PHYLLO PIE

To line the pan, place each sheet of phyllo at a slight angle to the last sheet so that the whole bottom and sides are covered, with an equal amount of overhang all around.

After placing the phyllo on top of the pie (again at a slight angle to one another), use scissors to trim the overhang to about 1 inch. Then tuck the overhang down the sides of the pan to seal the pie.

CHICKEN PHYLLO PIE

Chicken Biriyani

Here is Indian food at its simple, inviting best. Biriyanis are rice dishes layered with meat, poultry, or seafood. Add interest to the meal by serving a selection of Indian pickles and chutneys, along with an Indian bread, such as naan, which is sold in many supermarkets.

LOW FAT

Prep Time: 15 minutes plus
   marinating time
Cooking Time: 45 minutes
Makes 8 servings

6	cloves garlic, crushed and peeled
2	pickled jalapeño peppers
1	piece (3-inch) fresh ginger, peeled and thinly sliced
⅓	cup fresh lemon juice (about 3 lemons)
2	cups plain low-fat yogurt
2	tablespoons curry powder
2½	teaspoons ground cumin
1	teaspoon salt
16	bone-in chicken thighs or drumsticks (about 4 pounds), skin removed
⅓	cup vegetable oil
1	large onion, halved and thinly sliced
2	cups basmati rice
1	package (10 ounces) frozen peas, thawed

1. In food processor or blender, combine garlic, jalapeños, ginger, and lemon juice, and process to a paste. Transfer to large bowl and stir in yogurt, curry powder, cumin, and salt. With fork or small knife, pierce chicken pieces in several places. Add to yogurt mixture, turning pieces to coat. Cover and refrigerate at least 2 hours or up to 4 hours.

2. Preheat oven to 350°F. In 7- to 8-quart flameproof casserole or Dutch oven, heat oil over medium heat. Add onion and cook, stirring frequently, 10 minutes or until golden brown. Add chicken and its marinade, reduce heat to low, and bring to a simmer.

3. Stir rice into casserole. Cover, place in oven, and bake for 35 minutes or until rice is tender and chicken is cooked through. Remove from oven, uncover, stir in peas, and cook on stovetop until peas are heated through.

NUTRITION INFORMATION
Per Serving
Calories 477
Total Fat 16g
Saturated Fat 3g
Cholesterol 111mg
Sodium 561mg
Protein 36g
Carbohydrates 50g

Chinese Chicken with Walnuts

In China, this dish would be made with a deep red, very salty ham that is most commonly cut into slivers or dice and used as a flavoring. Virginia ham, slow-cured and wood-smoked, is the best American substitute for the Chinese ham.

Prep Time: 20 minutes
Cooking Time: 20 minutes
Makes 8 servings

1	cup walnuts
⅓	cup lower-sodium soy sauce
1	tablespoon dry sherry
1	tablespoon cornstarch
1	teaspoon sugar
½	teaspoon salt
2½	pounds skinless, boneless chicken breasts, cut into 1-inch chunks
4	tablespoons vegetable oil
3	leeks, cut into 2-inch-long strips
1	pound asparagus, cut on diagonal into 1-inch lengths
1	red bell pepper, cut into thin strips
¼	pound Virginia ham, cut into 2-inch matchsticks
3	cloves garlic, finely chopped
½	cup chicken broth

1. Preheat oven to 350°F. Place walnuts on baking sheet and bake for 7 minutes or until lightly crisped and fragrant.

2. Meanwhile, in large bowl, whisk together soy sauce, sherry, cornstarch, sugar, and salt. Add chicken and toss to coat well.

3. In large skillet, heat 2 tablespoons of oil over medium heat. Add chicken to pan and cook 5 minutes or until golden brown and almost cooked through. With slotted spoon, transfer chicken to plate.

4. Add remaining 2 tablespoons oil to pan and heat over medium heat. Add leeks, asparagus, bell pepper, ham, and garlic, and stir-fry 4 minutes or until asparagus is crisp-tender. Add broth and cook 2 minutes. Return chicken to pan and cook 2 minutes or until cooked through. Sprinkle with toasted walnuts to serve.

NUTRITION INFORMATION
Per Serving
Calories 399
Total Fat 19g
Saturated Fat 2.5g
Cholesterol 92mg
Sodium 1093mg
Protein 42g
Carbohydrates 14g

CHINESE CHICKEN WITH WALNUTS

CHICKEN & MUSHROOM RAGOUT OVER POLENTA

Prep Time: 20 minutes plus standing time for polenta

Cooking Time: 1 hour 40 minutes

Makes 8 servings

NUTRITION INFORMATION

Per Serving

Calories 475

Total Fat 19g

Saturated Fat 4g

Cholesterol 105mg

Sodium 999mg

Protein 48g

Carbohydrates 28g

TECHNIQUE

MAKING POLENTA

When polenta is cooked to the proper, stiff consistency, a wooden spoon will actually stand up in the mixture.

Chicken & Mushroom Ragout over Polenta

Contrary to popular opinion, not everyone in Italy dines daily on pasta. In northern Italy, polenta—a thick cornmeal mush—is preferred. Like pasta, polenta is bland, and an ideal underpinning for flavorful sauces. Cut into squares and sautéed, polenta develops a crisp crust.

- 1 cup yellow cornmeal
- 2 teaspoons salt
- ¾ cup grated Parmesan cheese
- 1 package (.35 ounce) dried porcini mushrooms
- ½ cup boiling water
- 8 tablespoons olive oil
- 8 skinless, boneless chicken breast halves (about 3 pounds), each cut crosswise into 4 pieces
- ⅓ cup flour
- 6 cloves garlic, finely chopped
- 1 pound button mushrooms, quartered
- ¾ pound shiitake mushrooms, stems trimmed and caps quartered
- ½ cup dry red wine
- 1 can (28 ounces) tomatoes, chopped with their juice

1. In small bowl, stir together cornmeal and 1½ cups of cold water until well combined. In medium saucepan, bring 2 cups of water to a boil over medium heat. Stir in 1 teaspoon of salt and cornmeal mixture, reduce heat to low, and cook, stirring frequently, 15 minutes or until mixture is very thick and begins to leave sides of pan (a wooden spoon will actually stand up; see technique photo, at left). Add Parmesan and stir to combine. Pour mixture into lightly greased 9-inch square baking dish and let stand 45 minutes until firm. (This can be done as much as a day ahead; cover and refrigerate until ready to use.)

2. In small bowl, combine porcini and boiling water, and let stand 20 minutes or until mushrooms are soft. With slotted spoon, scoop mushrooms out of their soaking liquid, rinse them, and coarsely chop. Strain soaking liquid through paper towel-lined sieve.

3. Meanwhile, in Dutch oven or 5-quart flameproof casserole, heat 2 tablespoons of oil over medium heat. Dredge chicken in flour, shaking off excess. Add half of chicken and sauté 3 minutes per side or until golden brown. Transfer chicken to plate. Repeat with 2 tablespoons of oil and remaining chicken.

4. Reduce heat to low, add garlic, and stir-fry 2 minutes or until tender. Add reconstituted porcini, and fresh button and shiitake mushrooms; cover and cook 10 minutes or until fresh mushrooms are soft. Uncover, increase heat to high, and cook 5 minutes or until liquid has evaporated.

5. Add red wine and cook 2 minutes. Add tomatoes, mushroom soaking liquid, and remaining 1 teaspoon salt, and bring to a boil. Return chicken to pan and bring to a boil; reduce to a simmer, cover, and cook 45 minutes or until chicken is tender.

6. Meanwhile, with metal spatula, cut around edges of polenta pan. Invert polenta onto work surface and cut into 16 squares. In large skillet, heat remaining 4 tablespoons of oil. Add polenta to skillet and sauté 4 minutes per side or until golden brown and crispy. Serve polenta squares topped with chicken and sauce.

IN A HURRY?

Substitute 1 pound precooked polenta (found in refrigerated compartment in many supermarkets) for homemade polenta (step 1). At serving time, cut polenta into 8 slices, sprinkle with 1 tablespoon Parmesan each, and broil for 1 minute.

TO REDUCE THE FAT

Omit step 6 and 4 tablespoons of oil. Instead, preheat broiler. Lightly grease baking sheet. Place polenta squares on baking sheet and spray tops of polenta lightly with nonstick cooking spray. Broil for 1 minute or until lightly browned.

Calories 427, Total Fat 13g, Saturated Fat 3g, Cholesterol 105mg, Sodium 999mg, Protein 48g, Carbohydrates 28g

CHICKEN & ORZO SALAD WITH SCALLIONS

Prep Time: 15 minutes plus
  standing time
Cooking Time: 35 minutes
Makes 8 servings

NUTRITION INFORMATION
Per Serving
Calories 411
Total Fat 23g
Saturated Fat 8.5g
Cholesterol 98mg
Sodium 494mg
Protein 28g
Carbohydrates 25g

Tortilla Torta with Chicken, Pepperjack & Tomato

This unexpected brunch dish, gooey with melted cheese, is of Mexican derivation: Corn tortillas are layered with shredded chicken bathed in a creamy but peppery sauce. Use a nice thick salsa, not a watery one. If the salsa seems too thin, place it into a strainer and let some of the liquid drain off.

2	tablespoons olive oil
2	scallions, thinly sliced
2	cloves garlic, finely chopped
1	red bell pepper, cut into ¼-inch dice
2	tablespoons flour
1¾	cups milk
½	pound pepperjack cheese, shredded (2 cups)
3	cups shredded cooked chicken thighs or breasts—leftover or poached (page 17)
½	cup chunky, mild or hot bottled salsa
12	corn tortillas (7-inch diameter)

1. Preheat oven to 400°F. In large saucepan, heat oil over medium heat. Add scallions and garlic, and cook, stirring frequently, 2 minutes or until scallions are tender. Add bell pepper and cook, stirring frequently, 4 minutes or until tender. Stir in flour and cook 1 minute. Gradually stir in milk and cook, stirring frequently, 5 minutes or until mixture has thickened. Remove from heat and stir in pepperjack until melted. Stir in chicken and salsa.

2. Lightly grease a 3- to 4-quart soufflé dish whose diameter is slightly larger than 7 inches. Place 1 tortilla on bottom. Spoon generous ¼ cup of chicken mixture over tortilla. Continue layering tortillas and chicken mixture until both have been used up. The top tortilla should be covered with chicken mixture as well. Cover with foil and bake for 20 minutes or until piping hot and bubbly. Let stand 20 minutes before spooning out.

Prep Time: 15 minutes
Cooking Time: 10 minutes
Makes 8 servings

NUTRITION INFORMATION
Per Serving
Calories 511
Total Fat 18g
Saturated Fat 2.5g
Cholesterol 60mg
Sodium 936mg
Protein 32g
Carbohydrates 54g

Chicken & Orzo Salad with Scallions

As a change from run-of-the-mill macaroni salad, bring this hearty chicken and pasta main-dish salad to your next potluck. No stodgy mayonnaise here: The dressing is a snappy lemon vinaigrette. Garbanzo beans add extra protein, and snipped dill contributes its wonderfully fresh flavor.

1	pound orzo
1	tablespoon grated lemon zest
⅔	cup fresh lemon juice (about 6 lemons)
½	cup olive oil
2¾	teaspoons salt
4	cups shredded cooked chicken breasts or thighs—leftover or poached (page 17)
2	red bell peppers, cut into ¼-inch dice
1	can (19 ounces) garbanzos (chick-peas), rinsed and drained
1	pint cherry tomatoes, halved
⅓	cup snipped fresh dill
6	scallions, thinly sliced

1. In large pot of boiling water, cook orzo according to package directions; drain.

2. Meanwhile, in large bowl, whisk together lemon zest, lemon juice, oil, and salt. Add hot orzo and toss to combine.

3. Add chicken, bell peppers, garbanzos, cherry tomatoes, dill, and scallions, and toss to combine. Serve at room temperature or chilled.

Focaccia Pizza
with Sausage & Spinach

Unless you grew up in an Italian neighborhood, focaccia is probably a recent addition to your culinary vocabulary. This thick flatbread, which resembles a pizza crust, can be baked with toppings, or used as a sandwich bread. Bake an extra batch of the focaccia and try it.

Prep Time: 20 minutes plus
  rising time
Cooking Time: 50 minutes
Makes 8 servings

- 3 tablespoons olive oil
- ¾ pound fresh chicken sausage
- 2 pounds store-bought pizza or bread dough
- 1 container (15 ounces) ricotta cheese
- 1 package (10 ounces) frozen chopped spinach, thawed and squeezed dry
- ½ teaspoon salt
- ¼ teaspoon ground nutmeg
- 4 cups shredded mozzarella cheese (1 pound)
- 1 red bell pepper, cut into thin slivers
- 1 green bell pepper, cut into thin slivers

1. In small skillet, heat 1 tablespoon of oil over medium heat. Add sausage and cook, turning occasionally, 10 minutes or until just done. Drain on paper towels. When cool enough to handle, thinly slice.

2. Pat dough into greased 10½ x 15-inch jelly-roll pan. With your fingers, dimple dough all over, pressing almost but not through dough. Drizzle remaining 2 tablespoons oil over dough. Cover with oiled plastic wrap and let stand in warm, draft-free spot 30 minutes or until puffy.

3. Meanwhile, preheat oven to 450°F. Uncover dough and bake 20 minutes or until golden brown and crisp. Cool to room temperature.

4. In medium bowl, stir together ricotta, spinach, salt, and nutmeg. Spread ricotta mixture over dough. Scatter mozzarella on top. Sprinkle sausage and peppers on top. Bake 15 to 20 minutes or until cheese has melted and pizza crust is browned and crisp. Cool 5 minutes before cutting.

IN A HURRY?

Use ¾ pound fully-cooked chicken sausage, sliced, and omit step 1 and the 1 tablespoon oil. Use a store-bought focaccia at least 10½ inches square and layer with sausage and toppings as directed. Bake in 450°F. oven for 15 minutes or until cheese has melted.

NUTRITION INFORMATION
Per Serving
Calories 634
Total Fat 30g
Saturated Fat 13g
Cholesterol 97mg
Sodium 1750mg
Protein 36g
Carbohydrates 56g

Chicken & Scallion Strata

Strata means "layers," and that's how this brunch favorite is made—by layering bread and filling, pouring on a mixture of milk and eggs, and then baking. If possible, let the strata sit overnight after pouring on the liquid; the bread will become saturated and bake up like a soufflé.

LEFTOVERS

Prep Time: 15 minutes plus
  standing time
Cooking Time: 50 minutes
Makes 8 servings

- 1 tablespoon olive oil
- 8 scallions, thinly sliced
- 1 red bell pepper, cut into ½-inch squares
- 3 cups milk
- 8 eggs
- 1 cup grated Parmesan cheese
- ¾ teaspoon salt
- ¾ teaspoon freshly ground black pepper
- 4 cups chunks (½-inch) cooked chicken thighs or breasts—leftover or poached (page 17)
- 6 slices (½-inch-thick) country bread (about 10 ounces), halved crosswise

1. In medium skillet, heat oil over medium heat. Add scallions and bell pepper, and cook 4 minutes or until pepper is crisp-tender. Cool to room temperature.

2. In large bowl, whisk together milk, eggs, Parmesan, salt, and black pepper. Stir in cooled scallion mixture. Lightly grease 9 x 13-inch glass baking dish. Place chicken in bottom of dish. Top chicken with bread and prick bread in several places. Pour egg mixture over bread. Cover and refrigerate 30 minutes or up to overnight.

3. Preheat oven to 325°F. Bake 45 minutes or until egg mixture is set and strata is puffed and golden. Let stand 10 minutes before serving.

NUTRITION INFORMATION
Per Serving
Calories 443
Total Fat 22g
Saturated Fat 8g
Cholesterol 301mg
Sodium 784mg
Protein 35g
Carbohydrates 25g

FOCACCIA PIZZA WITH SAUSAGE & SPINACH

Chicken Burritos
with Roasted Tomato Salsa

Roasting vegetables works a sort of alchemy that no other cooking technique can match. The direct heat concentrates the flavor and adds a rich, smoky note as well. Plum tomatoes are the best for roasting because the flesh is comparatively dry and will not turn to mush.

2   pounds plum tomatoes, halved lengthwise

2   tablespoons olive oil

1   red onion, finely chopped

3   cloves garlic, finely chopped

¾   teaspoon ground cumin

½   teaspoon dried oregano

½   teaspoon salt

¼   teaspoon crushed red pepper flakes

16   flour tortillas (7-inch diameter)

4   cups shredded cooked chicken thighs or breasts—leftover or poached (page 17)

6   ounces feta cheese, crumbled

32   sprigs of cilantro

2   tablespoons fresh lime juice

1. Preheat broiler. In large bowl, toss tomatoes with 1 tablespoon of oil. Place tomatoes, cut-side down, on broiler pan and broil 8 inches from heat for 3 minutes or until skin begins to blister. When cool enough to handle, coarsely chop tomatoes and transfer to large bowl.

2. In small skillet, heat remaining 1 tablespoon oil over medium heat. Add onion and garlic, and cook, stirring frequently, 10 minutes or until onion is golden brown. Stir in cumin, oregano, salt, and red pepper flakes, and cook 2 minutes. Transfer to bowl with tomatoes and stir to combine.

3. Place tortillas on work surface. Divide chicken, feta, cilantro, and roasted tomato salsa evenly among tortillas. Sprinkle with lime juice and roll up.

LEFTOVERS

Prep Time: 20 minutes
Cooking Time: 15 minutes
Makes 8 servings

NUTRITION INFORMATION
Per Serving
Calories 449
Total Fat 20g
Saturated Fat 6.5g
Cholesterol 86mg
Sodium 721mg
Protein 28g
Carbohydrates 40g

Chicken Tabbouleh Salad

Basic tabbouleh is a toss of fresh parsley and mint, tomatoes, onions, and bulgur (a type of cracked wheat) in a light, lemony dressing. The addition of shredded chicken makes it a meal. Look for bulgur on the shelves near the rice or in the Middle Eastern foods section of the supermarket.

3   green bell peppers, cut lengthwise into flat panels

1⅓   cups bulgur

1¼   cups fresh lemon juice (about 10 lemons)

⅔   cup olive oil

1½   teaspoons salt

½   teaspoon ground allspice

1½   cups chopped parsley

½   cup chopped fresh mint or 1 tablespoon dried

2   large tomatoes, cut into ½-inch chunks

1   large cucumber, peeled, halved lengthwise, seeded, and cut into ¼-inch-thick slices

4   cups shredded cooked chicken breasts or thighs—leftover or poached (page 17)

8   cups mixed salad greens (optional)

1. Preheat broiler. Place bell pepper pieces, skin-side up, on broiler pan and broil 4 inches from heat for 10 minutes or until skin is blackened. When cool enough to handle, peel peppers and cut into ½-inch squares.

2. Meanwhile, in large bowl, combine bulgur and 3 cups of hot water. Let stand 30 minutes. Drain through colander. Transfer bulgur to kitchen towel and press on bulgur to remove excess liquid.

3. In large bowl, whisk together lemon juice, oil, salt, and allspice. Add bulgur and toss well. Add parsley, mint, tomatoes, cucumber, chicken, and roasted peppers, and toss well. Cover and refrigerate at least 1 hour for flavors to blend. Serve over salad greens, if desired.

LEFTOVERS

Prep Time: 25 minutes plus soaking and chilling time
Cooking Time: 10 minutes
Makes 8 servings

NUTRITION INFORMATION
Per Serving
Calories 395
Total Fat 21g
Saturated Fat 3g
Cholesterol 60mg
Sodium 506mg
Protein 26g
Carbohydrates 28g

CHICKEN TABBOULEH SALAD

CHICKEN-STUFFED MANICOTTI WITH PORCINI CREAM SAUCE

Prep Time: 20 minutes plus
   mushroom soaking time
Cooking Time: 1 hour
Makes 8 servings

NUTRITION INFORMATION

Per Serving

Calories 600

Total Fat 29g

Saturated Fat 11g

Cholesterol 139mg

Sodium 857mg

Protein 32g

Carbohydrates 52g

HINTS & TIPS

➤ Dried mushrooms some-
times have a little grit
trapped in their folds, so it's
a good idea to strain the
soaking liquid through a
sieve lined with a paper
towel (or through a coffee
filter) to catch any grit.

➤ Porcini have a delicious
earthy flavor, but if you
can't find them—or would
prefer not to spend the
money—this dish would be
fine with the type of dried
mushroom found in most
supermarkets. The plastic
tub that holds the mush-
rooms is usually simply
labeled "Wild Mushrooms"
or "Dried Mushrooms."

➤ If you've baked the manicotti ahead of time and
frozen it, reheat it, covered
with foil, in a 350°F. oven (it
doesn't have to be thawed)
for 30 to 50 minutes, or
until the manicotti are piping hot. Ten minutes before
it's done, remove the foil
and sprinkle the manicotti
with the Parmesan.

Chicken-Stuffed Manicotti with Porcini Cream Sauce

The sauce for this upscale pasta bake looks deceptively delicate, but it's robustly flavored with dried porcini and fresh shiitake mushrooms, sage, and a bit of bourbon or brandy. If you don't need 8 servings all at once, bake one of the pans of manicotti to freeze for another day, with the following changes: Remove the pan from the oven before sprinkling with Parmesan (the cheese will be sprinkled on when the manicotti are reheated—see "Hints & Tips" below); cool to room temperature, cover with foil, and freeze.

 1 package (.35 ounce) dried porcini mushrooms
 1 cup boiling water
16 manicotti (about 1 pound)
 3 tablespoons olive oil
 2 large onions, finely chopped
 5 cloves garlic, finely chopped
 2 pounds ground chicken
 1 cup heavy or whipping cream
1¼ teaspoons salt
 ¾ teaspoon freshly ground black pepper
 ¾ teaspoon dried sage
 1 pound fresh shiitake mushrooms, stems trimmed and caps thinly sliced
 ¼ cup bourbon or brandy
 ¾ cup chicken broth
 ½ cup grated Parmesan cheese

1. In small bowl, combine dried porcini and boiling water, and let stand 20 minutes or until mushrooms are soft. With your fingers, scoop mushrooms out and rinse under running water. Coarsely chop; set aside. Strain soaking liquid through paper towel-lined sieve.

2. Meanwhile, in large pot of boiling water, cook manicotti according to package directions. Drain, rinse under running water, and set aside.

3. In large skillet, heat oil over medium heat. Add onions and garlic, and cook, stirring frequently, 7 minutes or until onions are soft. Transfer 1 cup of onion mixture to large bowl and cool to room temperature. Stir in chicken, ¼ cup of cream, ¾ teaspoon of salt, ½ teaspoon of pepper, ½ teaspoon of sage, and ⅓ cup of mushroom-soaking liquid. Mix well.

4. Preheat oven to 350°F. Fill a pastry bag or large sturdy zip-seal bag with chicken filling. Pipe into cooked manicotti (see technique photo, page 104). Place 8 manicotti in each of two 9 x 13-inch baking dishes.

5. Return skillet with onion to heat. Add fresh shiitakes and reconstituted porcini, and cook, stirring frequently, 5 minutes or until fresh mushrooms are tender. Add bourbon, bring to a boil, and cook 1 minute to evaporate alcohol. Add broth and remaining mushroom-soaking liquid; bring to a boil and boil 3 minutes. Add remaining ¾ cup cream, ½ teaspoon salt, ¼ teaspoon pepper, and ¼ teaspoon sage; bring to a boil and boil 1 minute.

6. Pour cream sauce over manicotti, cover, and bake for 30 minutes. Uncover, sprinkle with Parmesan, and bake for 10 minutes or until piping hot.

FROM THE FRIDGE

Use 3 cups minced cooked chicken instead of ground chicken and add as directed in step 3.

Coq au Vin

If France has a national comfort food, this is it. You'll find coq au vin on the menu at just about any self-respecting bistro. Serve it with plenty of crusty French bread.

- ½ pound bacon, cut crosswise into 1-inch pieces
- 2 whole chickens (about 3½ pounds each), each cut into 8 serving pieces (page 14), skin removed
- ⅓ cup plus 2 tablespoons flour
- 2 cups frozen pearl onions, thawed
- 3 cloves garlic, crushed and peeled
- 2 teaspoon sugar
- 1 pound mushrooms, quartered
- 2 cups dry red wine
- ¾ cup chicken broth
- 2 tablespoons tomato paste
- 1 teaspoon salt
- ½ teaspoon dried thyme
- ½ teaspoon freshly ground black pepper

1. Preheat oven to 350°F. In 8-quart flameproof casserole, sauté bacon over medium heat for 7 minutes or until bacon is crisp and fat is rendered. With slotted spoon, transfer bacon to paper towels to drain. Pour bacon fat into cup or bowl.

2. Return 4 tablespoons of bacon fat to casserole (discard any remaining fat). Dredge chicken in ⅓ cup of flour, shaking off excess. Working in batches, add chicken to pan and sauté 4 minutes per side or until golden brown. As chicken browns, transfer to bowl.

3. Add pearl onions and garlic to pan. Sprinkle with sugar and cook, stirring frequently, 7 minutes or until onions are lightly golden. Add mushrooms and cook, stirring frequently, 5 minutes or until tender. Add wine to pan, increase heat to high, and boil 2 minutes. Add broth, tomato paste, salt, thyme, and pepper, and return to a boil. Return chicken and bacon to pan and bring to a boil. Cover casserole, place in oven, and bake for 1 hour or until chicken is cooked through.

4. In small saucepan, combine remaining 2 tablespoons flour and ¼ cup of water. Ladle out 1 cup of cooking juices from casserole and add to saucepan. Bring to a boil over medium heat. Stir thickened sauce back into casserole.

Prep Time: 15 minutes
Cooking Time: 1 hour 40 minutes
Makes 8 servings

NUTRITION INFORMATION
Per Serving
Calories 392
Total Fat 15g
Saturated Fat 4.5g
Cholesterol 145mg
Sodium 738mg
Protein 46g
Carbohydrates 16g

Chicken Paella

Paella, its golden rice studded with tomatoes, chicken, and seafood, is one of Spain's proudest culinary traditions. Don't be shocked at the price of saffron—a little goes a very long way.

- ¼ cup olive oil
- 8 whole chicken legs (about 5 pounds), split into drumsticks and thighs (page 14), skin and any visible fat removed
- 1 large onion, finely chopped
- 5 cloves garlic, finely chopped
- 1 green bell pepper, cut into ½-inch chunks
- 1 red bell pepper, cut into ½-inch chunks
- 2 cups rice
- 3 cups chicken broth, canned or homemade (page 45)
- 1 can (14½ ounces) diced tomatoes, chopped with their juice
- 2 teaspoons salt
- ¼ teaspoon saffron threads
- 1½ pounds large shrimp, shelled and deveined

1. In large nonstick skillet, heat oil over medium heat. Working in batches, add chicken to pan and cook 4 minutes per side or until golden brown. As chicken browns, transfer to plate.

2. Add onion and garlic to pan and cook, stirring frequently, 10 minutes or until onion is soft and golden brown. Add bell peppers and cook, stirring frequently, 4 minutes or until peppers are crisp-tender.

3. Add rice to pan and cook, stirring frequently, 5 minutes or until rice is pale gold. Transfer mixture to 7- to 8-quart flameproof casserole or Dutch oven. Add broth, tomatoes, salt, saffron, and 1 cup of water, and bring to a boil. Reduce to a simmer, return chicken to pan, cover, and cook 30 minutes or until chicken is tender.

4. Place shrimp on top, cover, and cook 10 minutes or until shrimp are cooked through and rice is tender.

LOW FAT

Prep Time: 25 minutes
Cooking Time: 1 hour 20 minutes
Makes 8 servings

NUTRITION INFORMATION
Per Serving
Calories 534
Total Fat 15g
Saturated Fat 3g
Cholesterol 235mg
Sodium 1306mg
Protein 51g
Carbohydrates 44g

CHICKEN PAELLA

CHICKEN-RICOTTA NOODLE ROLL-UPS WITH SUN-DRIED TOMATO SAUCE

Prep Time: 35 minutes
Cooking Time: 50 minutes
Makes 8 servings

NUTRITION INFORMATION

Per Serving

Calories 493

Total Fat 20g

Saturated Fat 9g

Cholesterol 87mg

Sodium 1282mg

Protein 26g

Carbohydrates 53g

TECHNIQUE

MAKING LASAGNA ROLLS

After covering the cooked lasagna noodles with smoked chicken, spread with the ricotta-feta mixture, leaving a border along both sides to allow for spreading.

Roll up the lasagna noodles gently enough so the filling does not squeeze out, but firmly enough so the roll does not come apart.

Chicken-Ricotta Noodle Roll-Ups with Sun-Dried Tomato Sauce

Flat lasagna is fine, but ruffly, individually rolled noodles are more fun. A rich sauce made with sun-dried tomatoes adds zest to this appealing entrée, but to save time, you can use a good-quality bottled marinara or sun-dried tomato sauce. You'll need 5 cups of sauce for this recipe.

- 2 tablespoons olive oil
- 1 large onion, finely chopped
- 4 cloves garlic, finely chopped
- 1 can (35 ounces) tomatoes, chopped with their juice
- ½ cup oil-packed sun-dried tomatoes, drained and finely chopped
- ½ cup chopped fresh basil leaves
- ¾ teaspoon salt
- 16 lasagna noodles
- 1 container (15 ounces) ricotta cheese
- 6 ounces feta cheese, crumbled
- 1 large egg
- 10 ounces smoked chicken breast, thinly sliced crosswise and each slice halved lengthwise

1. In large skillet, heat oil over medium heat. Add onion and garlic, and cook, stirring frequently, 7 minutes or until onion is soft. Add canned tomatoes, sun-dried tomatoes, basil, and ¼ teaspoon of salt, and bring to a boil. Reduce to a simmer, cover, and cook 10 minutes to develop flavors.

2. Meanwhile, in large pot of boiling water, cook lasagna noodles according to package directions. Drain and rinse under running water.

3. Preheat oven to 400°F. In medium bowl, stir together ricotta, feta, egg, and remaining ½ teaspoon salt. Lay cooked lasagna out on work surface. Divide smoked chicken evenly among lasagna noodles, placing strips down length of noodles. Spoon ricotta mixture over chicken (see technique photo, top left). Starting at one short end, roll each noodle up (bottom photo).

4. Lightly grease two 7 x 11-inch glass baking dishes. Place 8 rolls, seam-side down, in each baking dish. Spoon sauce over each. Cover with foil and bake for 30 minutes or until cheese filling is set and pasta is piping hot.

CHICKEN & TOMATO ROLL-UPS WITH PESTO CREAM SAUCE

Omit step 1 and tomato sauce ingredients. Cook lasagna noodles as directed in step 2. In step 3, preheat oven as directed. To make filling: Omit ricotta, feta, and egg. Instead, in a food processor, combine 8 ounces cream cheese and ½ cup grated Parmesan. Spread mixture over one side of lasagna noodles. Increase smoked chicken to ¾ pound and divide evenly among lasagna noodles. Coarsely chop ½ cup oil-packed sun-dried tomatoes and sprinkle over chicken. Roll up and arrange in two baking dishes as directed. In food processor (no need to clean), combine 2 cups packed basil leaves, 1 cup heavy cream, ⅓ cup grated Parmesan cheese, 2 tablespoons pine nuts (or almonds), and ½ teaspoon salt; process until smooth. Spoon sauce over lasagna rolls and bake as in step 4.

Calories 537, Total Fat 29g, Saturated Fat 16g, Cholesterol 96mg, Sodium 1178mg, Protein 24g, Carbohydrates 47g

Chicken Breasts with Apple & Calvados Cream Sauce

Calvados is a strong apple brandy made in Normandy. America's own applejack is similar, and can stand in for the imported Calvados, which is considerably more expensive. The combination of apple brandy and heavy cream is quite wonderful, and very fitting for an autumn dinner party.

Prep Time: 20 minutes
Cooking Time: 30 minutes
Makes 8 servings

NUTRITION INFORMATION
Per Serving
Calories 383
Total Fat 14g
Saturated Fat 6g
Cholesterol 127mg
Sodium 431mg
Protein 41g
Carbohydrates 17g

- 8 skinless, boneless chicken breast halves (about 3 pounds), pounded to ½-inch thickness (page 15)
- ⅓ cup flour
- 2 tablespoons butter
- 2 tablespoons vegetable oil
- 1 small onion, finely chopped
- 4 red apples, cut into 8 wedges each
- 1½ teaspoons sugar
- ¼ cup Calvados or applejack
- ½ cup chicken broth
- ½ cup heavy or whipping cream
- ¾ teaspoon salt
- ½ teaspoon freshly ground black pepper
- ¼ cup chopped parsley

1. Dredge chicken in flour, shaking off excess. In large skillet, heat butter and oil over medium heat. Working in batches, add chicken cutlets to pan and sauté 3 minutes per side or until golden brown and just cooked through. As they are done, transfer cutlets to platter; cover and keep warm (or transfer to 250°F. oven to keep warm).

2. Add onion to skillet and cook, stirring frequently, 5 minutes or until onion is tender. Add apples and sugar, and cook, stirring frequently, 5 minutes or until apples are crisp-tender.

3. Add Calvados to pan and cook 1 minute to evaporate alcohol. Add broth and bring to a boil. Add cream, salt, and pepper, and boil 6 minutes or until slightly thickened. Stir in parsley. Spoon sauce and apples over chicken.

CHICKEN VÉRONIQUE Cook chicken as directed in step 1. In step 2, sauté onion as directed, but omit apples and sugar. Instead, add ¼ cup Cognac (or other grape brandy) to onion and cook 1 minute. In step 3, omit Calvados. Stir in broth, cream, salt, and pepper, and boil as directed. Substitute 2 tablespoons snipped chives for the parsley; add 3 cups seedless green grapes (or red grapes, or a mixture) at end, tossing until heated through.
Calories 381, Total Fat 14g, Saturated Fat 6g, Cholesterol 127mg, Sodium 431mg, Protein 41g, Carbohydrates 16g

HINTS & TIPS

➤ Sauté the floured chicken cutlets in batches to ensure that they develop a delicately crisp exterior. If they are crowded closely in the pan, the trapped steam will produce a soggy coating.

➤ If you don't want to buy apple brandy just for this recipe, you can use regular brandy instead. And if you prefer not to cook with alcohol, you can substitute apple cider for the Calvados or applejack.

➤ Use firm apples that won't turn to mush when they're sliced and sautéed. Some good choices are the Northern Spy, Cortland, and Rome varieties.

CHICKEN BREASTS WITH APPLE & CALVADOS CREAM SAUCE

CHICKEN ROLLATINE WITH PROVOLONE & ROASTED PEPPERS

Prep Time: 25 minutes
Cooking Time: 35 minutes
Makes 8 servings

NUTRITION INFORMATION
Per Serving
Calories 299
Total Fat 10g
Saturated Fat 4.5g
Cholesterol 113mg
Sodium 665mg
Protein 46g
Carbohydrates 5g

Chicken Rollatine with Provolone & Roasted Peppers

Serve these rolled, stuffed chicken cutlets whole, on a platter; or cut them crosswise and fan the slices on dinner plates. If you can't get fresh sage leaves, substitute fresh basil, which is more widely available. Serve the chicken with baby summer squash, steamed and glossed with melted butter.

2 red bell peppers, cut lengthwise into flat panels

8 skinless, boneless chicken breast halves (about 3 pounds), pounded to ¼-inch thickness (page 15)

¾ teaspoon salt

8 thin slices Provolone cheese, halved lengthwise (about 6 ounces)

16 fresh sage leaves

1 tablespoon olive oil

1 small onion, finely chopped

1 can (14½ ounces) diced tomatoes

½ cup chicken broth

¼ teaspoon crushed red pepper flakes

1. Preheat broiler. Place bell pepper pieces, skin-side up, on broiler pan and broil 4 inches from heat for 10 minutes or until skin is blackened. When peppers are cool enough to handle, peel and cut each piece in half lengthwise.

2. Place chicken on work surface. Sprinkle with ¼ teaspoon of salt. Place pepper slices crosswise down length of each chicken cutlet. Top with 1 slice of Provolone and 2 sage leaves. Starting at one short end, roll each cutlet up. Secure rolls with toothpicks.

3. In large skillet, heat oil over medium heat. Add onion and cook, stirring frequently, 7 minutes or until onion is soft. Stir in tomatoes, broth, red pepper flakes, and remaining ½ teaspoon salt. Bring to a boil, reduce to a simmer, and add chicken rolls. Cover and simmer 12 minutes or until chicken is cooked through. Transfer chicken to large serving platter. Remove toothpicks.

4. Return tomato mixture to a boil and boil 3 minutes or until slightly thickened. Spoon sauce over chicken.

IN A HURRY?
Omit peppers and broiling in step 1. Instead, use bottled roasted red peppers.

Prep Time: 15 minutes
Cooking Time: 15 minutes
Makes 8 servings

NUTRITION INFORMATION
Per Serving
Calories 314
Total Fat 12g
Saturated Fat 3g
Cholesterol 107mg
Sodium 332mg
Protein 41g
Carbohydrates 9g

Chicken Piccata Stir-Fry with Mushrooms

Here's a super-quick company dinner inspired by veal piccata. Strips of chicken breast dredged in cornstarch take the place of floured veal cutlets. The cornstarch gives the chicken a fine, golden crust, and sliced mushrooms round out the dish nicely. Serve the stir-fry over noodles or rice.

8 small skinless, boneless chicken breast halves (about 3 pounds), cut for stir-fry (page 15)

⅓ cup cornstarch

¼ cup olive oil

1 pound mushrooms, thinly sliced

6 cloves garlic, finely chopped

⅓ cup chicken broth

⅓ cup fresh lemon juice (about 3 lemons)

½ teaspoon salt

2 tablespoons butter, cut up

¼ cup chopped parsley

1. Dredge chicken in cornstarch, shaking off excess. In large skillet, heat oil over medium heat. Working in batches if necessary, add chicken and stir-fry 8 minutes or until golden brown and cooked through. As it browns, transfer chicken to plate.

2. Add mushrooms and garlic to pan, and cook, stirring frequently, 5 minutes or until mushrooms are tender. Add broth, lemon juice, and salt; increase heat to high and cook 3 minutes or until slightly reduced. Remove pan from heat and swirl in butter. Return chicken to pan and stir gently to coat. Stir in parsley.

Mahogany Chicken with Rice Stuffing

A soy sauce marinade, its taste and color further enhanced with brown sugar and cinnamon, yields a Chinese-style roast chicken with mahogany-brown skin. As an attractive glaze (and for an extra flavor dimension), the chicken is brushed with fragrant dark sesame oil after it comes out of the oven. The rice-and-vegetable stuffing honors the Asian origins of the recipe.

Prep Time: 10 minutes plus
  marinating time
Cooking Time: 1 hour 30 minutes
Makes 8 servings

NUTRITION INFORMATION
Per Serving
Calories 604
Total Fat 27g
Saturated Fat 7g
Cholesterol 134mg
Sodium 1017mg
Protein 46g
Carbohydrates 39g

- ½ cup lower-sodium soy sauce
- ¼ cup dry sherry
- ¼ cup packed light brown sugar
- 1 teaspoon ground cinnamon
- 1 whole roaster chicken (about 6 pounds), giblets removed and reserved for another use
- 1 tablespoon vegetable oil
- 4 scallions, thinly sliced
- 2 cloves garlic, finely chopped
- 2 carrots, quartered lengthwise and thinly sliced crosswise
- 1½ cups rice
- 1 cup chicken broth, canned or homemade (page 45)
- ½ teaspoon salt
- 2 teaspoons sesame oil

1. In small bowl, whisk together soy sauce, sherry, brown sugar, cinnamon, and ½ cup of water. Place chicken in large bowl, pour in soy-sauce mixture and refrigerate at least 1 hour or up to overnight, turning chicken 2 or 3 times to coat with marinade.

2. Meanwhile, in large saucepan, heat vegetable oil over low heat. Add scallions and garlic, and cook 2 minutes or until garlic is tender. Stir in carrots and cook 4 minutes or until crisp-tender. Stir in rice, broth, salt, and 2 cups of water, and bring to a boil. Reduce to a simmer, cover, and cook 17 minutes or until rice is tender. Cool to room temperature.

3. Preheat oven to 400°F. Lift chicken from its marinade; reserve marinade. Loosely stuff neck and body cavities of chicken with rice mixture. (If there is any rice remaining, spoon it into 8-inch square baking pan, cover with foil, and bake alongside chicken during last 15 minutes.) Tie chicken legs together with kitchen string. Lift wings up toward neck, then fold wing tips under back of chicken so wings stay in place.

4. Place chicken, breast-side up, on rack in 15 x 11-inch roasting pan and roast for 15 minutes. Brush with half of reserved marinade. Roast for 30 minutes. Brush with remaining marinade. Roast for 15 to 20 minutes, until chicken is cooked through. Check frequently to be sure chicken is not overbrowning. If it begins to get too brown, tent with foil.

5. Remove chicken from oven and transfer to platter or carving board. Brush sesame oil over chicken and let stand 10 minutes before carving.

SZECHUAN CHICKEN WITH VEGETABLE-RICE STUFFING
In step 1, reduce soy sauce to ⅓ cup and brown sugar to 1 tablespoon; omit cinnamon; add ¾ teaspoon freshly ground black pepper and ¼ teaspoon crushed red pepper flakes. Marinate as recipe directs. In step 2, increase oil to 2 tablespoons; increase scallions to 6; increase garlic to 3 cloves; increase carrots to 4, and add 1 red bell pepper, cut into ½-inch squares. Sauté as directed. Proceed with remainder of recipe as directed.

Calories 608, Total Fat 29g, Saturated Fat 7g, Cholesterol 134mg, Sodium 818mg, Protein 46g, Carbohydrates 36g

HINTS & TIPS

➤ Marinating a whole chicken is an unusual technique, but it's even easier to do if you place the chicken and marinade in a large zip-seal plastic bag. Place the bag in a bowl or baking dish (in case of leaks) and just turn the bag a few times during the marinating.

➤ Soy sauce contains so much sodium that you might want to make the lower-sodium variety your kitchen staple. Lower-sodium soy sauce has about one-third less sodium than regular soy sauce.

➤ Tenting a piece of foil over chicken as it roasts can help keep it from overbrowning. The foil should not tightly cover the roasting pan and the two ends should be unsealed—as the term "tenting" implies. This allows the chicken to maintain a crisp skin; a tightly sealed pan would steam the chicken and soften the skin.

MAHOGANY CHICKEN WITH RICE STUFFING

Main Index

Low-Fat Index

All of the entries in the Low-Fat Index are recipes that derive 30 percent or fewer of their calories from fat. In most cases, these recipes are also flagged as "Low-Fat" in the body of the book. Reduced-fat versions of no-flagged recipes are also included.

Quick-to-Fix Index

All of the entries in the Quick-to-Fix index are recipes that take 30 minutes or less, from start to finish.

METRIC CONVERSIONS

LENGTH

When you know:	If you multiply by:	You can find:
INCHES	25	MILLIMETERS
INCHES	2.5	CENTIMETERS
FEET	30	CENTIMETERS
YARDS	0.9	METERS
MILES	1.6	KILOMETERS
MILLIMETERS	0.04	INCHES
CENTIMETERS	0.4	INCHES
METERS	3.3	FEET
METERS	1.1	YARDS
KILOMETERS	0.6	MILES

VOLUME

When you know:	If you multiply by:	You can find:
TEASPOONS	4.9	MILLILITERS
TABLESPOONS	14.8	MILLILITERS
FLUID OUNCES	29.6	MILLILITERS
CUPS	0.24	LITERS
PINTS	0.47	LITERS
QUARTS	0.95	LITERS
GALLONS	3.79	LITERS
MILLILITERS	0.03	FLUID OUNCES
LITERS	4.22	CUPS
LITERS	2.11	PINTS
LITERS	1.06	QUARTS
LITERS	0.26	GALLONS

WEIGHT

When you know:	If you multiply by:	You can find:
OUNCES	28.4	GRAMS
POUNDS	0.45	KILOGRAMS
GRAMS	0.035	OUNCES
KILOGRAMS	2.2	POUNDS

TEMPERATURE

When you know:	If you multiply by:	You can find:
DEGREES FAHRENHEIT	0.56 (AFTER SUBTRACTING 32)	DEGREES CELSIUS
DEGREES CELSIUS	1.8 (THEN ADD 32)	DEGREES FAHRENHEIT

Metric Equivalents†

Linear

US	Metric
⅛ IN	3 MM
¼ IN	6 MM
½ IN	1.5 CM
¾ IN	2 CM
1 IN	2.5 CM
6 IN	15 CM
12 IN (1 FT)	30 CM
39 IN	1 M

Weight

US	Metric
¼ OZ	7 G
½ OZ	15 G
¾ OZ	20 G
1 OZ	30 G
8 OZ (½ LB)	225 G
12 OZ (1 LB)	340 G
16 OZ (1 LB)	455 G
35 OZ (2.2 LBS)	1 KG

Volume

US	Metric
1 TBSP (½ FL OZ)	15 ML
¼ CUP (2 FL OZ)	60 ML
⅓ CUP	80 ML
½ CUP (4 FL OZ)	120 ML
⅔ CUP	160 ML
¾ CUP (6 FL OZ)	180 ML
1 CUP (8 FL OZ)	235 ML
1 QT (32 FL OZ)	950 ML
1 QT + 3 TBSPS	1 L
1 GAL (128 FL OZ)	4 L

Temperature

US	Metric
0°F (FREEZER TEMPERATURE)	-18°C
32°F (WATER FREEZES)	0°C
98.6°F	37°C
180°F (WATER SIMMERS*)	82°C
212°F (WATER BOILS*)	100°C
250°F (LOW OVEN)	120°C
350°F (MODERATE OVEN)	175°C
425°F (HOT OVEN)	220°C
500°F (VERY HOT OVEN)	260°C
*AT SEA LEVEL	

† ALL NUMBERS HAVE BEEN ROUNDED. FOR MORE EXACT NUMBERS, USE METRIC CONVERSION CHART AT LEFT

MM	=	MILLIMETER	OZ	=	OUNCE
CM	=	CENTIMETER	FL OZ	=	FLUID OUNCE
M	=	METER	QT	=	QUART
IN	=	INCH	GAL	=	GALLON
FT	=	FOOT	G	=	GRAM
ML	=	MILLILITER	KG	=	KILOGRAM
L	=	LITER	LB	=	POUND
TSP	=	TEASPOON	C	=	CELSIUS
TBSP	=	TABLESPOON	F	=	FAHRENHEIT